Journey From India to Jamaica

Henry W. Jaghai O. D., J. P.

Pustak Bharati, Toronto, Canada

Author :
Henry W. Jaghai, O.D., J.P.

Title :
Journey from India to Jamaica

Published by :
Pustak Bharati, Toronto, Canada
pustak.bharati.canada@gmail.com
www.pustak-bharati-canada.com

Available at : www.amazon.com

ISBN : 978-1-989416-05-1

Colored Delux Edition : ISBN 978-1-897416-21-1

Copywrite 2020

© All rights reserved. No part of this book may be copied, reproduced or utilised in any manner or by any means, computerised, e-mail, scanning, photocopying or by recording in any information storage and retrieval system, without the permission in writing from the author.

I hope that as you read this book, it will shed some enlightenment upon the challenges of our forefathers and how they bravely overcame them to rise up as successful citizens of their new country (Pardes). It was my pleasure to put together the accounts and profiles and hope you find delight in reading the

""Journey From India to Jamaica."

Henry Jaghai O. D., J. P.

CONTENTS
Journey form India to Jamaica

Dedication	
Early Indentured Workers	
Foreword	1
Author's Prologue	4
Arjun's Journey from India to Jamaica	5
Arjun and his children in Jamaica	27
Jaitun	40
Alfred Arjun	41
Doris Arjun (Maragh)	42
Irene Arjun-Henry	45
Douglas Arjun	46
Rosetta and Michael Singh	48
Autaria and Jaghai	49
End of one journey ans start of another	57
To the Plantation, Journey to the Estate	62
Completion of indentureship	65
Cattle rearing and dairy	66
Indian settlements after indentureship	68
A better life	68
Commemoration Ceremony	71
Autaria's struggle	73
The Promise	77
The Trust Fund	80
Henry W. Jaghai, O.D. J.P	101
Business Success	106
Involvement in Sports	108
Cricket, Lovely Cricket !	135
Indo-Cultural Contribution	148
Pardes Book Launch	163
The Jaghai Family	165
Dax Reid	172
Ali and Barbara Bahadur	174
John Hill Suckie and wife Bhagwantie	176
Everal "Baba" Juggan and Catherine Suckie Juggan	178
Hagaroo's and Minnie's Grandchildren and Great Grandchildren	180
Phyllis Hill Sukie-Bijou	180
Faith Maragh	182
Bennet Family	184
Melvin Bennett	186
Sogun Beepat	189
Thaddeus Bessi	191

Cislyn Marie Brown	192
Wally Byroo	193
Mohinder Byrosingh	194
Derrick Denniser	195
Richard Francis	199
The Gallow Family	202
Cecil Suckram Gibbore	205
Donald Goluab	207
Franklyn Jaghroo	207
Violet Johnson and Tomlinson Sweetland	208
Ramlal and Sara Malgie	210
Olive Maragh, PhD, J.P.	212
Ramesh Maragh/Maharaj	214
Wendy Maragh	216
Ronald McDonald	217
Johnny Mykoo	219
Icilda Pandohie	220
Robert and Miriam Pancham	221
Ramesh Pershad Singh	224
George and Miriam Ragbar	225
Harold Ramcharan	229
Cecil Ramsamugh (Snr) and Family	230
Cecil Ramsamugh JR	231
Alvin Singh	232
Ganga Singh	234
Sukhdevi Singh	236
Lorna Sukie	238
Roy Sweetland	239
Wilbert Tallo J.P.	242
Vijay Thompson	243
Sonny Ward J.P. & Family	244
Albelto Ward & Family	245
Marley Kiah Agustus Williams	246
Vinroy Webb	248
Samuel Williams	249
Appendix I, Caribbean British Colonies	251
Appendix II, Ships which came to Jamaica (1845-1917)	252
Appendix III, Distribution of Indentured Workers to various Estates	255
Appendix IV, Last voyage back home	261
Appendix V, Distribution Rolls for SS Dahomey, 1903	262
Appendix VI, Vinery Estate Indentured Workers	264
Appendix VII, Workers distributed to Fort Stewart Estate in St. Mary	265
Appendix VIII, Distribution of workers by Parish Estates	266
Appendix IX, East Indian Settlements : information	269
Appendix X, Gorakhpur May 26, 1905; from Calcutta by SS Indus	271

Dedication

This book, inspired by Henry W. Jaghai, OD, JP, and compiled by Barbara Jaghai Bahadur, Donna Maragh, Andrea Jaghai Williams, Matthew Williams, Rosita Arjun Singh and Yasmin Henry is dedicated to the memory of Arjun, his family and the people of Rattapur, India. It is also dedicated to Jaghi, his family and the people of Bahadurpur, Basti.

Henry Jaghai

Barbara Bahadur

Andrea Williams

Yasmin Henry

Rosita Arjun Singh

Donna Maragh

Early Indentured Workers

Arjun left the village of Rattapur in Uttar Pradesh in 1911 aboard the ship S. S. Indus to Jamaica. He went to Hudson Dairy Farm, St. Catherine.

Ragbar left Bombay, India in 1913 aboard the S. S. Mutulah. He went to Orange Hill Estate, St. Mary.

KhunKhun Singh emigrated from the village BaralGanch in 1912.

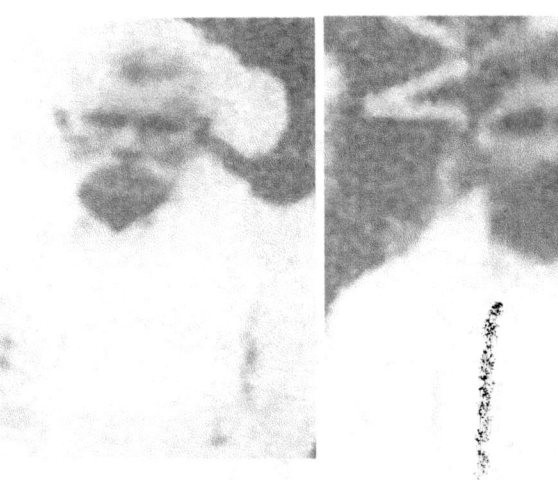

Soman arrived in Jamaica in 1912 aboard the S. S. Ganges from Lucknow, Uttar Pradesh.

Suckwar Maragharrivedin 1905 from Bast Uttar Pradesh   Bharat Maragh 1905

Patia Changur was aboard the S. S. Indus in 1911 to Jamaica. She went to Holland Estate, St. Elizabeth.

Bafatan arrived in Jamaica 1916 aboard the S. S. Dewa. She went to Grays Inn Estate, St. Mary.

Najeeran Mangaroo arrived in 1913 with her mother, Gafooran. Gafooran was indentured to an estate in St. Mary, after they moved to Clarendon.

Sortie 1913

Ramdeen 1915

Atwari Singh 1912

From the Desk of the Publisher

Pustak Bharati, Toronto, Canada

Sometimes divine coincidences (*Daivi Samyoga*) do occur. As the Editor-in-Chief of the Pustak Bharati Research Journal, Toronto, Canada, I am in the process of Editing and publishing our upcoming book "*Overseas Indians*" particularly focused on the old practice of voluntary agreement/indenture (*girmit*) to become a bonded labor, and with a wonderful divine coincidence the breathtaking book, "Journey from India to Jamaica," by Henry W. Jaghai, O.D., J.P. came to us for Editing and Publishing. Going through the awe-inspiring manuscript, and after fathoming the events of the life and achievements of Henry, it sinks in positively that, behind the astounding success of Henry, each relative of the greater Jaghai family, beginning with Arjun thorough Abrham, has played a role, direct or indirect, in this success story, beginning from an absolute scratch.

The book is a first hand narration of the chain of events and milestones by Jaghai's maternal grandmother Autaria of Bharatpur, about the saga that began with the travel of Arjun Jaghai of Rattapur (Uttar Pradesh, India) on March 16, 1911 from Calcutta on SS Indus for Jamaica. It is also a memorable account of achievements of this clan and how it contributed to the cultural, economic, educational, health, political, religious, social and sporting climate of Jamaica. Besides the overwhelming business success of Henry Jaghai, noteworthy are his passions and pastime in the sports activities of Pigeon breeding and Racing Championship, Horse breeding and racing championships, Cricket Matches and Team Captainship, Indo-Cultural contribution and International Travels through Florida, Illinois, New York and Pennsylvania in USA; London, Italy, Switzerland, France, Austria, Belgium, Pakistan, Trinidad and Tobago, Guyana, Puerto Rico and India through Delhi, Jaipur, Calcutta, Bombay, Agra and Kashmir. This precious book, written by Henry to fulfill the old promise he made to his grandmother Autaria, is a collectors item for those readers who are interested in the history, achievements and contributions of the Indian Diaspora.

Ratnakar Narale, Toronto, Canada[1]
Prof. Hindi, Ryerson University, Toronto, Canada

---

[1] Prof. Ratnakar Narale has Ph.D. from IIT. Kharagpur and Ph.D. from Kalidas Sanskrit University, Nagpur, India. He has proficiency in Hindi, Sanskrit, Music and Poetry. He is living in Toronto for last 50 years. He has taught Hindi at the three Universities and both the school boards of Greater Toronto. He is the Editor-in-chief of Pustak Bharati Research Journal and Bharat Saurabh e-Magazine. He has received such prestigious citations as "Vishva-Hindi-Samman" by the Ministry of External Affairs, Government of India (2018), Hindu Ratna Award from the City of Markham-Toronto (2017), Artist of the Year award by Panwar Music and Dance Productions, Toronto (2016), etc. He can be reached at pustak.bharati.canada@gmail.com.

Foreword

I am more than pleased that the author, Henry W. Jaghai, OD, JP, has asked me to write this foreword to his second book ... concerning the migration of *Indians* to *Jamaica*, and their experiences. I will briefly include a little of my own personal experience and thoughts on 'growing up Indian' in *Jamaica*.

When slavery ended in *Jamaica* in 1838, the sugar barons in there faced an immense shortage of labor, and the colonial masters, ever so concerned about the well being of their kindred folks abroad, turned to India and China for cheap labor. As pointed out by Mr. Jaghai in his book, '*Pardes*,' over 36, 000 Indians migrated to Jamaica as 'indentured servants.' The first migrants arrived in 1845 on the ship *Blondel* that embarked from *Calcutta* and landed at *Old Harbor Bay*. From there, the migrants were transported to various sugar estates in *Vere*. Migration continued until 1917.

The migrants were given 'five-year indentureship' contracts, and at the end of this period, they were afforded the opportunity to stay on the estates with incentives. Many accepted the offer and not quite a few were strong-armed in staying. Some returned to India, with repatriation in 1929 being the last one.

The migrants were segregated from others and were housed in 'barracks.' These barracks were mostly one-room row houses and thus migrants with families were crammed into each other. Monies for rent and other expenses were deducted from the meager wages of the migrants, and all reports indicated that health care and sanitary conditions were abominable. Water for drinking, cooking and other personal uses were likely obtained from polluted sources like rivers or gullies. Rainwater may have been an option for some.

The abominable living conditions and inhumane treatment of the migrants were unearthed and the Indian Raj, still under British jurisdiction, stopped the migration which officially ended in 1917. The 'Protector of Indians' in Jamaica may have had a hand in the matter.

As someone of Indian descent, I cannot help but feel the pain of my ancestors in this human tragedy. As someone put it, we have 'risen from the ashes.' But I must hasten to say that Indo-Jamaicans are not singular in this respect. So I still see my father and others toiling from dawn to dusk in the sugar cane fields of Vere, surviving mostly on 'dhal and bhat' and 'roti and callaloo.' I am proud of the fact that Indian migrants and their descendants have made considerable contributions to the advancement of Jamaica, and the West Indies in general, in spite of very many difficulties that were faced. Contributions have been made in the fields of agriculture, education, health care, sports, and politics, to mention a few areas. I cannot avoid mentioning *Dr. Winston Chutkan*, one of the very first Indo-Jamaican physician and a man of very humble background. Now there are very many such physicians and surgeons in Jamaica, including some from Guyana and Trinidad and Tobago.

The Indian culture has survived in Jamaica and has spread widely especially in the culinary field, as well as in music and dancing. 'Curried Goat and Rice,' is a Jamaican favorite, especially on joyful occasions. 'Chicken Roti' is also a favorite of many, even in far-flung places like the USA and Canada. *Hindustani (Hindi)*, and *Urdu* the main language of the migrants, have all but died out in Jamaica. Other languages spoken by the migrants include *Bojpuri*, which is close to *Hindi*, and *Bengali*. *Urdu* is very close to *Hindi* as well but it is written in *Arabic* characters. The learning curve for these languages is exceptionally steep very steep.

Unfortunately, I have known only a few original Indian migrants-maybe among those who arrived in the early 1900's. I remember *Dowansingh* whose children, grand- and great-grands, still live in Vere. Then there was *Karkar* who lived at *Springfield,* my birthplace. **Karkar** sang and danced for us on Friday evenings after taking a few drinks of 'leggarboot' (*Bootlegger,* a brand of rum then) while smoking 'onion bud,' ('*Humming Bird,*' cigarette brand then). In addition, how can I not mention *Sri Rattan* and his wife *Junya,* who lived at **Kemps Hill**, and *Bolasingh* and his wife who lived at *Race Course. Sri Rattan* taught English to the migrants, and *Junya* was a female Indian dancer of class. Their son *Edwin* was involved in Jamaican politics and is a well-known philanthropist in *Vere.* The name *Sri Rattan* was 'corrupted' to the surname *Suraton* at birth registration; *Sri Nanan* became *Sunanon/Sunanan;* and *Sri Baran* became *Subaran/Sybron,* and so on. The title *Sri* refers to a learned individual. As was the custom at that time and probably is still so, Indians had only one name because the family was a close-knit unit so two names were not necessary for identification purposes. Moving far away was not really an option. Moreover, I did know of some *Hindu* priests (pundits) who lived in *Vere* during my boyhood days, but I cannot recall their names. We called them '*Maragh*' men. The word *Maragh* is a corruption of *Maharaj,* a *Hindi* word for a revered ruler. The pundits officiated at weddings and funerals. The Mosque in Spanish Town served the Muslim (Mussulman) community.

My maternal grandfather, who may have been a *Punjabi,* lived at Toll Gate with wife, Jane, and their children. His name is listed as *Alexander Mitchell* on my mother's birth certificate, so he must have worked on one of the many sugar estates in Vere owned by *Mitchell* as listed in Henry Jaghai's book '*Pardes.*' But my grandfather was also called *Karkar Budhoo,* and *'Coolie' Jimmy.* The word *'Coolie'* is a derogatory term that is used in many places to refer to people of the Indian sub-continent. It is not unusual for some patients to refer to Indo-West Indian physicians and surgeons, and those from the *Indian* subcontinent as well, as '*coolie doctors.*'

Anyway, my grandfather *Jimmy* must have been an enterprising person as he bought land in Toll Gate and nearby in Decoy. My father and others from Springfield cultivated rice at Decoy on my grandfather's land. I remember helping with the rice farming and found the reaping and threshing back-breaking work. However, planting and weeding were much easier but not for the lazy. We slept in my grandparents old houses at Toll Gate during the reaping season, or in huts at Decoy. We made the huts ourselves and the bagged rice was transported to Springfield on drays. Kissoon, a first cousin, was the dray driver. A lantern suspended from the bottom of the dray provided light at night.

However, we reaped enough rice to serve the family until next season. The rice seeds (dhan) were steamed overnight in a large 'kerosene' pan, sun dried on tarpaulins, beaten in a mortar, and then fanned to remove the chaff. Sometimes hulling was done using a foot operated 'dienkhi' owned by Sagar Williams at Gimme-me-bit in Vere. Later milling was done on a machine owned by Mr. Hayman at Kemps Hill. Split peas (matar dhal), hardi (yellow ginger), coriander, (dhanya), meeti, geera, lesun (garlic) and a few other ingredients were ground to a moist paste on a (grinding stone) and ready for the pot.

My paternal grandmother was *Miriam Bajue* ('*Maa*') and she helped with caring for us young ones. However, I did not know my paternal grandfather who was known as variously as *'Bajue,' ''Badjue,'* or '*Bajou,*' depending on the mood of the *Post Mistress* recording births. **Bajue's** father, *Ganase,* was a migrant. So too were *Maa's* parents, *Somra and Cookan.* The men worked at *Sevens Plantation,* and lived with their family in barracks nearby.

The Indian society is *maternal* in nature, so us boys of Indian origin did not help much with house hold chores. Some boys would help their parents with work on the estates during the holidays from school, but most of us spent our spare time playing cricket, fishing, or hunting birds with slingshots in the hunting season. We were hardly successful at bird hunting or fishing but there was more success at crab hunting. Crabs were plentiful during the rainy season in Vere, in May and again from August to October. Housework, a thankless job, was left to mothers and their daughters.

Most of us boys enjoyed playing cricket or going to cricket matches at fields in *Vere*, especially at *Monymusk*. At that time sugar was 'king' and our local Indo-Jamaican 'soil' heroes were the *Harold Deena*, *Sydney Johnson*, the *Budhoo* brothers-*Manny, Willie,* V*innie,* '*Kaise*' (Hubert Mitchell), *Rex Suckoo*. And *Bob Maragh* from Kingston of course. In addition, at the international level *Rohan Kanhai, Joe Solomon, Alvin Kalicharan Sonny Ramadhin* (of '*Ramadhin and Valentine*' fame), and *Nyron Asgarali,* all of Indian origin. The feeling of being 'Indian' apparently fades away much too slowly I think, so I remember rooting silently for India and Pakistan in Test matches versus the West Indies, except when *Kanhai* was playing. To me there seems to be something unique in being Indo-Jamaican. What it is, I do not know although I am aware that Indian migrants and their descendants would not be welcome with open arms in high class society in India. Maybe it is has to do with the close-knit nature of the Indian family, as well as their caring nature and their preference for a quiet rural way of life. Or is it the fear for aggressors? Or a combination of all? I suppose the answer will never be known, or even told.

Most second and third generation Indo-Jamaican children excelled in elementary schools, but unfortunately, only a few went to high school (college) because of the associated expenses. There was only enough money to buy food, meet other expenses, and save to buy land and build a house of their own. So we owe much to our parents who sacrificed much in seeing us through the formative years and after. Much too is owed to many of our older siblings who stayed at home to care for the young ones while our parents toiled away in the cane fields. Moreover, many first generation Indo-Jamaican children served as translators for their Hindi or Urdu-speaking parents, so they were unable to attend school regularly. In addition, we have to thank former Chief Minister Norman Manley, who many years ago legalized Hindu and Muslim marriages. Prior to this the birth certificates of many of the children of Indo-Jamaicans show only the mother's name-the fathers name is missing. So these children had only one name-*Bajue, Mohan, Ramlal, Gobind, Budhoo, Bachue,* for example. Later on children were given two names-Stanley Bajue, Henry Jaghai, Roy Singh and so on.

This history needs to be told in much greater detail and taught in the schools as well. So I say 'well played Henry Jaghai.' I look forward to your third book on Indian migration to Jamaica.

Stanley. A. Bajue, Ph. D.

I sincerely thank, acknowledge and appreciate the Jamaica Archive, mangers, staff and everyone whom provided the opportunity and help in our research for the historical data required.

Likewise Professor Ratnakar Narale PhD. for his diligence, patience in his tremendous effort and input in editing and publishing The Journey From India to Jamaica.

Henry W. Jaghai OD, JP

AUTHOR'S PROLOGUE

My paternal grandfather (Aaja), Jaghai, left his native country India in 1905 to work in Jamaica, which he always referred to as pardes (foreign country). He and his wife Autaria (Aaji), became pardesi-jan (a term I heard them use repeatedly) - strangers in a new country, as did my maternal grandparents, Jaitun, Ragbar and Arjun. The stories they told me about the Motherland, the lifestyle they brought over and the culture and religion they practiced, gave insight into the way of life in India. It was this strong cultural influence that impacted me most of all and created the fervour and passion in me to keep my grandparents' stories and cultural heritage alive.

To reconnect with my roots, I visited my ancestral home in 1987, which proved to be one of the most rewarding experiences of my life. With the help of Dr. Ajai Mansingh, his wife Laxmi Mansingh and Dr. Mansingh's brother, I was able to locate the village of Bahadurpur from which my paternal grandparents originated.

While I was excited to trace back my roots, at the same time I was saddened at the state in which the people lived. I enquired about any surviving relatives and was told of a cousin who had married and relocated to another village.

After this enlightening trip, Dr. Ajai Mansingh proposed writing a book together about the East Indians' journey to Jamaica as indentured labourers and what happened thereafter. In my role as researcher and financier, and the Mansingh's as authors, ***Home Away from Home: 150 Years of Indian Presence in Jamaica***, was published in1999.

Over the ensuing years, I became motivated to build up on ***Home Away from Home***, focusing on the stories of pardesi-jan (strangers in a new country) and their descendants.

Pardes: Stories through the Eyes of a Pardesi's Grandson recaptures oral stories, cultural heritage and highlights of Indo-Jamaicans' accomplishments in Jamaica. After tracing the roots of my Nana in January of last year, through the help of Richard Francis and my friend, Ashutosh Diljun and his brother Avnindar Diljun and friend Lovey Dayal, I decided to write another book highlighting Arjun's story.

This book and its contents were inspired by my origins as a poor boy who made a promise to my Aaji (grandmother) Autaria, to one day travel to her home village of Bahadurpur and help the villagers living in squalor.

I must acknowledge the assistance of Dr. Stanley Bajue and all the people who gave me profiles.

I was able to help the villagers of Bahadurpur through the JAHBLESS Foundation (founded by Rajesh Jaghai and his wife Dr. Kiranjit Bedi), by providing scholarships and school sweaters for fifty children, thirty blankets and donations for the elderly, and constructing a Lord Shiva temple.

I must acknowledge the assistance of Anil Kumar, his relatives, the village head, the school principal and all the villagers who assisted with all the Bahadurpur projects.

The influence that my Nana Arjun had on me, motivated me to provide assistance to his home village of Rattapur in Faizabad. Arjun arrived in Jamaica in 1911, and I lived with him as young boy in 1940 until I became a young man in 1960. He was instrumental in my development as an adolescent, enabling me to develop skills as a mechanic. The debt of gratitude I owe him, I attempt to repay by honoring his memory by improving the lives of the villagers of Rattapur, which include the descendants of his relatives he left behind.

Similarly to what I did for the villagers in Bahadurpur, I have done for the villagers in Rattapur. The residents designed a Hannuman temple, the building of which I financed. The JAHBLESS Foundation will continue to offer assistance each year to both villages.

I must acknowledge the assistance of Tilak Raam (Arjun's grand nephew), Arjun's other relatives, the village head and all the villagers who assisted with all the projects.

The book comprises two sections:
Section 1 focuses on the *Pardesi-Jan Stories* which I have recounted based on what my grandparents told me and what I have observed myself and the accounts of their descendants.
Section 2 outlines East Indians' and Indo-Jamaicans' achievements and how these individuals have contributed to the cultural, economic, educational, health, political, religious, social and sporting climate of Jamaica. These articles were contributed by the individuals or written based on information that was received from them or gathered from other published sources.

I want to thank all the individuals who were supportive in helping me source information and photos. My gratitude goes to: Irene Arjun Henry, Donna Maragh, John Khan, Patrick Jaghai, Roy Sweetland, Richard Francis, Audrey Arjun, Rosita Arjun Singh, Yasmin Henry, Matthew Williams, and Andrea Williams. Many thanks to the villagers of Rattapur and Bahardurpur especially Anil Kumar, Gharilal Chaudhari (village head), Mohammad Aslam (school teacher), Chaornisyin, Chaaudhari, Sirpat Kumar, Rajpat Kumar, Ram Simpat, Kanik Ram Chaudhari, Kapil Dev and Gyandas Yadav.

I am also appreciative of all the people who allowed me to feature them and share their family histories.

This book would not have been possible without the support of my family members who were instrumental in organizing the content.

Finally, I would like to give special recognition to Myrtle (nee Suckie), my wife of 65 years, who has supported me in all my endeavours.

ARJUN'S JOURNEY FROM INDIA TO JAMACA

MAN'S EMIGRATION PASS.

HEALTH CLASS,

Depôt No. 292.
For Ship "INDUS," S.S. PROCEEDING TO JAMAICA.
No. 232

Jamaica Government Emigration Agency,
21, Garden Reach,
Calcutta, the MAR 15 1911 19

PARTICULARS OF REGISTRATION,	Place,	Cawnpur
	Date,	16 . 1 . 11
	No. in Register,	23

Name, Arjun
Father's Name, Ari
Age, 19
Caste, Ahir
Name of Next-of-kin, Prasati, Brother
If married, name of Wife, Sukhdai at Rattipur
District, Faizabad
Thana, Miltipur
Village, or Town & Mahalla, Rattapur
Bodily Marks, Scar on right Knee
Occupation in India, Cultivation
Height, 5 Feet 1½ Inches.

CERTIFIED that we have examined and passed the above-named Man as fit to emigrate; that he is free from all bodily and mental disease; and that he has been vaccinated since engaging to emigrate.

DATED
The   19 .

Depôt Surgeon.

Surgeon Superintendent.

CERTIFIED that the Man above described has appeared before me and has been engaged by me on behalf of the Government of JAMAICA as willing to proceed to that country to work for hire; and that I have explained to him all matters concerning his engagement and duties. This has also been done at the time of registration by the Registering Officer appointed by the Indian Government.

DATED

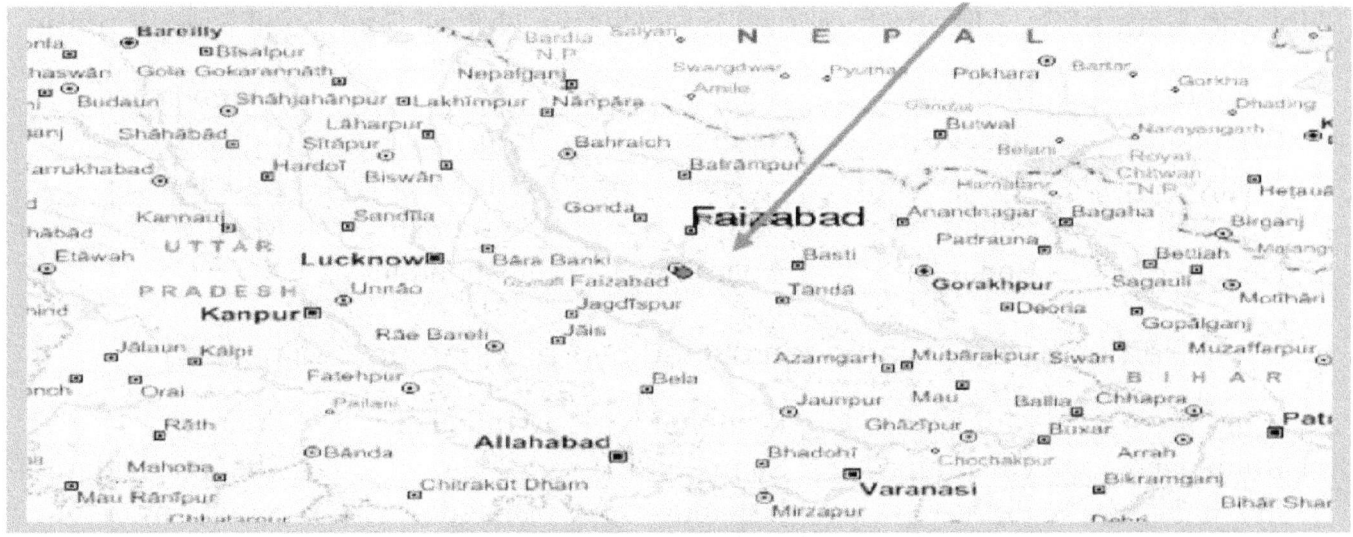

Map showing the city of Faizabad.

http://www. bing. com/images/search?q=faizabad+map&view=detailv2&id=BF-90D45285A20BB7AE4F6B3A063711DB51360ED3&selectedindex=2&c-cid=r7l52W%2Bs&simid=608010427307262845&thid=JN. PGTJfaQxn1WjDVP- 4c%2Fv4LA&mode=overlay &first=1

Arjun's Jahajis (Shipmates) on S. S. Indus from Calcutta arrived at Kingston on May 5, 1911

Golden Grove Estate, St. Thomas owned by United Fruit Company

Jaganath	Kali Pershad	Sahadeo	Kusuru	Harpal
Mathura	Ghurahu	Balbhadar	Jagai	Saitu
Hausildar	Rajaram	Santu	Ramlal	Jasodra f
Ashraf	Ramautar	Kishun	Abdul	Mathura
Dalla	Rukmin f	Bindeswar	Somni f	Sattan

Hopewell Estate, St. Mary owned John Pringle

Sheonarain	Sukhrani f	Husain Bux	Parbati f	Sheonath
Parbati f	Jailal	Banskalia f	Piroo	Bakhti f
Narbadia f	Maharajia f	Magghu	Bhajan	Ramnath
Idoo	Mohabir	Musai	Bahadur	Maharajwa
Sheobhik				

Holland Estate, St. Elizabeth owned by Williams Nuttall Campbell Farquharson

Ramphal	Mulheri f	Sohana	Sundar	Sheopershad
Pershadi	Bahadur	Sahibdin	Ramkali f	Bekaru
Jhaga	Bhagwanti f	Roshan	Jadi f	Balkaran
Dhanraji f	Patia f	Batohi	Sadubhan	Matti f
Nepal	Sonia f	Anardaiya f	Kishundutt	

Perrins Estate, Clarendon owned by Farquharson &Milholland

Ramlal	Mohadai f	Ramphal	Mulheri f	Sohana
Ramanand	Dhanrajia f	Sampatia f	Sundar	Sheopershad
Pershadi	Pirthi	Bahadur	Bhagoo	Sahibdin
Ramkali f	Bekaru	Ramkalia f	Shoenarain	Jhaga
Bhagwanti f				

L-R Ashutosh Diljun, Jiyaram Yadav (Arjun's grand-nephew), Richard Francis, Lovey Dayal

Arjun's journey started one early morning in January, in the small village named Rattapur in India. Arjun was sent by his father Ori, to attend to his usual chores, of rounding up the cows, leading them to the milking shed and milking them to provide milk for the family, to start their day.

In the evenings, he would gather the cows from the pasture and lead them to their pen. Arjun had a faithful cow, who he affectionately named, "Baroda." He would tie her to the verandah post in the evenings, in preparation for the morning milking. On this unforgettable morning, Ori told Arjun to "go get the dude for breakfast," when Arjun went outside, his favorite cow Baroda was missing. Arjun began to panic and went in search of his cow. The search was in vain, Baroda was no where to be found. Frightened that his father would punish him, Arjun decided to stay away and did not return home. Hungry and tired, he eventually stopped to rest under a Neem tree, and started eating some of the berries from the tree. After a while a group of young people were passing by and saw Arjun eating the berries. They stopped and questioned Arjun, who related his story to them. Seeing a frightened, hungry boy, fearful of punishment, they felt sorry for him and decided to stop and share their food with him. In their conversation, Arjun learned that the British were recruiting workers to go abroad to work as Indentured laborers. His newly found friends were on their way to Faizabad, to sign up for the Indentureship program.

Arjun saw this as an opportunity to make a future for himself. He decided to take a risk, and went with his friends, on their journey to Faizabad. This journey, on foot took him through Milkipur, before arriving at this destination. On arrival, they were met by the British recruiters, who painted a glowing picture of life, as an Indentured laborer. This was very enticing to Arjun, who became very excited about his future. He made the decision to travel by train to Cawnpur to register as a labourer. The British Government provided temporary housing and food for all the recruits at the holding depot, until they reached the desired amount of workers they needed. Eventually, all the recruits were transported to Garden Reach, Calcutta, where the registration process was completed.

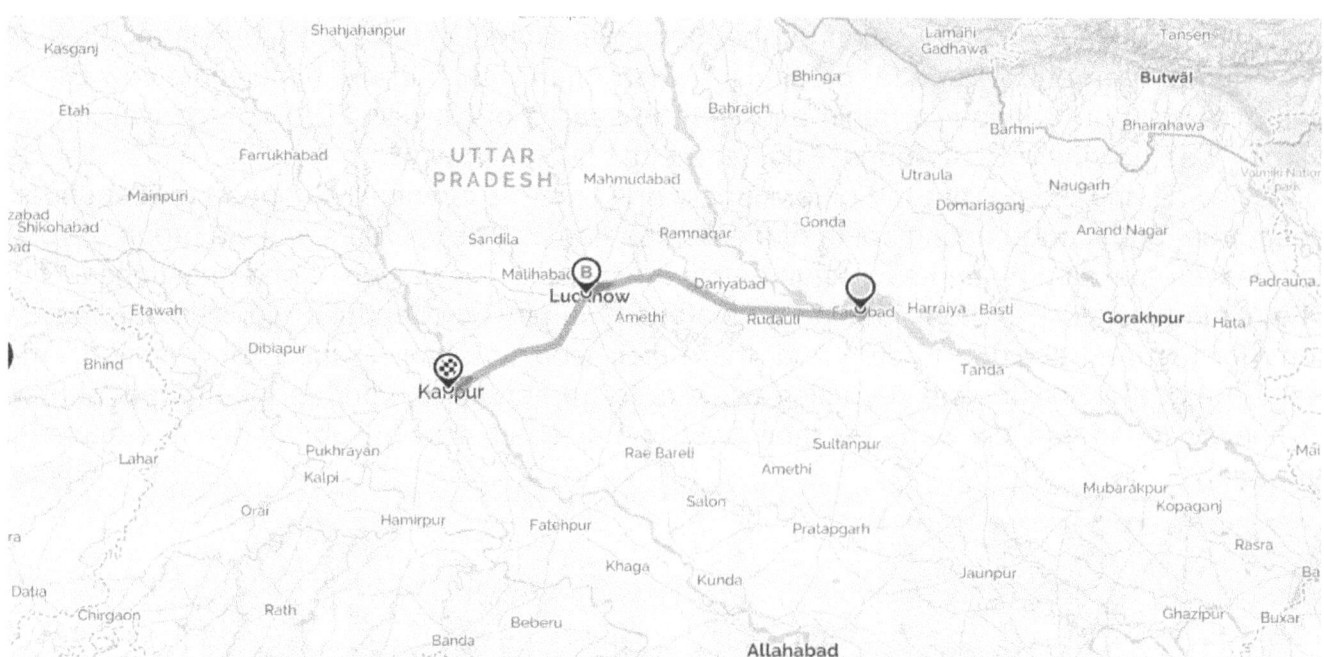

Arjun's journey from Faizabad, to Lucknow and then to Kanpur
https://www. mapquest. com/directions/list/1/india/faizabad-282476010/to/india/lucknow-282476232/to/india/kanpur-282476815

L-R AvnindraDiljun, Ashutosh Diljun, Lovey Dayal, Richard Francis, on the way to Rattapur

As part of the screening the recruits were also examined by the medical doctor to ensure they were in good health to travel. As part of the agreement they had to swear that they were going voluntarily and were asked questions that formed the terms of the five-year indentureship contract. Once they agreed to this stipulation their thumbprint was stamped on the form. A few days before they sailed, they had another physical examination and then brought down to the river to have a bath. They were supplied with a set of new clothing, blankets, eating and drinking utensils. The recruits were allowed to bring their vegetable and fruit seeds and their musical instruments. Arjun made sure to bring his janghia pants. On the historical day of March 20, 1911, Arjun along with his 812 shipmates (jahaji) departed the port of Calcutta on SS Indus in route to Jamaica West Indies.

Arjun's journey on the SS Indus was described as perilous at times, especially when the sea was rough and the ship would sway back and forth on the high waves. At times Arjun would find himself questioning his decision to leave his homeland. He would become very sad when he would recall his family that he left behind. Other times he would entertain himself by dancing and singing with his shipmates. On May 5, 1911 the SS Indus docked at the port in Kingston Jamaica. Arjun along with his shipmates, four of which were female by the name of Gobinda, Sarsutta, Sheerujia and Sitaram. The five males were Bhawani, Bipat, Chedi, Lalta and Raghu. All were assigned to work on Charles Gilpin Hudson's plantation and dairy farm, located on Marchpen road in Blairpen, Spanish Town St. Catherine. The farm was located 14 miles from Kingston to Spanish Town. The workers were transported by horse driven cart to the plantation.

For the first five years Arjun worked very hard and was proficient at dairy farming job. Arjun worked with a similar breed of cows that he was accustomed to in India.

Typical setting in Rattapur, India

His days started out at 2 am. He would gather the milk containers and head toward the cow pen where he would milk the cow one by one in the stall. As he collected the milk, he would pour it in a large container, after several hours he would have accumulated enough milk to fill about 12 huge containers. He and his coworkers would then carry the containers to the side of the road where they would be picked up by the milk truck. The milk from these containers would be poured into a milk tank on the truck. The workers would collect the containers and return them to the stall. The milk truck would then travel to the condensery which was about a 10mile radius. By midmorning Arjun and his coworkers would take the cows out to the pasture and return to the dairy farm to clean up. By 4:30-5pm they would round up the cows and return them to the cow pen next to the milking stall. Arjun and his coworkers would then return to their barracks where the females would cook food for everyone while the men gathered around to relax and smoked their Chilum pipes and singing the Biraha. He knew how to read and write Hindi well. He would often receive letters from India and would sing about those stories. He would offer his assistance to his friends to write letters for them to send to their relatives in India. Arjun would dress up in his janghia pants and perform his traditional dance entertaining the crowd.

At the end of the first five-year indentureship, Arjun proved to be a very diligent worker who had impressed the busha. He was promoted to headman on the dairy farm. Arjun made the decision to sign up for a second five-year indentureship work. In 1924, he left the farm and went to brick hill on Spanish town road in Kingston where he lived one year before starting his family.

As good as he was with his hands milking the cows; Arjun was even more skilful with his feet. He was an exceptional janghia dancer and had made sure to carry his colourful and patterned janghia pants from India. His combination of dancing skills and colourful costume always attracted attention and he soon formed a group called Arjun's Janghia Group. The dancers were Gaghai Hadeen, Bagaloo, Munesar, Jaggersah, Ramasrei, Saathai, and Salamatt. Accompanying drummers were Panchan and Sumai, and the singer was Kaka Ramdeen. Arjun and Mai complemented each other culturally. He liked to dance and she to sing. Jaitun boasted of being one of the best singers of Indian folk and wedding songs of her time.

After three years of being together, Jaitun gave birth to Rosetta (my aunt) and shortly after, the family moved to a leased property at 58 1/2 Spanish Town Road owned by Dhanuk Dhari Tewari. Nani and Nana took over the house of Mahoney "Moonshine" Bola (Jaitun's god sister), who had moved to a seven-acre property on Whitehall Avenue, St. Andrew.

Mr. Tewari had sub-divided about 75 acres of property (which ran along Spanish Town Road to May Pen Cemetery, bordering the train line in Western Kingston) and leased it to the ex-indentured Indians. The area which was called Kingston Pen consisted of five sections known as: Ackee Walk, Back O' Wall, Grassyard, Maranga Lane, and Newland (Appendix IX).

In addition to living there, residents could plant crops and set up cottage industries. Some Indians specialized in barbering, carpentry, jewellery making, shoemaking, and tailoring. Kingston Pen soon became the headquarters for commercial, cultural and religious activities for the pardesjan and their descendants.

We lived between the Ackee Walk and Newland sections. After the 1944 hurricane, our neighbour Abi Bulla died and my grandfather bought the goodwill (house and garden) for 40 pounds. He allowed his daughter Rosetta, her husband Cleveland Black and their daughter Marjorie to live in the house.

While we lived in the area, I remember, the Caucasian Christian missionaries who traveled on bicycles who would visit us every Sunday. Under the big East Indian mango tree in the yard, they would hold Sunday school sessions to Christianize us, as they thought the religion of our Hindu parents was pagan. Each year, they took us to a fair and picnic, where we traveled by tramcar to a huge field at Shortwood Road and Constant Spring Road. It was an event that we always looked forward to.

Maie told me that they had to pay one pound a month for the lease of the property. Mr. Tewari provided water from a well to help with the irrigation of the lands. My grandparents continued their backyard gardening and also began animal rearing. They sold their produce to the local markets.

Nani and Nana had another daughter, Elizabeth (my aunt) and four sons, Alfred, Adolphus, Aston, and Leslie (my uncles). Although my uncles, aunts and mother had to help with the cultivation and animals, my grandparents insisted that they also attend school. They went to Ebenezer School located on Darling Street.

Ashutosh Diljun Speaking to Rattapur Pradhan (Village Leader) Sukhraj Yadav

My Nana Arjun said that after the indentureship period ended in 1917 and the last 5-year contract ended in 1922, the East Indians who decided to remain in Jamaica had a hard time sustaining themselves. To alleviate the situation the Governor Sir Arthur Richards, introduced The Government Relief Program (Bollo Work). The government employed ex-indentured Indians and their children to cultivate vegetable gardens on allotted lands that were divided into four sections. They were called Family Pen, Kingston Pen, Majestic Pen and Tinson Pen. These lands commenced at West Kingston at the end of Industrial Terrace and Marcus Garvey Drive and extended into the border of Hunts Bay Lane. The first land to be allotted, which was situated in the east, was known as Kingston Pen and continuing westward were Tinson Pen, Family Pen and Majestic Pen. There were several secured entrances to the premises. They were enclosed with black wooden gates. One entrance was at East Avenue and First Street; another at Spanish Town Road opposite Hagley Park Road and the third, opposite Oakland Road. There was also an unsecured entrance accessible from Pechon Street and West Street.

The produce from the fields would supply government institutions such as hospitals and prisons. Surplus crops were sold at the government retail station, which was located on Spanish Town Road in the vicinity of Three Miles.

Arjun said workers on the farm were placed in groups of twelve to fifteen and supervised by a headman. My own father, Abraham Jaghai, Gam Bankasingh and James Purai worked as Bollo labourers. My grandfather Arjun and John Sankar were employed as headmen. They earned one pound and two shillings per week plus a free lunch daily. The other labourers received a salary of fifteen shillings weekly and also received free lunch every day. All workers were paid on Fridays. Nana said his salary from Bollo Work, in addition to his earnings from personal cultivation and animal rearing, made his family comfortable.

In addition to vegetables, other crops that were supplied were guinea grass, rice, sorghum (guinea corn), and sweet corn. Water from underground was extracted to fill gadhas (catchment area) - a process the Indians were accustomed to for irrigating their vegetable gardens. Women were employed to take around water in buckets to quench the thirst of the farmers. The water was collected from standpipes that were placed in different sections of the fields.

Just as how workers' thirst had to be quenched, so too their stomachs had to be filled. One advantage of working on the farm was the guarantee of a cooked meal every day. The government provided kitchen facilities where hot lunches were prepared for the workers on a daily basis. My mother Ambrozine (Daata) cooked for the labourers. She cooked both Jamaican and Indian food. The workers were given food tickets which valued one shilling, and which could be used at any one of the kitchens in any of the 'Pens' they chose.

Once my mother collected these tickets, she would send them down to the local office at the end of the day. They were counted and sent to the Labour Office at East Race Course in Kingston. On Saturdays, Daata went to the Labour Office where she collected her pay based on the total amount of tickets she had sent in for the week.

After living at Ackee Walk for several years, my grandfather Arjun related that in 1945, Mr. Tewari sold all his property, except the section in which he had built his house at 48 Spanish

Town Road in the Grass Yard area to a developer, Allan Blissett. All tenants received six months notice to vacate the premises.

Like wandering sheep trying to find suitable grazing pastures, the East Indians sought other areas to live. They formed new Indian communities in Denham Town, Bachan Pen, Granton Pen, Maxfield Avenue, Greenwich Farm, Waltham Park, Whit- field Town, Two Miles, Payne Land, Three Miles, Four Miles (Hindu Town), Cockburn Pen, Kencot, Red Hills Road, Cassia Park Road, Mountain View Avenue, Franklyn Town, Vineyard Town, Chisolm Avenue, Omara Road, Seaward Drive and Olympic Way.

Some even went further away to Bushy Park, Featherbed Lane, Fellowship Hall, Job's Lane, Old Harbour Road, Sydenham, St. John's Road and Winter's Pen in Spanish Town, St. Catherine to plant rice. There was a rice mill in Spanish Town at the inter- section of Oxford Road and Windsor Road.

After the sale of Tewari's land, Mai, Arjun and their family, which included me, had to move again. We relocated at the intersection of Red Hills Road and Cassia Park Road, to a one-acre property, which Nana had purchased for one hundred pounds- his life savings.

Villagers of Rattapur congregate after Richard Francis delivers Henry Jaghai's book Pardes to villager seated in center.

We settled down, re-established our crop cultivation and animal rearing as a supplemental source of income. After living and working on the property for one year, my grandparents realized that the person who sold them the property was not the rightful owner. It turned out the sale of this property was illegal.

Maie and Arjun's hard-earned money had gone down the drain. Again, we had to relocate. In 1947, my grandparents bought a one-acre plot of land, in Simmons Pen at 66 1/2 Chisholm Avenue for one hundred and sixty pounds. This became our family home for years to come. My aunts, uncles and I grew up learning various trades and eventually started our own families creating a second generation of Indo-Jamaicans.

From 1950 to 1960 was a turbulent time in Arjun's life. He was faced with a lot of hardship and bad luck. In 1950, he lost his job as headman at the relief site. In order to provide for his family, he started a vegetable garden and continued his dairy farming business, providing milk for his neighbors. He had acquired eight cows after completion of his indentureship program.

In 1951 Arjun and his family was faced with a natural disaster. It was a Friday night in August, Hurricane Charlie hit Jamaica resulting in devastation to the community and caused massive damages. His wattle and daub house was flattened by the hurricane. He and his family became homeless. They had to start all over again. He built a make shift temporary house from remnants of the storm and he had to obtain a loan from lawyer Aires using the title from his land to get a loan of a hundred pound. He worked very hard to rebuild a home for his family and return to their daily routines.

In 1952, one of his prized milking cows, which he also named Baroda which unfortunately was fatally hit by a car. The driver demanded compensation for the damages done to his vehicle. Arjun had no choice but to sell two more of his milking cows to pay for the repairs. This misfortune forced his wife, Jaitun to seek employment to help with household expenses. Jaitun worked as a laborer in a vegetable garden which paid her three schillings per day. Both Arjun and Jaitun worked together totaling their earnings to pay the mortgage and provided food for the family. Arjun again sought employment as a headman at Ernest Ray Dairy Farm in Signam, Spanish Town. Arjun had made arrangements with his son, Alfred to pick up the pay bills on Friday and deliver them to the dairy farm.

In 1952, bad luck followed Arjun once again when his big son, Alfred was robbed of the weeks pay bill for the laborers traveling from Church street on the bus to Signam in Spanish town. He was robbed of the total amount of 10 pounds. Arjun had to borrow the 10 pounds from a money lender, Mr. William Bailey, which he had to repay with two schilling on every pound weekly. In 1953, the owner of Signam decided to sell the dairy farm which was later used for residential housing development which resulted in Arjun's unemployment yet once again. In 1954, Arjun was invited by his friend, Bagaloo to perform the Janghia dance in St Mary. The Janghia dance was performed by Arjun, Bagaloo and Munesar. On his journey home on Monday to Kingston, the country bus that he was traveling on was involved in an accident with another vehicle. Arjun sustained multiple rib fractures and also punctured his lung. His injuries resulted in him having a lot of pain preventing him from doing his normal work. With time on his hands, Arjun would reflect more on his life. He would reminisce about his father, Ori and his brother, Barati. He would often rest on his Katia under the shades of the grape tree and would often be heard singing his favorite Biraha song, with tears rolling down his face. He would sing about his life in India, his family, his father, brother and the villages where he came from namely Rattapur, Milkipur and Faizabad. His health gradually declined. Arjun required weekly respiratory treatments at the clinic on Slipe Pen road. In October1960, his final health crisis was a massive heart attack when he was rushed to the University Hospital in Papine. He was hospitalized for two weeks before he succumbed to his injuries and died at the age of 68 years old. Arjun remains were laid to his final rest at May Pen Cemetery on Spanish Town Road.

Grave of Arjun

Arjun's relatives among Villagers of Rattapur

Arjun's relatives in Rattapur

L-R Jiyaram Yadav, Sits Pati, Shiv Sharan Yadav, Sumit Yadav

Original Temple in Rattapur

Preparation of foundation for new temple by Laxman Kumar (standing) and Krishna Kumar (bending)

Half finished temple. Temple funded by Henry Jaghai and Irene Arjun Henry (Arjun's grandchildren) The temple is designed by the villagers of Rattapur.

Sheetla Parshad Sharma hands out sweets to villagers in celebration of building of new temple

Completed temple welcomed by the villagers of Rattapur

Memorial plaque for temple

Special thanks to Tilak Raam (4th from left) and all the villagers of Rattapur who helped to complete the temple

Richard Francis (at right, representing the Arjun family of Jamaica) and Sumit Yadav cutting the ribbon to the computer center

Inside the computer center

Ramabarranthum Yadav (front right - grandson of Arjun's bother) and his wife Soorkali Yadav (stooping in center) distribute donation on behalf of the Jahbless Foundation to the villagers.

A female villager receives her donation

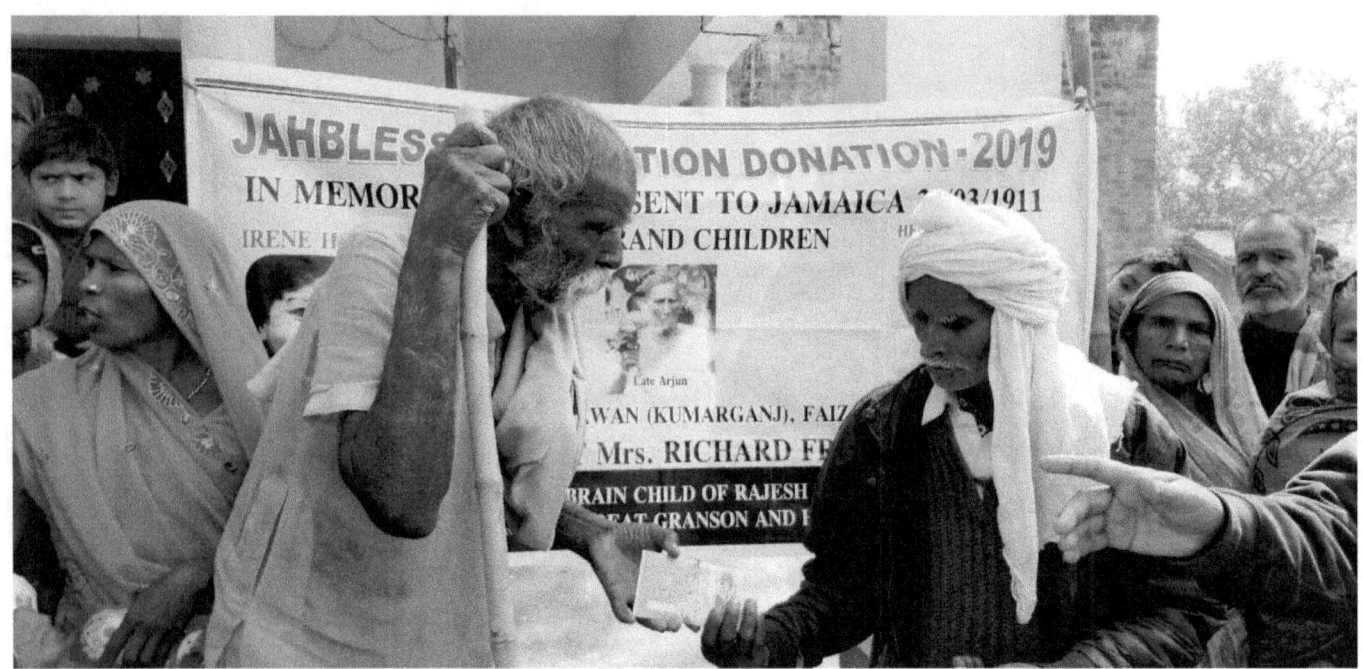

An elderly male receives his donation

Family members of Arjun

Arjun and his children in Jamaica

Arjun

Elizabeth

Alfred

Adolphus

Aston

Leslie

Cleveland Black, Arjun's son-in-law by his marriage to Arjun's daughter, Rosie.

Arjun's Grand and Great Grandchildren

Arjun's Grand and Great Grandchildren L to R: At back: Douglas Arjun, Irene Arjun Henry, Henry Jaghai, Rose Arjun Singh, Barry Goolgar, Rudolph Arjun, Rada Arjun. At Front: Brian Arjun, Jayla, Michael Singh

L to R: Dully Martin, Henry Jaghai, Connie Kadoo, Peaches Deans – Arjun's descendants

Arjun's Granddaughters L to R Audrey Arjun and Rosetta Arjun-Singh at the launch of Pardes by Henry Jaghai, (Arjun's Grandson)

Arjun's Grandsons Fitzroy Arjun and Henry Jaghai with Fitzroy's wife Flo

Arjun's descendants Rosetta Arjun-Singh, Irene Arjun-Henry, Donna Maragh, Henrietta Jadusingh

L-R : Sunita, Erick, Destiny, Elijah, Sasha, Jayla, Rosita, Sam, Janice, Stephen, Christopher, Joshua, Aiden, Dymitri and Kingston

Members of Arjun's descendants gather at the wedding reception of Joshua Singh, Arjun's great great grandson (in marine uniform) and wife Ariana, in Sacramento, California on Saturday, October 5, 2019. <u>Back Row L-R</u>: Barry Goljar, Danny Henry, Yasmin Henry, Sasha Jaghai, Brian Arjun, Christopher Arjun, Chloe Arjun, Tifanny Jaghai, Destiny Singh. <u>Front Row L-R</u>: Shana Henry Barton, Angela Lumley, Sunita Singh, Janise Orihuela, Kingston, Kaylee Arjun

Joshua Singh and wife Ariana gather with family member Janise Orihuela (Joshua's mother), Stephen Orihuela (Joshua's step father) and step brothers, Aiden and Dymitri. The wedding took place on October 5, 2019 in Sacramento, California.

Newly weds Joshua Singh, (great great grandson of Arjunn) and Ariana pose with family members. Back Row L-R: Danny Henry, Angela Lumley, Ali Bahadur, George Martin, Elijah Singh, Patrick Jaghai, Barry Goljar, Audley Arjun, Rudy Arjun, Peter Jaghai. Front Row L-R: Thelma Matin, Barbara Bahadur, Henrietta Jadusingh, Sasha Jaghai, Tiffany Jaghai, Rosetta Arjun Singh, Charmaine Jaghai, Irene Arjun Henry Audrey Arjun, Yasmin Henry

Front Row : L-R Patrick Jaghai, Irene Henry, Rosita Singh, Angella Lumley
Back Row: Rupert Bennett, Barry Gooljar, Myrtle Jaghai, Rudolph Arjun, Donna Maragh, Leslie Arjun, Henry Jaghai, Douglas Arjun, Fitzroy Arjun, Ambrozine Jaghai (daughter of Jaitun), Keith Arjun

Arjun's and Jaitun

Arjun

Jaitun (His Wife)

Jaitun with her Grandchildren

At Taj Mahal in Agra, India January 2018: Irene Arjun Henry (Granddaughter), Yasmin (Great-Granddaughter), Catherine (Great-Great-Granddaughter)

**JAHBLESS FOUNDATION DONATION 2018
IN MEMORY OF ARJUN SENT TO JAMAICA 03/20/1911
BY HIS GRAND CHILDREN**

IRENE HENRY   **HENRY JAGHAI FOUNDER**

AT RATTAPUR VILLAGE, POST- BAWAN (KUMAR GANJ) FAIZABAD UP
CHIEF GUEST ASUTOSH DILJUN- ADVOCATE HIGH COURT ALLAHABAD
JAHBLESS FOUNDATION IS THE BRAIN CHILD OF RAJESH & KIRANJIT BEDI- JAGHAI
ARJUN'S GREAT GRANSON AND HIS WIFE

Irene Henry   *Arjun*   *Henry Jaghai*

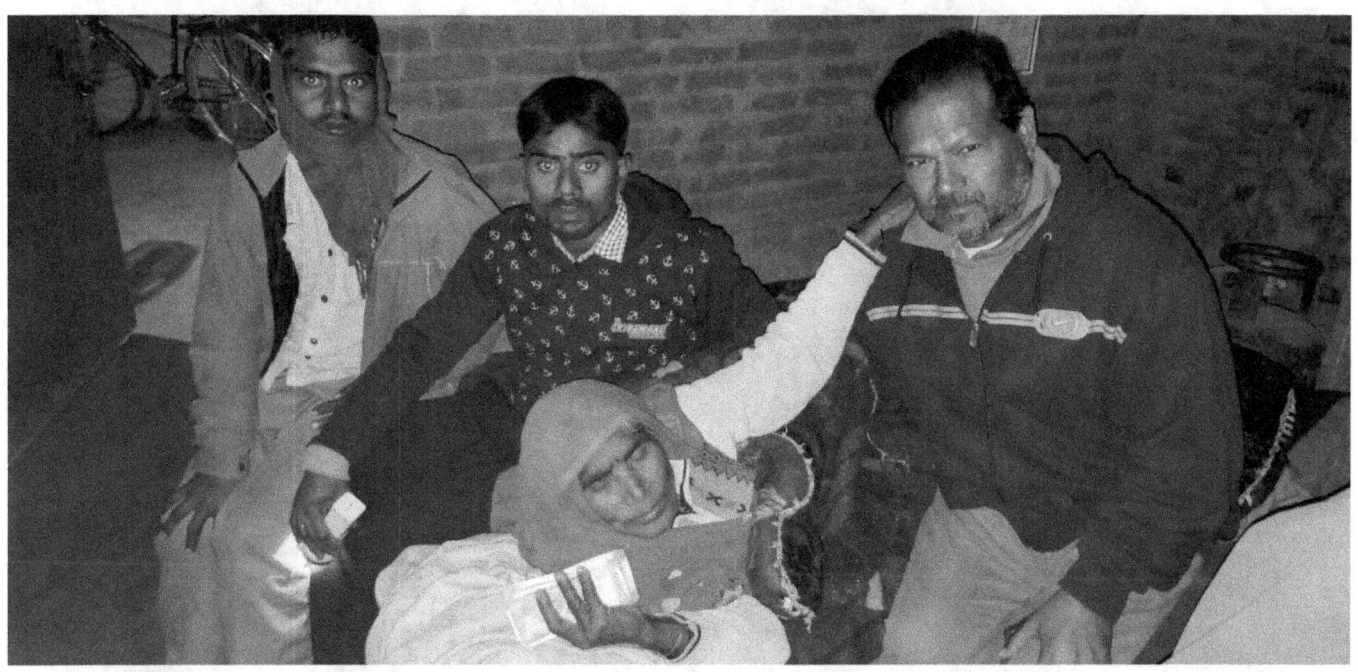

Arjun's Grandniece-in-law, Rajdeaiand her sons Hari Prasad Yadav and Kali Prasad Yadavin Rattapur, Faizabad receiving benefits from Richard Francis of JAHBLESS Foundation

Arjun's Grandnephew Hriday Yadav   Arjun's Grandnephew Jiyaram Yadav

Seated from Left to Right: Sukhraj Yadav, Ashutosh Diljun, Richard Francis, Jiyaram Yadav, Sits Pati. Standing is Shiv Saran Yadav, his sons and other villagers. There are 90 houses in the area of Rattapur.

Rattapur Beneficiaries of JAHBLESS Foundation – January 28, 2018

Journey From India to Jamaica

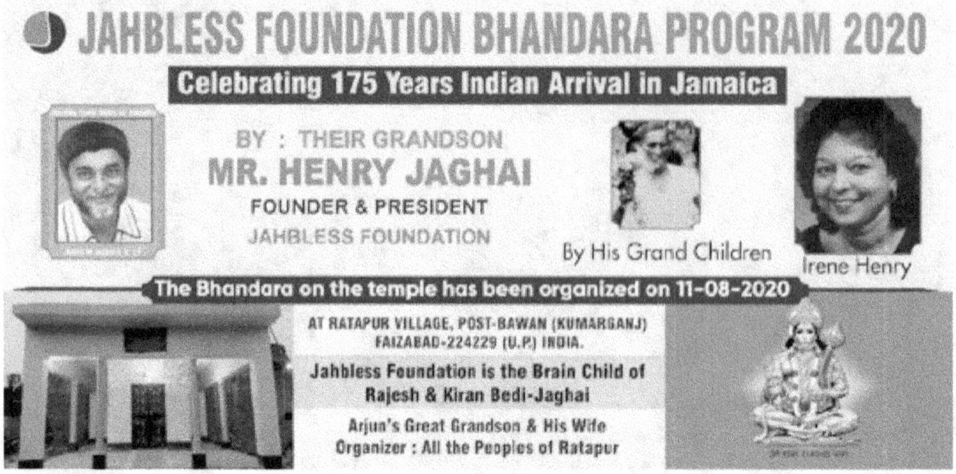
JAHBLESS FOUNDATION BHANDARA PROGRAM 2020
Celebrating 175 Years Indian Arrival in Jamaica
BY : THEIR GRANDSON
MR. HENRY JAGHAI
FOUNDER & PRESIDENT
JAHBLESS FOUNDATION
By His Grand Children
Irene Henry
The Bhandara on the temple has been organized on 11-08-2020
AT RATAPUR VILLAGE, POST-BAWAN (KUMARGANJ)
FAIZABAD-224229 (U.P.) INDIA.
Jahbless Foundation is the Brain Child of
Rajesh & Kiran Bedi-Jaghai
Arjun's Great Grandson & His Wife
Organizer : All the Peoples of Ratapur

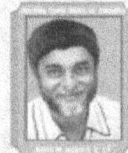

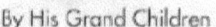

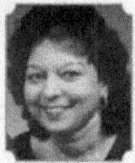

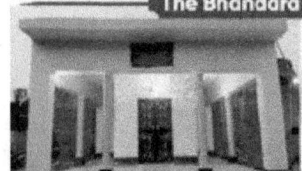

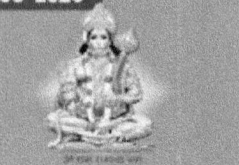

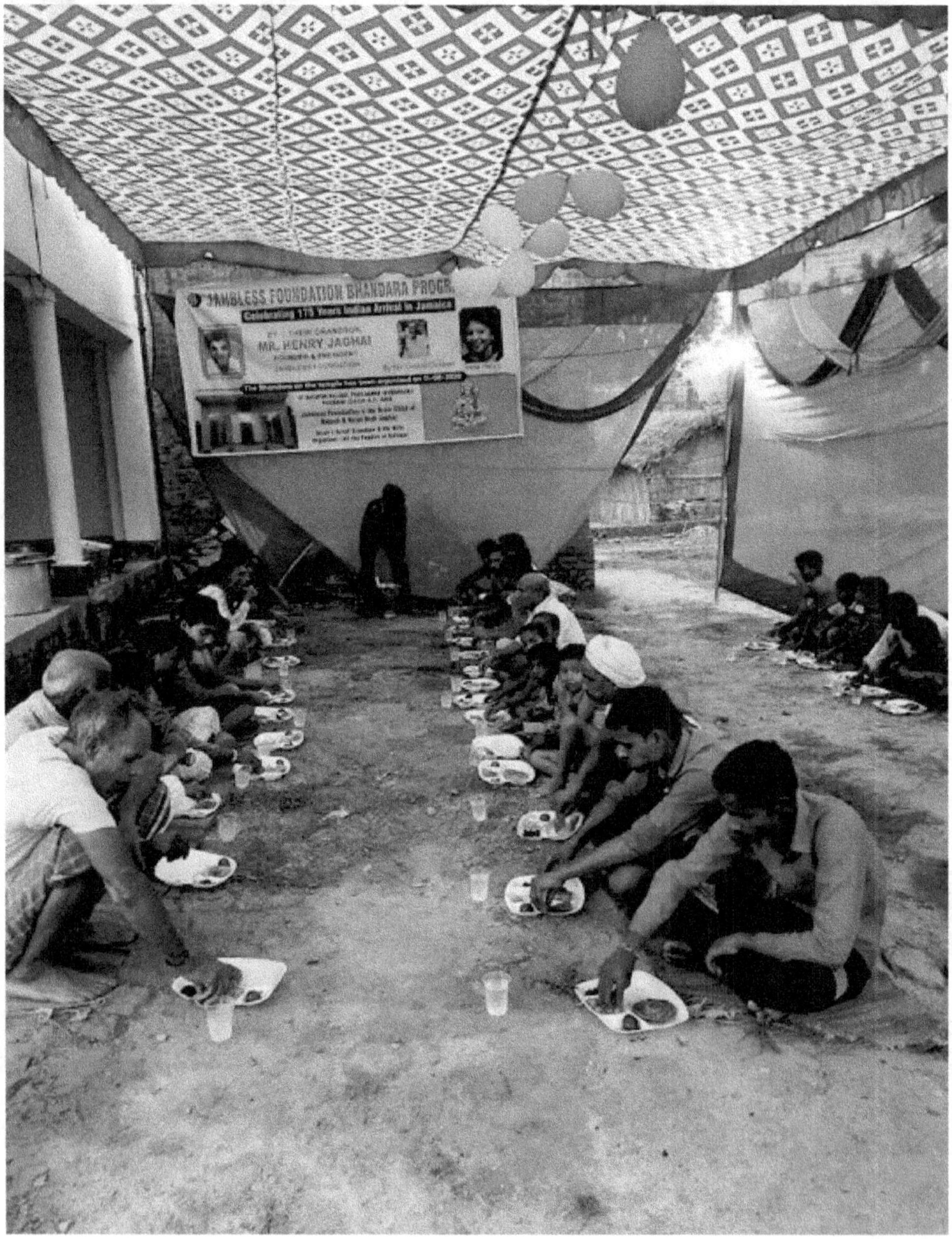

Journey From India to Jamaica

JAITUN

I lived with my Aaji Autaria until I was five years of age after which I went to live with my mother and her parents. My maternal grandmother, my Nani, Jaitun Coolie, or Maie, as she was affectionately called, told me kissa just like my Aaji. Maie's parents were pardesijan, (indentured labourers), who had come from India to Jamaica to work on the plantations. My Nani was born in Orange Hills, St. Mary in 1908. Like all the other indentured servants' children, Maie grew up on the plantation, helping her parents in the fields.

Grandmother Jaitun told me that when she was fourteen her parents and siblings decided to return to India but she refused to go as she was newlywed and did not want to leave her husband Ragnaught, who had made Jamaica his permanent home. Ragnaught however, began to mistreat Maie, but she refused to tolerate the abuse. They separated and she went back to Orange Hill Plantation, St. Mary to work.

It was during this time, she met Ragbar, whom she fell in love with. She told Methat Ragbar, also called Bapee, was twenty when he left India on April 4, 1913 on the SS Mutulah. The ship arrived on May 12, 1913 and he was assigned to the Orange Hill Estate where Jaitun worked. The estate was owned and operated by Sir John Pringle. Some of his jahaji-bhai were: Binda, Changur, Fuela, Herdai, Maharajie, Nandlal, Paragia, Pharoo, Rampershad and Sobrati.

The union between Jaitun and Ragbar produced their daughter, Ambrozine (Daata) my mother, who was born on March 13, 1921 in Orange Hill, St. Mary. A year later, Ragbar left Orange Hill Plantation, and went to White River in Portland, where he purchased one square of land. Maie said he worked long and hard cultivating his land because he wanted to give them a better life. Soon after, he was able to purchase two acres of land in Whitehall, Portland for four pounds each. This land however, proved to be a big challenge as the soil was rocky; there was no running water and no roads. Pandit Surrat Maragh, his godfather, had encouraged him to purchase this land (which was next to Belvedere- the adjacent district to Whitehall), so that he could be nearer to him. Despite the obstacles, Ragbar continued to work very hard, cultivating the land. He would visit his daughter periodically, bringing produce and money to help Jaitun. Over time, his visits however, became less and less frequent.

It has been said that 'absence makes the heart grow fonder, but there could also be a flip side to this idiom, 'absence makes the heart become lonelier. ' The latter is precisely what happened to Ragbar. Being away from Jaitun for such long periods, created a void in his life that was soon filled by another woman, Madeline Bagwandeen.

Maie said, when Ragbar and Madeline had their son, George, on July10, 1926, they legalized their union by getting married. They had two more sons, Joseph and Isaac, who were born in the mid-1930s but unfortunately both of them died in their teenage years.

My Nani, a fiercely independent woman, stated that she did not wallow in her loss of a partner and a father to her child. She continued working harder than ever - ploughing, planting, reaping and doing any other menial work that was available on the Orange Hill Plantation. Maie met Arjun shortly after and started a family.

My Nani became a cripple as a result of an illness and lost her husband Arjun after he suffered a massive heart attack. Days after, she lost her son Aston, who upon taking home friends from Arjun's wake, met in a fatal accident. Later that night, my Nani received the horrible news that Uncle Aston, her son, was involved in a motor vehicle accident, which took his life. My Nana was buried on the Sunday and my uncle, the Wednesday after. Many times when all alone and in the stillness of the night, I would hear Maie cry out to her God asking for help and mercy in her time of need.

My grandmother continued to have hope, continued to work in her vegetable garden moving about on her bottom, and lived to see sixty-eight years when she went to her final rest in 1976.

ALFRED ARJUN

Alfred "BG (Baya Gee)" Arjun, was born on February 6, 1931, in Kingston, Jamaica to Arjun (the only name Alfred's father registered after immigrating to Jamaica from India) and Susan Jaitun (from Jamaica). Alfred was the oldest son out of eight children, with his other siblings consisting of three brothers; Adolphus, Aston and Leslie and three sisters; Ambrozine, Rosetta and Elizabeth. At the age of seven, Alfred began attending the Ebenezer School and continued his schooling until the age of 15. He then found work as a tradesman in Molding at the Henrickitts Foundry on Darling Street, in Kingston Jamaica. In 1948, Alfred married Doris Maragh, as part of an arranged marriage. Alfred and Doris conceived eight children together; four boys; Keith, Karl, Rudy and Douglas and four girls; Irene, Yvonne, Rosetta and Antoinette. Although life in Kingston was difficult, with poverty being a constant concern, Alfred remained a strong father figure, and led by example, working hard to earn money for his household and always putting his children and family first. Alfred eventually moved from working in the foundry to working as a gardener for an English family. Alfred quickly proved his worth by always going above and beyond what was asked of him, with a keen attention to detail and strong work ethic, all the while learning.

Eventually, Alfred turned his passion for gardening and botany into a new work endeavor, creating beautiful flower and plant arrangements for local florists. Alfred gradually ended his work as a gardener and started to train in motion picture technology, eventually becoming the Chief Projectionist at Kingston's Regal Theater and later, the Ritz Theater. Alfred quickly became a prominent figure in the motion picture industry in Jamaica, as he was directly involved in the planning of entertainment venues and even concerts, with some featuring talented artists such as The Drifters and Jim Nabors, among many others. Alfred attended film shoots for such films as the famous James Bond movie "Dr. No," in 1962.

In 1979, Alfred immigrated to the Sacramento, California. Sacramento was where most of his children had settled, and where Alfred's grandchildren resided. Alfred found work, as a Front Desk Clerk, working for his eldest daughter Irene and her husband, Ron Henry at one of the hotel properties they owned. Alfred spent his non-working hours with his family, especially with his grandchildren.

DORIS ARJUN (MARAGH)

Doris Arjun (Maragh), born September 24, 1931, in Kingston, Jamaica, daughter of Gopal and Rhoda Maragh. Doris was blessed with eight siblings, three brothers; Baya, Massaman and Bisraam and five sisters: Amy, Ramsudar, Luloo, Enid and Roslyn. At the age of seven, Doris began attending the Ebenezer School where she first met Alfred Arjun, her schoolmate, who would also later become her future husband. In 1948 Doris and Alfred were wed in an arranged marriage. The union ultimately produced eight children, four boys; Keith, Karl, Rudy and Douglas and four girls; Irene, Yvonne, Rosetta and Antoinette. Doris was a proud mother and housewife, spending her time taking care of her household, her eight children and her husband. Doris's daily regimen consisted of ensuring that the house was cleaned, clothes washed and food was cooked; Doris loved to cook and would routinely cook big pots for food, so that her family and other family members who lived near their home on Chisholm Avenue in Kingston would also be able to eat as well. This daily routine normally took Doris from the wee hours of the morning until the late hours of the evening. Doris was a caring, humble, kindhearted and loving woman, who was known to make sure that everyone who came to her home was greeted warmly and was able to eat a meal and eat well; after they were full, Doris would take a scraping of leftovers for herself. Doris took pride in being a mother, in being a wife, and especially in being a friend, always willing to lend a helping hand or an ear to problems, and hardly ever taking time to herself. Doris spent her rare free time taking herself and her children to Kidd Lane to visit with her siblings. Doris and the children enjoyed going by Kidd Lane, as they were surrounded by their big, close knit family, with all of Doris's sisters regularly visiting with their kids.

Sitting L-R: Douglas, Doris, Alfred, Antoinette
Standing L-R: Rudy, Karl, Keith, Irene, Yvonne, Rosetta

Shana Henry Barton (standing), great granddaughter of Arjun pose with husband Mark, mother Irene Henry (Arjun's granddaughter) seated L-R, sister Yasmin Henry and son Nathaniel after receiving the award of 2019 Middle School Principal of the Year for the State of California.

Henrietta Jadusingh (granddaughter or Arjun) 3rd from left, pose with other members of Arjun's family at the celebration of her 75th birthday in Pembroke Pines, Florida on November 16, 2019. L-R Myrtle Jaghai, Henry Jaghai, Henrietta Jadusingh, Andrea Jaghai Williams, Shari Williams Mendel, Ari Mendel and Mark Williams.
Back Row: Matthew Williams

Back Row left-right: Douglas Arjun, Rudy Arjun, Audrey Arjun, Barry Goljar. Middle Row: Alverene Arjun, Irene Arjun Henry, Henrietta Jadusingh, Rosetta Arjun Singh, Audrey Arjun. Front Row: Jayla Arjun, Kaylee Arjun

IRENE ARJUN-HENRY

Irene Arjun was born in Kingston, Jamaica on May 18, 1949. She is the eldest daughter of Alfred Arjun and Doris Maragh. Irene attended the prestigious Wolmer's Girls High School.

Irene Arjun was married to Ronald Henry, oldest son of Daniel and Esther Henry on March 5, 1966 in Kingston, Jamaica.

Prior to this marriage, Ronald Henry, was a citizen of the United States, and resided in Sacramento, California.

In August 1966, Irene joined Ronald in Sacramento, after receiving legal residency from the U. S. Embassy in Kingston.

Ronald was a very ambitious, dedicated, hard worker. His main goals were to use the opportunity given to him, to be in America, to reach as far as possible to excel at whatever he chooses. He worked three jobs, seven days a week. These were low-paying jobs, since his education was limited. However, he was very determined.

Irene worked at A. T. &T. Telephone Company as a computer operator. Their lifestyle was quite low-key and economical because their goal was to invest in real estate.

Their first property was only a single-family house which they rented out rooms to four occupants. Both Ron and Irene continued their jobs. Their goal was to save as much as possible, without having to give up a comfortable lifestyle.

In July 1967, Yasmin, their first daughter was born. Ron continued to work his jobs and Irene stayed home with the baby. After six months, Irene changed to working the night shift at A. T. &T., and Ron took care of Yasmin during the evening.

In September 1971, their son, Ronald Jr. was born, and they both planned and worked out the same schedule so they can both work and raise a family at the same time. Ron and Irene purchased their first home that year.

During these times, Ron never forgot his vowed goal. They saved everything possible and in 1976, they purchased an 80-room hotel in downtown Sacramento. It was very scary, but very exciting, because they never thought it was possible, to own such a large parcel of real estate. They had put their entire savings into this venture.

Shana, their third child was born September of 1976. The hotel was always full and business was very good. Irene had to leave her job at A. T. &T. to work at the hotel and take care of three children. In 1977, they purchased a 9-room hotel in 1977 and 180-room hotel in1978. The investments were very successful and surpassed any goals they had. Since the late 1970s, Ron and Irene purchased over 35 real-estate parcels in the Sacramento area.

Daniel, their youngest son, was born in July 1980. Ronald and Irene continued to raise the family and purchase more real estate as the years went by.

The children are all very successful adults now. Yasmin is a science teacher on the high school level. She has earned her Bachelor of Arts in Biological Science and Chemistry as well as a Master's Degree in Education. She possesses California credentials in biology, chemistry, and physics. She is a very-respected teacher in the Sacramento City Unified School District. She is married to Mark Harris who is from the United Kingdom and they have a daughter, Katherine, who is entering her senior year of high school. Katherine would like to study law as a career.

Ronald Jr. is a real estate broker. He earned his Bachelor's and Master's Degree in Real Estate and Finance. He now manages the properties for the family business. The Henry family owns over 350 apartment units and four shopping strip centers. He has two daughters. Jacqueline has completed her freshman year at San Francisco State University. Jacqueline is focusing on a teaching career. Alexandra is entering her senior year of high school and wants to enter the world of fashion design.

Shana is a principal on the middle school level. She earned a Bachelor's degree in business and marketing. She also possesses a Master's and Doctorate in Education. Shana is married to Mark Barton and they have one son, Nathaniel, who is in elementary school and enjoys science.

Daniel is a very successful heating and air conditioning technician. He earned his contractor's license and possesses an Associate's Degree in Mechanical Engineering. He owns and operates his own company. In addition to this, he also owns a restaurant that focuses on authentic Mexican food. He is married to Candida Escobar and has two children, Daniel Jr. – age 10, and Arabella, age 8.

Ron passed away on September 14, 2014 at 77 years old. Irene continues to operate all the rental properties and businesses.

DOUGLAS ARJUN

Douglas (Dougie/Doug) Arjun was born in Kingston, Jamaica on August 2, 1960 to parents Alfred and Doris Arjun. Douglas' siblings includes three (3) brothers, Keith, Karl, Rudy and four (4) sisters, Irene, Yvonne, Rosetta (Rose) and Antoinette.

Douglas grew up at 66 ½ Chisholm Avenue, in Kingston 13, he attended Rousseau Primary and Norman Manley High School, as a young man, Doug had many interests, one of which was a love for music, he grew up on listening to Engelbert Humperdinck, Tom Jones, Jim Reeves just to name a few, at the age of 14 he decided to learn a little more about his culture so he attended the newly formed Prema Satsangh on Sunday mornings. Douglas met and interacted with the members, which over time grew steadily. It was while attending satsangh that he met Alverene (Radha) Dookie and the two quickly became friends, they later got married on December 24, 1983. They are blessed with three (3) children, Richard, Keisha and Brian.

Douglas and Radha are proud grandparents to Brianna, Jayla and Jahmir.

On October 1981, Douglas migrated to the United States and lived in Sacramento California with his father and siblings, he worked as Building Maintenance Supervisor for a Hotel, a 100 unit Apartment complex as well as the State of California.

In 2006, the family relocated to Florida and Douglas started to work with the Florida Department of Transportation, he is currently a Bridge Maintenance Technician and Heavy Equipment Operator, he drives and operates one of the biggest trucks owned by the department.

Douglas' love for music never faded, he introduced reggae music to his friends in Sacramento. He put a very basic house set together and would be the official DJ for family and very close friends. Over time he updated to a set of professional DJ equipment and named his set Supersonic, shortly thereafter, he was hired to play at the Paul Bunyan Hotel every Saturday night and gained the reputation as Sacramento's #1 DJ. Supersonic has played at concerts featuring Bob Marley's sons, The Mighty Diamonds and other local events, his biggest event was for the State of California Wine and Jazz festival and was featured in the Sacramento newspaper for that event. The Jamaican community in Sacramento was very small, as such, whenever the Jamaican artists would be performing in town, they welcome the sight of other "yardies" so after the concert they would end up at Douglas' house for food and drinks. He has entertained Sugar Minott, Delroy Wilson, Don Carlos, just to name a few, as a matter of fact, on one of Sugar Minott's visit to the house, he recorded a special song for Supersonic which Douglas would play at the start of his weekly events. After moving to Florida in 2006 he decided to retire from playing at events and now entertains his wife on Sunday mornings with Engelbert Humperdinck.

ROSETTA AND MICHAEL SINGH

Rosetta "Rose" Victoria (Arjun) Singh was born in Kingston, Jamaica on October 10, 1958, to proud parents, Alfred and Doris Arjun. Rosetta's siblings also include four (4) brothers, Keith, Karl, Rudy and Douglas, and three (3) sisters, Irene, Yvonne and Antoinette.

In her younger years, Rosetta attended Rousseau Primary School and Norman Manley High School. Rosetta further continued her education by attending Henderson Secretarial College in Kingston, Jamaica.

In April 1980, Rosetta immigrated to the United States and settled down in California. Rosetta later returned to Jamaica, where she married Michael "Sam" Roy Singh on November 5, 1980, returning to the United States a short time later.

Upon returning to California, Rosetta enrolled herself in school, attending classes for nine months until she accepted her first position in the Title Company (Housing Industries) in 1982. Rosetta is now a Senior Title Examiner, and has worked in the industry for the past thirty-five (35) years. Rosetta has received several awards during that time, including the Presidential Award for her professionalism and utmost dedication to her career.

Rosetta loves to be around her family, relatives and friends, and always encourages them to keep in touch, Rosetta is a firm believer in the saying "reach out and touch someone."

Michael "Sam" Roy Singh was born in Kingston, Jamaica on September 27, 1958, to parents James Singh and Irene Singh. Michael's siblings include two (2) brothers, Albert and Clive, and five (5) sisters, Cynthia, Joyce, Blossom, Sharon and Juliet.

Michael's father, James Singh, who was also known as Lapp Singh, was considered to be one of the greatest Indian chefs of his time on the island of Jamaica, at one point overseeing the culinary staff and cooking duties for dignitaries of the island, including the Prime Minister of Jamaica.

Michael assisted his father and siblings with the business for a short time before marrying Rosetta "Rose" Victoria Singh in 1980, eventually immigrating to the United States, settling in California.

Michael continues to tend to the cooking for his family and friends in California, and infuses his dedication and love for food into the meals he prepares. Michael currently works in a linen factory, as a Lead Supervisor in his department. He has worked in the industry for the last twenty-eight (28) years.

Michael and Rosetta are blessed with three (3) children, two daughters, Sunita and Janise and a son, Christopher. Michael and Rosetta also are blessed to have four (4) grandchildren, Joshua, Elijah, Destiny and Kingston. We love them all so much.

Autaria and Jaghai, my paternal-grandparents

I was only five, but at that age when stories make your eyes widen with amazement, and provoke wondering thoughts, which become forever etched in the corners of your minds as memories, and the accompanying emotions live for ever in your heart. I did not know my grandfather Jaghi, but the stories told to me by his wife, my grandmother, Autaria, made me feel that I knew him personally. I felt as if I were always surrounded by his presence, when I relived the kissa (stories) as my Aaji (grandmother) would call them. Jaghi became my hero, my motivator. He is my ancestral legacy.

Aaji told me that Jaghi's parents, Seogolan and Ramdularie, practicing Hindus, belonged to the Ahir caste - who by profession were cultivators, cattle herders and farmers. They lived in the northern state of Uttar Pradesh in India. The village they lived in was called Bahadurpur which falls in the Basti district, in the city of Lucknow. Jaghi was born in 1880 and his brother Mahabali, in1884.

Autaria, my Aaji, who was from the same district and also belonged to the Ahir caste, was betrothed to my grandfather when she was only twelve. She told me that in India girls were married very young and every one had to marry within his or her caste. Aaji said that Jaghi (the only name I ever heard her use to refer to him), had many responsibilities as the firstborn. In addition to his daily chores of cattle rearing, dairy farming, and planting crops, Jaghi also handled the house finances, which were falling short to meet their daily living expenses. Seogolan and Ramdularie became ill, and young Jaghi had another responsibility added to his list - that of looking after his parents. Autaria said her newlywed husband and soon-to-be father was buckling under the pressures facing him.

Aaji told me that one particular trip to the drug store in the local town (thana), Rudhauli, in January 1905 to purchase medicine for his mother would change Jaghi's life forever. He noticed a large gathering in the town centre and his curiosity led him right in to the midst of the crowd. Arecruiter (arkatia as she called him) was advertising for villagers to sign up to become labourers to work on plantations in far away countries. The arkatia said that the new workers would be paid well; they would have good housing, access to excellent healthcare, and have many recreational facilities.

The arkatia painted a perfect picture of life in the new world. Aaji said that the offerings of excellent wages and a free passage back to India after the five-year contract period ended were very enticing to Aaja. It was like a dream come true for Jaghi; away out to end his family's financial difficulties and to provide a more comfortable life for them.

Aaji said that Jaghi's head was in a spin as he hurried back to Bahadurpur to discuss the day's events with his parents, Seogolan and Ramdularie. His parents though, would not agree to this venture he wanted to embark upon, and Aaji reminded me that in India parents always had the last say. However, my grandfather was not willing to let an opportunity of possible success pass by. Aaji said he pleaded and persuaded until Maie and Baap (his mother and father) agreed to give their blessings. Aaja promised them that he would return with enough money so that they could have a better life. Aaji however, confessed that she was scared of the new move but in Hindu culture, she had no say in the matter and as a subservient wife, the only option was to follow her husband.

The first part of the process of becoming an indentured labourer was to register their names. They had to travel by rail to Gorakhpur, the city to the east of Lucknow where they lived, to complete this initial step. It was the first time they would both be traveling outside of their village and Aaji was already five months pregnant, but my Aaja was determined that this was the only way out of their financial misery.

Their departure from their village and especially their home was a heart wrenching one. Seogolan wept bitterly. Ramdularie hugged Jaghai tightly, not wanting to let go. Mahabali walked them out of the village, constantly patting his dada (older brother) on his back with tears streaming down his face.

Aaji Autaria said after the registration in Gorakhpur they were held there for several days. They then traveled by train, along with other prospective emigrants to Kolkata (Calcutta). She said they came to a place with high walls all around. This is where she, Aaja and the others would remain until it was time for them to board the ship. She confessed it was a difficult and a dark time in their lives. The confinement was alien to them, the interaction with other castes lower and above was against all their cultural beliefs, the living space was crammed and the constant monitoring of their every move was overwhelming.

Gorakhpur train station where Jaghi and Autaria and other indentured servants registered and boarded the train from there to Calcutta to catch the ship to Jamaica.

Years later through my research, I found out that this was a holding depot at 21 Garden Reach, Calcutta, an address that was evident on my grandparents' Emigration Pass. At Garden Reach, the rest of the registration process was completed. Autaria said the medical doctor inspected them several times - she more than others, because of her advanced state of pregnancy. They had to be determined fit to travel. They were requested to confirm that they were there voluntarily. They were also asked questions that formed the terms of the five-year indentureship contract. Once they agreed to the stipulations, they placed their thumbprints on the form.

```
COLONIAL EMIGRATION FORM No. 44.
                    MAN'S
            EMIGRATION PASS.              HEALTH CLASS.
Depôt No.  563.
For Ship _____   PROCEEDING TO JAMAICA.
No.   383
                    Jamaica Government Emigration Agency,
                         21, GARDEN REACH,
              CALCUTTA, the    26/5    1905

PARTICULARS   { Place,         Gorakhpur.
OF            { Date,          24. 3. 05.
REGISTRATION, { No. in Register,  1.
NAME,                          Jagai.
Father's Name,                 Sisgolam.
Age,                           25.
Caste,                         Ahir.
Name of Next-of-kin,           Mahabali  Brother.
If married, name of Wife,      —
District,                      Basti.
Thana,                         Rudhauli.
Village, or Town & Mahalla,    Bahadurpur.
Bodily Marks,                  Scars on back.
Occupation in India,           Labourer.
Height,                        5 Feet     4½ Inches.
```

Emigration Pass for Jaghi, grandfather of Henry W. Jaghai, OD, JP, which authorized his departure from Calcutta to Jamaica, for the journey into indentureship. May 26, 1905

Aaji said a few days before they set sail, the doctor came and examined them again. Before the sailing date, they were brought down to a nearby river to have a bath. In addition to the personal supplies and clothing that they brought with them, they were given supplies of new clothing, blankets, and eating and drinking utensils (thali and lota – brass plate and mug). She said they had brought along with them, vegetable and fruit seeds and the manjeera (cymbals) that Aaja liked to play. Other emigrants brought dholaks and nagaras (drums), sarangies (fiddles) and their dancing costumes.

> COLONIAL EMIGRATION FORM No. 44.
>
> ## WOMAN'S EMIGRATION PASS.
>
> HEALTH CLASS.
>
> Depôt No. 564.
> For Ship _____ Proceeding to Jamaica.
> No. 384
>
> Jamaica Government Emigration Agency,
> 21, Garden Reach,
> Calcutta, the 26/5 1905
>
> Particulars of Registration,
> - Place, Gorakhpur.
> - Date, 24. 3. 05.
> - No. in Register, 2.
>
> Name, Autaria.
> Father's Name, Biobalak.
> Age, 23.
> Caste, Ahir.
> Name of Next-of-kin, Laubar. Brother.
> If married, name of Husband, —
> District, Basti.
> Thana, Rudhauli.
> Village, or Town & Mahalla, Bahadarpur.
> Bodily Marks, Scar on left side of back.
> Occupation in India, Labour.
> Height, 5 Feet 2 1/4 Inches.
>
> Certified that we have examined and passed the above-named Woman as fit to emigrate; that she is free from all bodily and mental disease; and that she has been vaccinated since engaging to emigrate.
> Dated The 190.
>
> _____ Depôt Surgeon.
> _____ Surgeon Superintendent.
>
> Certified that the Woman above described has appeared before me and has been engaged by me on behalf of the Government of Jamaica as willing to proceed to that country to work for hire; and that I have explained to her all matters concerning her engagement and duties. This has also been done at the time of registration by the Registering Officer appointed by the Indian Government.
> Dated The 6. 4. 1905.
>
> _____ Government Emigration Agent for Jamaica.
>
> Permitted to proceed as in a fit state of health to undertake the voyage to Jamaica.
> Dated The 2. 6. 1905.
>
> _____ Protector of Emigrants.
>
> J. N. Banerjee & Son, Printers, Calcutta.—300—1-1905.

Emigration Pass for Autaria, grandmother of Henry W. Jaghai, OD, JP, which authorized her departure from Calcutta to Jamaica, for the journey into indentureship. May 26, 1905.

They boarded the SS Hindus destined for Jamaica on May 26, 1905. They had no idea which strange country (pardes) they were going to. Even if they were told the name, they would not possess the faintest clue where it was located on a map as they were uneducated and unaware of anything else around them but the simple agricultural village life that they had lived. Along with eight hundred and twenty jahaji-bhai (shipmates), Aaji and Aaja began their 2-month journey to pardes-Jamaica.

Abdulla	Adhin	Antar	Arjun
Babraji	Bachai	Bachan	Bachan
Bachmee	Badal	Baggo	Baichu
Baiju	Balai	Baldeo	Bandhoo
Bandhu	Baychoo	Behari	Bhagia
Bhagwan	Bhagwandeen	Bhagwandin	Bhola
Bhulai	Bismill	Bisoni	Buddhai
Budhai	Budhram	Budhu	Bulakan
Chatkan	Cheda	Chhatkan	Chhedi
Chintaman	Counsiia	Dalat	Dhouraj
Doohnath	Doojai	Dukhee	Durga
Durgasingh	Ganesh	Gazi	Ghoorao
Giridhari	Gopal	Gopi	Gujari
Gulab	Gulaba	Guptar	Jagasar
Jagessar	Jagmohan	Jagnandan	Jagrani
Jagroop	Jummi	Kandhai	Kanhai
Katarroo	Khubhur	Kulsuman.	Lachhu
Lachmin	Ladar	Lala	Laltoo
Mahabir	Mangari	Mangari	Manraj
Matai	Mathura	Mohan	Munesar
Munna	Munsi	Nageshar	Naipal
Narain	Narpat	Nirahu	Panchan
Pandohi	Parandi	Parbatia	Parsad
Puran	Puran	Raamautar	Raghubir
Rahiman	Raghunath	Ramautar	Rambali
Ramcharan	Ramdass	Ramdat	Ramdeo
Ramdhin	Ramdial	Ramdulari	Rameswar
Ramguli	Ramharakh	Ramjas	Ramkhelawan
Ramkunwar	Ramlall	Rammangal	Ramsaran
Ramsarup	Ramsunder	Roshan	Rupa
Saddal	Sadhai	Sampat	Samser
Sangam	Sapalia	Sardhar	Sarjoo
Sarju	Seosahai	Shankar	Sitalia
Sitaraam	Sitaram	Sitloo	Sookia
Sookraj	Soondar	Suddhoo	Suenaught
Sukhai	Sundaria	Surajbali	Sutal

Reference. : The Data of Names are retrieved from Archives of Jamaica

There was an interpreter on board to help with the communication process. Aaji described how they were placed into groups of 20 and a sardar (leader) was appointed from each group. Unmarried men were separated from unmarried women by placing each group in separate cabins on either end of the ship while married couples occupied the middle cabins.

The first time she and Aaja were seeing the sea and they were scared. They were anxious about the passage, worried about the families they left behind and uncomfortable with the every day life on the ship. Aaji related the ship story over and over and every time the information sunk deeper and deeper in to my brain just like anchored separately trying to find as strong hold in to the sand.

As time passed, my grandparents became more comfortable with the daily routine aboard the vessel. They also formed new friendships with other jahaji-bhai (ship- mates) in their group. Caste barriers had broken down in this environment of communal living that the emigrants were exposed to. Aaji would call out names of their ship mates and later through my research; I retrieved the list of their jahaji-bhai from the Jamaica Archives (Appendix X).

My grandmother said everyone was homesick, but the camaraderie among the jahaji-bhai and the practice of their cultural and religious activities kept them going. My Hindu grandparents chanted their morning and evening prayers, sang birha (lamentation songs), danced nachania and janghia, and told kissa to their jahaji-bhai to make life more tolerable.

When the seas were calm, the husbands would congregate on the deck, interacting with their fellow jahajis. At this time, the wives would be together below deck. They told stories to comfort one another, sang, played instruments and danced. This time spent led the wives to form lifelong bonds.

Autaria	Ajnasia	Anandi	Balwanti	Balwantia	Batasoo	Bipti
Biranjen	Bitta	Brichitra	Buddhai	Chuni	Elaichi	Fahima
Gangajali	Gayarsi	Geni	Gugli	Hubraja	Husrani	Indrani
Jagdai	Jagrani	Jamuna	Jhinki	Kabastra	Kaonli	Kubitra
Lagni	Lakhrani	Luchminia	Maharaji	Mahraji	Manraj	Mitania
Nasiban	Parandai	Patia	Raghuni	Rajdai	Rajwanti	Ramdai
Ramdaiya	Ramkali	Rukhma	Rukhrarn	Rupa	Sahjadi	Sheorani
Shewrani	Sirpalia	Sukhdai	Sukhdia	Sunia		

List of Married Women aboard SS Indus.

As Aaji's pregnancy progressed, she became more and more uncomfortable and prayed for a quick end to the journey. Three weeks before the ship reached Jamaica, my Uncle Ramjas was born. My Aaja told Autaria that it was a good sign for the star to a new and successful life. The birth of Ramjas had replaced my grandparents' anxieties and worries with happiness and hopes of a bright future.

On July 27, 1905, the vessel docked at Port Maria, St. Mary, Jamaica. A Protector of Immigration came on board to inspect the ship's conditions and question the immigrants about their journey. My grandparents along with their jahaji-bhai were taken ashore.

End of one journey and the start of another

Boat carrying few Indian indentured workers from ship to Old Harbour Coast while hundreds of liberated slaves look on (recreated scene, 1995, courtesy of JCDC.

Tasa Group performs

Henry Jaghai and Ramadhar Maragh enjoying the entertainment

A large section of the crowd.

PremaSatsangh Group performs

Priest (Ramnarain Maragh) encouraging the immigrants (Henry Jaghai, Maniram Prashad, Mattai family and others) recreated scene 1995.

To the plantation

Autaria told me that once they were on shore, they went through further processing. She and Jaghai, along with twenty of their jahaji-bhai were assigned to work at Hillside Estate in Vere, Clarendon, owned by James Harvey. They were taken to the estate by horse and mule driven carts.

The married ladies began to weep due to the anticipation of no longer seeing each other and having others to relate to. Despite the distances between plantations, these ladies were often able to meet again during cultural gatherings.

Journey to the estate

CRe-enactment commemorating the 150th Anniversary in 1995 of the first landing of East Indians in Jamaica on May 10, 1845. The first set of immigrants who came to Jamaica, arrived on May 9, 1845 on the Blundell Hunter which docked in Morant Bay and on the next day, sailed to Old Harbour Bay for disembarkation. They were then transported to various sugare states (Recreated scenes, 1995; courtesy JCDC.)

On arrival at the estate, Aaji said she and Jaghai were happy to see familiar faces. Some of the workers there were villagers from their hometown who had been recruited two years earlier. These workers were Ahrull, Bhanna, Chatkan, Dataram, Hukamarain, Ibrahuni, Isar, Janki, Kalu, Lalwai, Lukha, Llolal, Lomdari, Lalig, Lorrhisingh, Mohansingh, Nala Bakhsh, Nano, Naurla, Rupan, and Sardarsingh. The other immigrants were sent to other plantations in different parishes. (Appendix III).

Plantation life

East Indians Cutting Sugar Cane
Courtsey : Dr. Rakesh Kumar Dubey, Varanasi, India

Indian Banana Farmer
http://www.thehindu.com/news/national/karnataka/when-a-businessman-takes-to-farming/article3474098.ece

East Indians carrying bananas
http://www. cookiesound. com/2013/04/in-the-middle-of-the-fruit-vegetable-wholesalemarket-of-kolkata-india/

By the second week in the new country, Aaji said she and Aaja realized that things were not turning out to be what the arkatia (recruiter) had promised.

She lamented that from Monday to Saturday they had to work for nine hours every day. They had to clear and weed the land, plant and harvest not only sugarcane but also banana, cocoa, and coffee. They also planted rice . They were paid weekly; Aaja received one shilling and Autaria nine pence.

Rice field in Bahadurpur, India

During the indentureship period, Autaria and Jaghai along with other immigrants lived in barracks, high off the ground. Aaji complained that it was a very uncomfortable situation. Their barrack was overcrowded, hot, and lacked proper ventilation and proper sanitation. She said many nights she would cry and lament about the life she left behind. Jaghai, though also disappointed, never complained. Instead, he wished for the five years to finish quickly so that he could return home.

Indian barrack in Golden Grove, St. Thomas

A union hospital built in the 1870s in Golden Grove, St Thomas addressed the health needs of the indentured workers

Autaria said they were allowed to do backyard gardening which provided them with the fruits and vegetables they were used to eating. The seeds they had brought with them were shared among each other. Soon, they had thriving gardens with ban ghobi (cabbage), bodi (long bean), caraillie (bitter melon), bagie (callaloo), matar (peas), and baigan(eggplant).

Since they worked for such long hours six days a week, Autaria related that on Sundays, the immigrants and their families would go to the nearby Salt River in Clarendon to wash their clothes and have a proper bath.

Indian Women Washing Clothes In River
http://blogs. dnvgl. com/sustainability/2015/02/sustainable-development-reflections-ranging-winter-clad-switzerland-buzzing-vibrant-india/

Completion of indentureship

Aaji related that in 1910 when the contract was up for their batch, some of the workers returned to India, others migrated to Cuba and Trinidad, but the majority remained in Jamaica and started families. She said Jaghai signed up for another five- year period. Although they had been disillusioned at the beginning, after having spent the first five years, they agreed that by spending another five, they would earn more money to go back home and live comfortably. The rest of the jahaji-bhai who remained with Autaria and Jaghai, formed a close bond and became life-long friends.

Jaghai was frugal and had saved most of his indentureship pay. By the end of his second contract, he was able to purchase two heifers. Both the busha and the headman on the estate where he worked gave their permission for his cattle to graze on the canal bank. Soon his cattle rearing business was growing and so was his family. Aaja and Aaji had three more children: two sons, Chunmun and Abraham and a daughter, Ethlyn.

Cattle rearing and dairying

Jaghai was from the Ahir caste, known for their expertise in cattle rearing and dairy farming business and he applied his expert skills to his own business. My grand- mother would always remind me of the cow's sacredness and that to eat the meat was forbidden; Jo cheez hume zinda rakhti hai us cheez ko hum kaise maar saktehai? ("How could you want to kill and eat something that keeps you alive?") She would ask. It is interesting to note that although she spoke in Hindi, I could perfectly understand her and when I spoke in English she could perfectly understand me, but neither could she speak fluent English, nor could I speak fluent Hindi.

The revered cow, which took nine months just like humans to reproduce, provided in so many ways. First and foremost, the milk gave sustenance to the body. The bullocks ploughed the land; they also pulled the carts to accomplish daily tasks. The cow's urine was used as a natural pesticide and its manure as a natural fertilizer. The goobar(cow's dung) mixed with clay was used to plaster the walls of houses. The dung was also lit as a repellent against mosquitoes. The goobar was used as fuel for cooking.

There were other Indians involved in cattle rearing and/or dairying apart from my grandfather Jaghai, including Adbul, Arjun, Badal, Bagaloo, Bankasingh, Bhalai, Bho- la, Budram, Chutkan, Fray, Gallow, Gulgul, Guptal, Guyahdeen, Hagaroo, Harpaul, Hoorie, Jagasar, Jumai, Malgie, Maragh, Muckutt, Persaud, Purranda, Raamdanie, Raamotar, Rajie, Ramragh, Samai, Sarjue, Siddo, Soberan, Suckie, and Sunaugth.

Indian Woman Milking Cow

Indian settlements after indentureship

Aaji spoke about other Indian settlements which had developed after the indentureship period had ended. She had heard about them from her jahaji-bhai. The largest settlements were in St. Mary and Westmoreland followed by Clarendon (where they lived), then St. Thomas and Portland.

Aaji said all of the immigrants made their houses similar to the ones in India. They intertwined bamboo to form the framework of the building, then, mixed goobar (cow dung) with clay and covered the structure with this paste. They used this same mixture to paste the floors. The roof was made of thatch. I learned later that the term used for this finishing process, was wattle and daub.

A better life

Aaji smiled as she recalled how their fate turned around and they were finally beginning to see some light at the end of a dark tunnel. Aaja's cattle business flourished and he needed more space for his animals. From his savings throughout the years, he bought fifteen acres of land in Mitchell Town, Clarendon, not too far from the estate where he had worked. Here, he settled with his family.

A few years later, although Jaghai was doing well, he wanted to move into the urban area where he could command better prices for his goods. Accustomed to taking risks, he sold what he had established in Mitchell Town and relocated to Mona Commons, St. Andrew. Busha Davis, the landowner there leased him property that extended from Hope Road to Mona Road. Accompanied by his family, workers and herd of cattle, Aaja made the arduous journey by mule carts from Mitchell Town to Mona. The trip lasted two days and two nights.

Once there, work immediately resumed, with Jaghi supervising the dairy farming and Autaria, the planting of vegetables namely matar (cowpeas), and tambaku (tobacco). When there was adrought in the area, all the other immigrant farmers would congregate at Jaghai's place and along with the pandit, sing and pray all night for rain to come.

Aqueduct at te University of the West Indies, Mona, Jamaica

My grandfather increased his workforce by employing six ex-indentured workers who had decided to remain in Jamaica but who did not want to enter into another contract with plantation owners. These workers were Bansee, Bhola, Guru, Jabur, Juhlur and Ragu. Jaghi allowed them to live on his property while they tended to his cattle. These workers also belonged to the Ahir caste. After a hard day's work, they would gather to entertain Jaghai, his family and friends by playing the nagara drums and singing birha songs, reminiscent of their life in India.

Eventually, other Indians moved into the area and became Jaghai's neighbours, namely: Badal, Abibulha, Amair (Hosay maker), Andhu, Cayman, Cohen, Gaghee, Gajhai, Gidya, Gulfarm, Guyadeen, Latchman, Kaldhal, Kanhai, Kibia, Kon, Magal, Madhu Singh, Malahoo, Malgie, Mannie, Manowgie, Munnu, RamBaccas, Ramdeen, Ramjeawhan(Sammy), Ramlakan, Sudial, Tantia, Willie and Cohen (sons of Andru).

With this newly developed Indian community, they kept the culture alive by celebrating traditional Diwali and Phagwah festivals of their motherland.

Aaji said Aaja was finally feeling that he was achieving his dream of economic prosperity. He constantly thought about his parents and his brother, but having his own family and having adapted to the ways of this pardes (strange country), going back to India to live, did not seem as a possibility anymore.

Autaria chuckled as she related a kissa. She said ever since his arrival from India, Jaghai always wore a dhoti (a white rectangular piece of cloth wrapped about the waist and legs).

One Saturday evening, he decided to be daring and dress like an Englishman. He dressed in a pair of trousers borrowed from his son, Ramjas, and went out to Papine Square for his usual social evening drink of dharu (rum).

Aaji says she does not know what happened to him. It might have been the influence of the dharu or the strange sensation of the unfamiliar pants or both - who knows? He lost control of his usual calm composure and became very unruly, resulting in the police at Papine Square locking him up.

On Monday, he was tried at Half-Way Tree Petty Session Court and fined 5 shillings, which was paid by Ramjas, his eldest son.

My grandfather was so annoyed with his behaviour and believing that pants were responsible for his rowdy action, went home and burned them. He never wore another pair again.

An East Indian man dressed in dhoti

My Aaja and his family prospered at Mona until his death in 1929 at the age of 49. He was buried on the land where he lived and worked. His grave lies under a Guinep tree, near Taylor Hall at the University of the West Indies, Mona.

Seventy-eight years after his death, the university held a service to commemorate the life of my Aaja, who had contributed to the historical landscape of the campus.

Commemoration ceremony

Grand and great grandchildren of Jaghai in attendance at the commemoration ceremony held in honour of Jaghai, at the University of the West Indies, Mona, Jamaica in 2007

Back Row (L-R): Tira Jaghai (great great granddaughter), Marcia Jaghai (great granddaughter - in -law).
Front Row (L-R): Shari Williams (great great granddaughter), Alex Jaghai (great great grandson), Mark Williams (great grandson - in -law).

Back Row (L-R): Matthew Williams (great great grandson), Andrea Williams (great granddaughter), Tira Jaghai (great great granddaughter), Alex Jaghai (great great grandson), Mark Williams (great grandson – in –law). Front Row (L-R): Alicia Bahadur (great great granddaughter), Barbara Bahadur (great granddaughter), Ali Bahadur (great grandson – in –law), Audrey Arjun (great granddaughter).

Henry W. Jaghai, grandson of Jaghi and his three colleague Justices of the Peace at the Commemoration Ceremony held in honour of Jaghi, at the University of the West Indies, Mona, Jamaica in 2007 (L-R): Wilbert Taloo J, Henry W Jaghai, O. J, Elvena Reittie, JP, Richard Pandohie JP

Grand and greatgrand children of Jaghi in Attendance at his Commemoration Ceremony held at the University of the West Indies, Mona, Jamaica in 2007.
Front Row (L-R): Harry Jaghai (grand-son), Derrick Edwards (greatgrandson), Myrtle Jaghai (granddaughter-in-law).
Back Row (L-R): Doreen Sirjue (great granddaughter), Miriam Edwards (granddaughter).

Autaria's struggle

After Jaghai's death, Busha Dolphie, the new land owner gave Aaji and Ramjas notice to leave the land as he wanted it to rear and breed racehorses. With Aaja gone, my Aaji and my uncle had to carry on the family business. They leased 50 acres of land in Cherry Gardens from Mr. Drurie. The land extended from Barbican Road to Norbrook. There they reestablished their cultivation and dairying.

Eventually, my uncles started their own families. Ramjas got married to Sarne and had Gina, their daughter. Chunmun, his brother, got married shortly afterwards to Adelyn Bhalai. Their union produced a daughter Miriam, who was born in April 1926 and subsequently Viola, Fenk, Roy and Richard were born.

After a few years, Chunmun decided to leave the extended family home to go to Kemps Hill, Clarendon with his family. He gained employment with a plantation owner of a sugar estate.

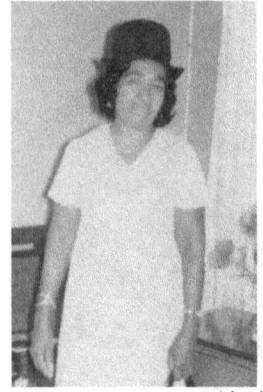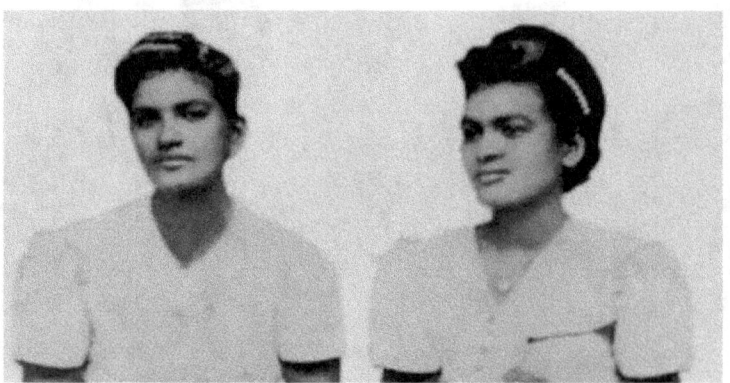

Jaghi's descendants: three of Chunmun's children. L to R: Viola Jaghai and daughter), Miriam Jaghai (granddaughter), Richard Jaghai (grandson) Virgini Jaghai (Gina - daughter of Ramjas) lived at Mona Estate with her parents and grandfather, Abrham Jaghi, in the 1920s.

Abraham, father of Henry W. Jaghai   *Henry W. Jaghai, son of Abraham*

In 1935, Abraham, Jaghai's youngest son, got married to Ambrozine Arjun, who joined family.

home in Cherry Gardens. As customary in Hindu culture, a stand-in father for the groom was required for the marriage ceremony to take place. Since Jaghai had passed away, his good friend and jahaji-bhai, Jaggernauth filled this role. With Chunmun's departure, Ramjas continued to care for the livestock, while the female family members prepared the land for planting, and cultivated ground produce. The latter activity helped to bring in extra income.

In 1935, Mr. Drurie gave Aaji notice to vacate the property. She moved again with her family and livestock to Waddle Pen, located behind King's House on Barbican Road. By then business had slowed down considerably and as a result, Aaji had to start selling out the livestock. Seeing their plight, that there was no guaranteed source of income and no permanent abode, Jaggernaut, the stand-in father for Abraham, offered to sell one of his properties at a reduced price of one hundred pounds to Aaji. This property was eight and a half(81/2) acres at 7Ford Pen Lane in Barbican, now known as Castle Heights.

Shortly after, misfortune befell Aaji's family. Ramjas, while riding his horse on the road, collided with a motor vehicle and sustained a serious injury that left him handicapped for the remainder of his life. His wife Sarne had died a few years before and now he was faced with this permanent disability. He had to use a walkng cane to move around.

With the loss of his ability to be productive, the onus was on the Jaghai women to bring in the income. My father, Abraham, was more of a carefree character and could not perceive the seriousness of the family's situation. Autaria and my mother began cultivating garden vegetables on her new land at Ford Pen Lane.

In January 1936, Abraham and Ambrozine had heir first son, Henry(me). Their second son, Harry, was born in 1938. After a few years, my father in search of his self-fulfillment decided to sign up or farm work in the United States. He secured a contract to work for six months at a time in Connecticut, USA.

Jaghai Family

From Left to Right: Charmela Esther Jaghai, Myrtle Jaghai, Ambrozine Jaghai, Abraham Jaghai, Henry W. Jaghai
Photograph showing three generations of Jaghi's descendants. Abraham's family from L-R Charmela Esther (daughter of Henry & Myrtle), Myrtle (grand daughter in law of Jaghi), Ambrozine (daughter-in-law of Jaghi, Abraham (son of Jaghi) and Henry (grandson of Jaghi)

Autaria's extended family structure was crumbling. In 1938, my Aunt Ethlyn got married to BiyaDaybedeen, but unfortunately, she died during childbirth.

With Autaria advancing in age and Ramjas handicapped, Ambrozine (Daata), my mother, decided to seek employment out side of the home to support the family. She worked with Mr. Cox, whose plantation was in Jacks Hill. Her earnings amounted to one shilling per day. Every

Friday when she got paid, on her way home she would stop at the local grocery store owned and operated by Mr. Yapp in Barbican Square and buy enough grocery to feed the family for one week.

Daata was the main income earner for Autaria's household. She worked day and night to make ends meet. Her responsibilities however, became so unbearable that in 1940, she took Harry (my brother) and moved to her parents' home in Ackee Walk, Denham Town. Arjun, her stepfather, who was a foreman with the Government Relief Program, promised her a job in the kitchen where she could earn more money. Daata, wanted to take me too, but my Aaji who I was attached to, refused to let me go.

Within a year, my mother came back and took me to live with her. The following year, Aaji Autaria died. She left me with so many kissa (stories), so many memories. When my father completed his farm work program, he reunited with my mother. The final addition to the family came with the birth of my sister, Henrietta, in 1944.

Descendants of Jaghi, Abraham's son Harry Jaghai and his family
Standing (L-R): Howard (great grandson), Harry (grand-son), Herman (great grandson), and Hanif (great grandson).

Henrietta (granddaughter of Jaghi) and her daughters (L-R) Donna and Karen (great granddaughters of Jaghi)

The Promise

As I conclude my dear Aaji's story-story of a pardesi shown through my eyes, I have flashbacks; flashbacks of her working hard all day planting crops, cooking, cleaning, and caring for her family. When the sun went down, and after dinner, she would sit under the maaro, (thatched roof) on her khatia (wooden stool) with me, the youngest, sitting in her lap and surrounded by my cousins, Miriam, Gina and Vie. It was at those times she would tell us kissa (stories).

My Aaji, had made me realize how poverty-stricken her village was and how hard life was for her and my Aaja. As young as I was, even then, I possessed that same impulsive and determined drive of my grandfather. I promised my grandmother that when I grew up, I was going back to their village in India. I wanted to see where she and Aaja had lived. I became committed to helping the people of her village.

To my Aaji Autaria: It may have taken me 46 years since I told you I would visit your home in India and another 27 years after, to help your village. However long it took, I still kept my promise.

Henry W. Jaghai and wife Myrtle standing in front of Jaghi's and Autaria's house in Bahadurpur, India, during their visit to the motherland in 1987

Henry W. Jagahai and wife Myrtle (standing beside Henry), surrounded by villagers of Bahadurpur, in the district of Basti, India, the place of origin of Jaghi and Autaria, (Henry's paternal grandparents). This was during their 1987 visit to the motherland.

Mind play

The promise was forever in my mind. It surfaced, it submerged, it resurfaced, it re-submerged. Throughout my entire life, this mind action kept repeating itself. How could I possibly achieve this? I was young, I was penniless. As the years passed by and the promise would come to my mind from time to time, I became more adept at keeping it at bay, so it wouldn't bother my conscience.

As fortune had shone on my grandfather in his midyears, it started to shine on me too. I could indulge in pastimes I loved, like horseracing and cricket without compromising my family's lifestyle. Every summer, I would travel to England for business and pleasure.

I watched the World Cup 60-Overs Series in 1975, 1979, and 1983 at Lords, England. When the announcement was made that the 1987 World Cup final would be played in India and Pakistan, the promise flashed across my mind bolder than t have ever done before. I played back scenes of my cousins and me listening intently to Aaji's kissa. I played back the scene of my telling her that I was going to India and that I would help her village. How could I ever find where they lived? In what way could I help the people of the Bahadurpur Village?

You could say it was divine intervention or some would say it was luck, but shortly after, Dr. Ajay Mansingh and Laxmi Mansingh, researchers and historians from India entered into my life. Through archive research, we were able to locate the immigration passes for Jaghai and Autaria, which detailed where they were from. The Mansingh's, along with their connections in India helped me find the village. The 1987 trip was definitely one filled with excitement about the cricket match but more so with anxiety and anticipation to finally see where my Aaji and Aaja had come from and where they had lived.

THE TRIP

In October 1987, my wife and I boarded a flight on British Airways to Heathrow, England. We did an overnight in London then took a flight on Air India, to Delhi Airport. At the cricket match in Delhi, we met up with Professor Mansingh and his brother in Lucknow. They escorted my wife and me to Bahadurpur village. As interpreters, they facilitated the communication process between us and the villagers of Bahadurpur.

As we began our journey from Lucknow, the first city we passed was an old one, Barabanki, which is about 25 kilo meters from Lucknow. After Barabanki, we passed through Faizabad, which is about 125 kilometres from Lucknow, then Ayodhya which is in the district of Faizabad. From there, we entered in to the district of Basti, which starts when you cross River Saryu.

Vikram Jot, Chawni, Harraiya, Kapath Ganj, and Maharaj Ganj were various small towns which we had passed along the way. After crossing Basti, we travelled on Bansi and Dumariya Ganj Roads up to 20 kilometres north, where we reached Bishun Purwa, which is 2 kilometres before we reached the town of Rudhauli.

Once we reached Rudhauli, we turned left. There were cane fields on both side of the road. After traveling another two kilometers we came upon the small village of Bahadurpur. I remember asking the driver to stop, so I could walk on the unpaved dirt road, to get a clear view of the place. The driver proceeded ahead of me while I continued walking towards the village. The car came to a stop where an elderly man was sitting on a khatia (wooden stool) on the side of the road, before the village's entrance.

I eventually caught up with them. We learned that the old man was the village councilor, also known as a Panchayat. Dr. Mansingh spoke with him in his native language, making inquiries about the whereabouts of the Jaghai family. He responded, pointing towards one of the houses. He said the house was unoccupied, as many years before, one of the Jaghai's son and his wife (my grandparents) had traveled out of the district. He told us that the other brother who remained behind had one son and one daughter, but the son died at an early age from a snake bite, the daughter had married and moved away from the village.

My wife and I decided to look around and meet some of the villagers. We were very saddened by the state of poverty that the people were living in, and felt the need to reach out and help these people. We met mostly women and children as the male villagers had gone to work in the fields. The Panchayat spoke to the villagers and advised them that we were visiting from another country. He related that we were there to inquire about our ancestors who had traveled to Jamaica in the 1800's. He gathered the women and children under a huge shady tree. My wife and I started distributing food items and money to the people. They were so grateful and thanked us repeatedly.

A relative of Jaghai and his mother, pose with Richard Francis of Jamaica receiving a copy of the book Pardes.

The trust fund

The East Indian counter parts who helped to establish the Jaghi-Autaria Scholarship Trust, pose for the camera in 2014. From L to R-Raghupati Kannaujiya (Gram Pradhan- elected village head), Rama Nand Yadav Mulayam (village elder), Ashutosh Dijan (coordinator) & Aleem Akhtar (politician and parliamentary election organizer)

After seeing the impoverished state of the village, I remembered the promise I had made to my grandmother and right there and then pledged to help the people. This came to fruition in December 2014. With the help and guidance of a loyal friend and advocate in India, Ashutosh Diljun, I have arranged for 12 scholarships of 5,000 rupees each to be awarded annually to children in need.

I have also arranged for a plaque to be erected in Bahadurpur, on a piece of land donated by Mr. Raghupati Kannaujiya (Gram Pradhan – village head). This plaque will be erected in honor of Jaghai and Autaria. I have also set up a trust fund to ensure that the money will be available for the next ten years to assist the children's educational needs. The following is a list of eligible candidates who were selected to receive the first scholarships from the Jaghai Trust Fund. These students were chosen from among farmers working in Bahadurpur.

The 12 pioneer recipients of the Jaghi & Autaria Scholarship

Dugesh Kumar; son of Gyan Das, 9 years old, Ahir caste
Ankit Kumar; son of Sanjay Kumar, 10 years old, Badhai caste
Anita Kumari; daughter of Jai Prakash, 11years old, Dhobi caste
Mohit Ram; son of late Ganga Ram, 13 years old, Dhobi caste
Raj Kumar; son of Rajendra Prasad, 10 years old, Dhobi caste
Ajay Kumar; son of Anil Kumar, 13years old, Kurmi caste
Amit Kumar; son of Ram Kewal; 10 years old, Chamar caste
Anoop Kumar; son of Ram Sajeeva, 7 years old, Chamar caste
Shalini Prakash; daughter of Om Prakash, 9 years old, Dhobi caste
Puja Mohan; daughter of Brij Mohan, 10 years old, Barai caste
Imran Waris; son of Kawmaal Waris, 6 years old, Muslim
Aafreen Waris; daughter of Ghulam Waris, 7 years old, Muslim

Ahir – cattle herders, Badhai – carpenter, Barai – cultivators, Chamar– leather tanners, Dhobi – washer people, Kurmi–farmers,

I am eternally grateful to the Mansingh family for all the time and effort they put in helping me to locate my ancestral village in India.

The scholarship awardees and their parents

We were very fortunate to have met a number of very kind and cooperative persons to guide us during our explorative visit, especially in the search of the village of my ancestors. Unfortunately, we did not make contact with any family members.

I could not have accomplished this task without the great assistance of four outstanding gentlemen. One is Raghupati Kannaujiya, the elected village head, also known as Gram Pradhan, who was very helpful in organizing the villagers and gained their cooperation in the selection of students for the scholarship. Another is Rama Nand Yadav Mulayam, village elder for the Ahir families in Bahadurpur. He is greatly respected by all the villagers who seek his advice on all matters of the village. The next gentleman to whom I am grateful, is Aleem Akhtar, politician and parliamentary election organizer. He was born in Bahadurpur, Gram Sabha, and was instrumental in gaining the cooperation of the Pradhans, in Bahadurpur.

Special thanks to my loyal friend and advocate Ashutosh Diljun, lawyer of Allahabad High Court, and son of Ravindra Nath Singh, for taking time out of his busy schedule to research and advise me on the best ways to assist the villagers in Bahadurpur. If it weren't for his help and guidance, I would not have been able to fulfill the promise I made to my Aaji.

Jaghai and autaria's memory live on in their home village of Bahadurpur, india

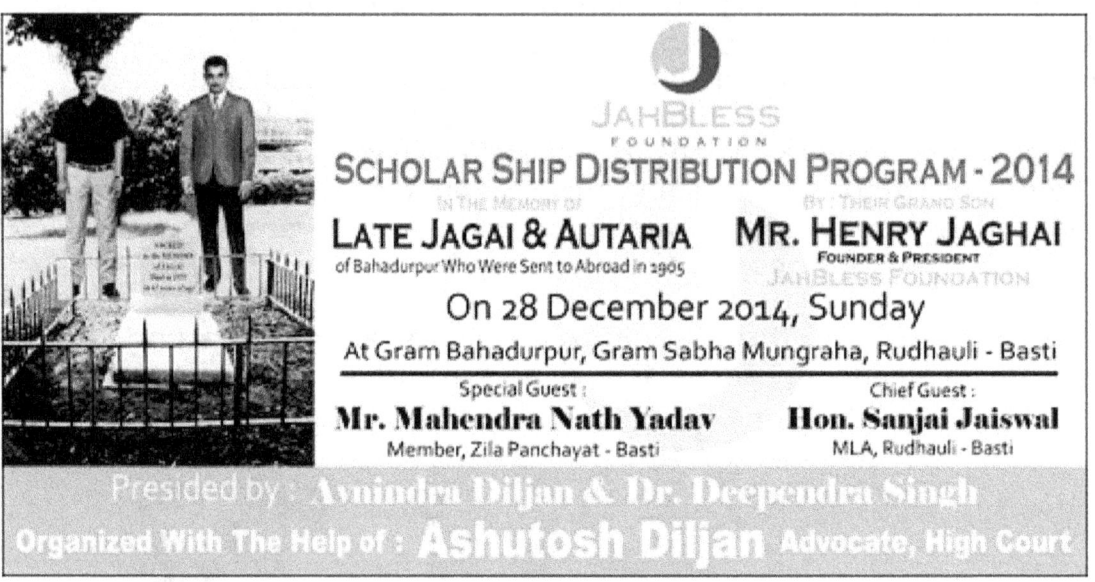

The Jahbless Foundation, brainchild of Rajesh and Kiranjit Bedi-Jaghai, great great grandson and great, great, granddaughter-in-law of Jaghi and Autaria, is responsible for the disbursement of scholar-ships to twelve children. The first disbursement was made on December 28, 2014.

Mr. Santosh Singh hands out scholarship money to one of the twelve recipients

Of the twelve recipients, one boy who is visually challenged received 5,000 more rupees than the other children did. This will help to pay for medical expenses for his upcoming surgery. Due to the great need for school supplies in the village, an additional 20 children were given 500 rupees each.

Several dignitaries attended the disbursement of scholarships on December 28, 2014 in the village of Bahadurpur, Lucknow, Uttar Pradesh, India.

In attendance were (L-R): The chief guest, Honourable Sanjai Pratsp Jaiswal (Member of Legisla- tive Assembly at U.P), Mahendra Nath Yadav (from Rudhauli), Member of Zila Panchay at Basti and President of Samajwadi Yuvjan Sabha at Basti (a youth outfit of the ruling Samajwadi Party in U.P), Avnindra Diljan (brother of Ashutosh Diljan coordinators of the event): Dr. Deependra Singh, Santosh Singh, Pradhan Raghupati Kannaujiya, Alim Akhtar Majhjhan and many others of Bahadurpur village.

NEWS PAPER ARTICLE ABOUT DISBURSEMENT OF SPONSORSHIP

Picture1: Daily News Paper "Amar Ujala" dated 29.12.2014. Article published in local news paper
Picture2: Enlarged image of article clipping

Lord Shiva Temple in Bahadurpur

Villagers in Bahadurpur

Female Villagers of Bahadurpur

Left to Right: Amravati Chaudhari, Tanu Chaudhari, Saloni Chaudhari, Mahima Chaurasia, Indravati Devi

Amarnath distributing sweets to the children of Bahadurpur

Female recipients: Krishana Devi, Indrawati Devi, Anara Devi, Radhika Devi, Gayattri Devi, Reeta Devi, Vidyawati Devi, Vittan Devi, Parvati Devi, Urmila Devi, Parvati Devi, Kismati Devi, Nirmala Devi, Manju Devi, Vidyawati Devi, Kislawati Devi, Keshav Devi

Male recipients: Gayan Das Yadev, Rajpat Kumar, Vans Raj Chaurasiya, Ram Milan Sharma, Ram Sabad, Mithailal Chaudhari, Hari Parshad Chaudhari, Shiv Parshad Chaudhari, Ram Naresh Chaudhari, Beepat Kannujiya, Ganpat Ram, Kapil Dev, Gharilal Chaudhari Pardhan

Children who received sweaters through the courtesy of Jaghai and Autaria's grandson Henry Jaghai O.D. J.P.: Shadab Rja, Meraj Aalam, Mo. Aarif, Palak, Shiv kumar, Arun kumar, Priyanka, Madhuri Sharma, Mamta, Payal, Anuj Kumar, Ramu, Anesh Kumar, Raj, Adersh Kumar, Durgesh Kumar, Mo. Sahil, Uma Bharti, Sheema Bharti, Priya, Ranya, Shalu, Raj Kumar, Aftab Rja, Nandini, Shasi Kumari, Shuhani, Kajal, Sufia, Anewar Rja, Adersh Kumar, Yuraj, Kishan Kumar, Nilam, Muskan, Anushka Sharma, Aman, Reema, Seraj, Nitesh Kumar, Kuldeep, Abhisekh, Rajesh Kumar, Kanchan, Nida, Jishan, Deepak Kumar, Mahek, Sumit Kumar, Shamu, at right is the school headmaster Mohamed Aslam.

Left to Right: Ganpat Ram Ji and Ghari Lal Pradhanji

Left to Right: BeepatKannujiya, Ghari Lal Pradhanji, Sunil

Head of Bahadurpur Village Gharilal Chaudhary presenting donation from JAHBLESS Foundation to from Left to Right: Gaytree Sharma, Seeja Devi, Priya Sharma, Rajesh Sharma, Mahavir Sharma, Dinesh Sharma

Bahadurpur Villagers

Richard Francis receiving gifts on behalf of Henry Jaghai from Ganpat Ram, Keshav Devi, Sadhana Devi, Parshuram Sharma

Ganpat Ram and Richard Francis of Jamaica with Akala Devi, the caretaker of the temple.

Wedding ceremony of Sunil and Laxmi June 20, 2018 at temple in Bahadurur Post Kohra district, In Basti village Bodwal Post Munerwa District Settlement

Sunil and Laxmi

Sunil and Laxmi with family members

Anil Kumar (extreme right) and family at his brother Sunil's wedding

Anil and his family in Bahadurpur which has 80 houses in the area

2019 Scholarship recipients pose for the camera. The circular stage around the peepal tree that the students are standing on also serve as a rest area for weary villagers.

A group of villagers standing next to peepal tree

Memorial plaque in front of temple construced by Henry W. Jaghai O.D., J.P

Villagers worshipping at the temple

Henry Jaghai and his wife Myrtle with Children of Bahadurpr Village, 1987

Journey From India to Jamaica

JAHBLESS FOUNDATION BHANDARA PROGRAM 2020

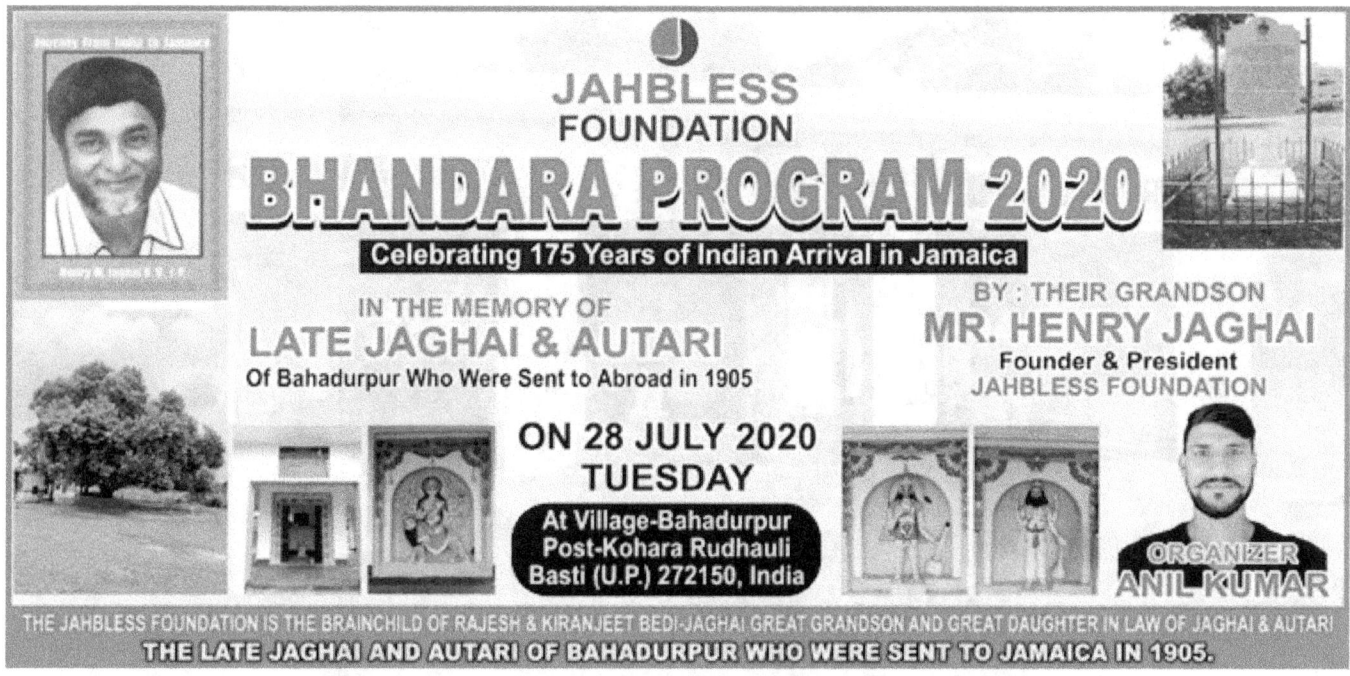

"Poverty was the greatest motivating factor in my life"
- Jimmy Dean
Henry W. Jaghai, O.D., J.P

I was born on January 5, 1936, to parents Abraham Jaghai of Cherry Gardens and Ambrozine Arjun of 58 & 1/2 Spanish Town Road in Western Kingston. When the midwife delivered me, she told my mother that I was going to be called Money Man because of the size of my large ears. It is uncanny to think that her words have come true. Since then, I have often wondered if people really have the gift to predict the future.

At the tender age of six weeks old, my mother and I relocated to 7 Fort Penn Lane in Barbican to live with my paternal grandmother, Atwari. She cared for me during the day while my mother ventured out to work. My mother worked tirelessly to give me the best life she could. Two years later, in 1938, with the birth of my little brother Harry, my mother decided to move back to her parents' home in Tewarie Land, now known as Tivoli Gardens. My mother was finding life to be increasingly difficult with my father's absence from home, as he was not involved in my upbringing. He was a sportsman who was more interested in his friends and enjoyed a single man's lifestyle. Just before our departure, my grandmother became very emotional and held tightly onto my hand, begging my mother to take only the little one and leave me behind with her. My mother agreed, and I remained behind with my grandmother, Atwari. In December 1940, at the age of four, my mother learned that my father was planning to give me away to the Alpha Orphanage. He'd decided to send me there, as it appeared I was now becoming a burden to my grandmother. Distressed to hear this news, she and my maternal grandfather, Nana Arjun, hired a car and went to the Smith Village Police Station, in Denham Town, to report this. The police gave my mother a letter and instructed them to go to the Halfway Tree Police Station and request a police officer to escort them to my grandmother's home to retrieve me. As they approached the house, I saw them and ran to my grandmother Atwari, and told her, "Daata come with police for me." When they came into the yard, they found me barefoot, dressed in an oversized shirt that reached my ankles, and drinking mar (the strained water of boiled rice) with rice. I was surrounded by poverty and squalor. Though my grandmother cared deeply for me and did the best that she could with the resources she had, she was getting up in age, and was very frail and sickly. When she learned the group was there to take me back to live with my mother, she held on to me fiercely and declared she would not let me go. The police explained that I needed to attend school for my education very soon, and that my mother also missed me. So, I went to live with my mother once again.

In 1942, my grandmother died. My mother and I, and two neighbors, Surajee and Gathai Dammar, took the tram car from the intersection of North Street and Orange Street, to King's House Road. We then walked through grassland to Barbican, where we attended the funeral. I can vividly remember someone lifting me up and passing me over her coffin three times. This was very heart-wrenching for me, as I was extremely close to her. Looking on, I recalled to memory that many a night, as a small child, she would reminisce about her life in India and the village she came from, Bahadurpur in Basti. She'd recount the many hardships she'd endured as well as the poverty that existed there. After listening to her many heartfelt stories, I made a promise to my grandmother that I would visit her village in India and help the children there. With the help of God I was able to fulfill my promise by awarding scholarships annually to the poor children, provided bedding supplies to the elderly, and built a temple in her and honor which is erected in her village.

My mother continued to work very hard and struggled to send me and my siblings to school. I acquired my rudimentary literacy skills at Ebenezer Elementary and St. Thomas Aquinas, now known as St. Richards. As the eldest, I had to assume greater responsibilities than my younger siblings. My academic progress suffered because of this, and at the age of 14 I stopped attending school. I started working around the house. My chores included working in the garden and caring for our livestock. I milked the cows, and Sunday mornings I would accompany my grandmother, Jaitun, to the shop piazza between Barry and Highborn Street, owned by Mr. Duhaney who had given us permission to use the space to sell callaloo, and other vegetables from Jaitun's garden. By 9 o'clock, we would walk along Laws Street to sell the remaining produce and then return to Parade to take the bus back to Chisolm Avenue.

I had always had an interest in law and would read the court cases in the local newspaper weekly. I would hustle selling bottles to earn money to buy the paper once a week. There were two prominent lawyers that I had come to admire. They were Norman Washington Manley and Jag Smith. The crown prosecutor was an Indian man by the name of Harold Ballysingh. It was my lifelong dream to become a lawyer, but unfortunately I could not pursue this dream due to poverty. Instead I decided to learn a trade in auto mechanics. This career path was due in large part to my grandfather Arjun, who encouraged me to become an apprentice mechanic at

Houranay's Garage. While working at the garage, I had to take the public bus service to go back and forth from work. I was often ridiculed by the passengers on the bus who would heckle me because of my dirty appearance from working with oil and grease during the day. I would often be told to go to the back of the bus. To avoid the shame and scorn I experienced during those trips, I decided to purchase a bicycle and told my mother of my plans. She said she would help me if I got some of the money, so I inquired about working next door at the Zaidie Tobacco Shop, on my lunch break. I got the job there sharpening the knives they used to cut the tobacco. I was able to earn extra money towards the purchase of my bicycle.

I continued working at the garage, earning two shillings a week. At the end of one year I decided to ask my employer if he would be willing to pay me a little bit more, as I was now more advanced in my craft. He promptly turned me out of his establishment, saying "don't come back!" I was now out of a job. "This was pure sufferation."

My grandfather, Arjun, began to get older, become sickly, and he wanted better for his family. So, I started searching again for work. I noticed an advertisement in the Gleaner newspaper by the British Honduras government, now known as Belize, for an agricultural program. It offered 50 to 100 acres of land for purchase to then cultivate. I was accepted into the program, but this required an initial investment that I could not afford, so I had to abandon that idea. .

Another subsequent venture was pursued by my grandfather Arjun, when he learned of an opportunity to attain two farm work tickets for myself and my uncle, Alfred. The cost was 100 pounds each. He did not have the necessary funds to purchase these tickets. Instead, he made the decision to mortgage his land to obtain the funds needed for us to go abroad to pursue the farm work opportunity. After waiting for over six months, we were not called to go abroad. He reported it to the police, then went to a lawyer, and was able to reclaim the title for his property, and this plan too was unsuccessful.

Still without a job, I had no other recourse but to hustle to make some money. I would go to my relatives' home in Barbican, and pick fruits such as mangoes and ackee. I would then peddle my produce to a local vendor who would in turn sell them to customers on the street side. This was how I was able to earn some money to help out the family at home.

In 1953, a spark of luck hit me when I met an Indian gentleman by the name of Herbert Maragh. Herbert knew of my difficulties finding work and knew of my auto mechanic skills. He was able to secure a job for me at John Crook Limited. There I earned 15 shillings per week. Finally, I'd found a reliable job that paid me a steady salary. Now I was able to start saving one pound per week at the Government Savings Bank on Tower Street. I was also able to save money by going to my mother's kitchen at lunchtime to get free lunch. By then, my mother was working in the kitchen as a cook, providing lunch to government workers. Her customers were laborers who worked the plantation fields, and the government compensated her for the meals they consumed. After leaving work at 5pm, I would continue to do odd jobs to earn extra money. I also worked privately fixing cars which further contributed to my savings. On one occasion, I recall that I had gotten a car to work on. When the work was complete, some friends and I decided to take it for a drive to Port Royal to enjoy a fish and bammy meal. On our trip back, I was at the wheel as we were going around Lightburn Corner, and the car suddenly flipped over. I sustained a fractured arm in the accident, and this marked the beginning of another streak of bad luck for me. With the hand still injured, I couldn't perform adequately, so I was soon terminated. From the end of 1953, I was out of a job, until 1966, when Herbert Maragh, for the second time, got me a job at Motor Sales as a full fledged mechanic. I was there for 11 years. From then, I never looked back. I must give thanks to my mother Ambrozine, my Nana Arjun, my Nani Mai and Herbert Butty Maragh who supported me during that period of unemployment.

My affiliation with St. Thomas Aquinas as an altar server of the church paved the way for a significant milestone in my life. It was there that I laid eyes on a church attendee, the fair maiden, Myrtle Hill Suckie of Whitehall Avenue, and was smitten by her beauty. I, at the young age of 18, asked Myrtle, at the tender age of 17, to marry me. We were wed on April 25, 1954.

Soon after, Myrtle and I were blessed with our first child, Charmela Esther. Sadly, Charmela was quickly called away from this mortal life in 1959. She was only five years old. We were devastated by the loss of our child, but we slowly found a way to resume our daily activities, while the pain lived on in our hearts. We later completed our family unit with the births of Barbara, Patrick, Andrew, Andrea, Peter and Paul.

Henry and Myrtle pose with their children
Standing L-R: Patrick, Henry, Andrew, Peter Sitting L-R: Andrea, Myrtle, Barbara

Marleykiah Agustus Williams (King) was instrumental in caring for Henry's and Myrtle's children and grandchildren. He was greatly loved by all family members. Back Row L-R Alicia holding Tiffany, Stacy holding Adam, Tira, Rajesh, Front Row L-R : Kingie, Shari, Sasha, Alex

BUSINESS SUCCESS

I was determined that my children would have an easier life than I did. In 1968, I worked hard and diligently and finally was able to establish my own garage and auto parts business, Jaghai's Garage Ltd. Initially, the company dealt exclusively with the sale of new and used auto parts for British made cars but as the global market changed, I extended the business operations to the sale of Japanese auto parts. The company, which over time engaged the services of all of my sons, flourished to become the leading auto parts dealer between 1970 and early 1990.

PASTIMES

With the business successfully established, I could finally afford to spend time on a hobby I loved - cricket. I had started playing schoolboy cricket when I was ten years old. This passion has remained with me throughout my life. In 1954, I formed the All Indian Cricket Team, assuming the roles of financier, manager and captain for a few years. The team competed in many local competitions and won several trophies - the most prestigious being the Rankin Cup.

In 1973, accompanied by a large contingent of family and friends as supporters, the team toured Trinidad and Guyana, where we won most of our matches. It was a good occasion where sporting, cultural and social activities merged to make the tour an unforgettable experience.

During my 1973 Trinidad and Guyana cricket tour with the Balraam Championship team, I met Dr Cheddie Jaggan, President of Guyana. Dr Jaggan and Dr Balwant Singh were particularly helpful in accommodating the team at the Ghandi Youth Organisation Center in Georgeton, Guyana.

In August 1973, my wife Myrtle and I, along with friends, went to Guyana, where we visited the homes of famous West Indian cricketers Rohan Kanhai and Alvin Kalicharan, in Port Morant in Berbice. The cricketers were away on tour, but we met with their families.

TRAVELLERS

Another well-loved pastime which Myrtle and I share is traveling. In fact, we are accomplished travelers - having toured London for twenty-five consecutive years.

In 1977 we visited the Leaning Tower of Pisa in Italy, rode the Gondola in Venice, stood before the Alps in Switzerland, went to the Eiffel Tower in France, passed through Austria and Belgium. Our North American sojourn took us to the states of Florida, Illinois, New York, and Pennsylvania.

Other international visits included India, Pakistan, the Republic of Trinidad & Tobago, the sunny isle of Puerto Rico and the lush South American country of Guyana.

My most memorable travel experience was my 1987 two-week trip to India. Myrtle and I watched World Cup Cricket in India and Pakistan. The matches were played at Delhi, Jaipur, Karachi, Kolkata, Lahore and Mumbai.

The trip also provided the opportunity to visit the ancestral home of my grandfather Jaghai.

Myrtle and I visited metropolitan city of Mumbai (Bombay), the Taj Mahal and Bird Sanctuary in Agra, the Maharani ace in the Pink City of the cultural capital Kolkata (Calcutta), the crowded city of Delhi, the picturesque Kashmir. Enjoyed musical show well performed by my Rakhi sister Polly Sookraj, whom I sponsored for voice training along with other overseas students in Delhi.

In Jaipur, we watched cricket, rode an elephant to the lookout point that used to be an English Fort and also rode a camel.

In Mumbai (Bombay), we watched the second cricket match, walked along the riverbank where we saw the Dhobi caste washing clothes. We also visited the horse racing track. We took a tourist boat from the Gateway of India and sailed across the Arabian Sea to Monkey Island.

Our next trip was to the mountainous region of Kashmir. We spent three days there on a houseboat. At nights it would get so cold, that we slept on hot water bags.

We went on to Pakistan where we watched the next cricket match in Karachi and another match in Lahore. We returned to the developed city of Delhi, watched more cricket and visited the horse racing track there.

Our last itinerary stop was Kolkata (Calcutta). At the Eden Garden Cricket Grounds, we watched the World Cup finals between England and Australia, with Australia emerging the winners. We visited the charitable Mother Theresa Orphanage, where we gave an offering. We paid a sentimental visit to the Calcutta (Kolkata) port from which my grandparents had sailed on the S.S. Indus in 1905.

Involvement in Sports

PIGEON RACING CHAMPION

Another hobby of mine was pigeon racing. I joined the Pigeon Club in the 1960's and remained an active member until it became defunct in the 1970's due to the mass migration of many of its members.

I had over 300 pigeons, which I bred and raced. In the 1960's, my pigeon, Chantilly, clocked the fastest time of 58 minutes, flying from Mandeville to Rosalie Avenue, Kingston, a record which to date has not been broken. In 1999, I, along with other pigeon racing enthusiasts decided to form a new club, which we named Jamaica Racing Pigeon Club (JRPC). Meetings were held at my Bombay Stud Farm. In 2000, the Jamaica Racing Pigeon Club was revived and I served as its president for that year. I contributed financially towards the purchase of the racing clocks for the club and assisted members with the transportation for the training of the birds.

I made my office on the farm available for meetings and special occasions during the life of the JRPC. I competed in several races spanning the length and breadth of Jamaica. In 2009, I entered and won most of the races organized by the club and was awarded the Champion Loft Trophy for the year. The Staff Van Reet and Black Diamond strains of pigeon were helpful in my winning the championship.

My other notable interest is my love for horses. My interest in horses was sparked, when my parents relocated to the intersection of Red Hills Road and Cassia Park Road in 1946. Every day as a youngster, I had to pass the stables of Tewfik Zaidie at 51 Red Hills Road and Reggie McKenzie, also on Red Hills Road across from the location of what is now Calabar High School. Reggie McKenzie was a jockey and trainer, whose daughter, Lola, also attended St. Thomas Aquinas Catholic School, now St. Richards. In the mornings on the way to school my group of friends and I would see horses grazing, and in the evenings, Lola would accompany us in to her father's stable and we would play with the horses. We became friends with the stable jockey, J. Latty and the grooms at the stable. Horse races were primarily held on holiday festivals, and we would walk behind the horses on the way to Knutsford Park to watch them race. Only top-class horses went to the races by truck. Some members of our group became jockeys: Lloyd Roberts, Pascal Brown, Bobby Graham, John Russell, Harry Jaghai, Cleveland Suckie, and Horatio Nelson, a champion jockey in 1960.

My father returned to Jamaica, and secured a job at Knutsford Park, and then in 1959 he relocated to the newly opened Caymanas Park under similar ownership. He would procure passes for us to watch the races. He became good friends with many trainers, even clocking horses during the morning. I told him my friends and I would like to purchase a horse. He identified a horse trained by Allan "Billy" Williams and owned by Dr. John Maserton, named Smiling by Clonleason-Chuckle. She was a three-year-old E class horse. Billy offered her to my father and we purchased her for £150 and renamed her Latchmie Ranee, she won six races for us. At this point we attended races very regularly.

I acquired my first horse farm on 25 acres in Spring Gardens, St. Catherine known as Rockmore Farm from trainer Ren Gonsalves in 1968. I already boarded Latchmie Ranee, Dainty Petal and Tuneful Goddess there. When I purchased the farm, I bought it with the stallion Jobber Bill along with two mares, Sheila and Scapper Floor. I then bought True Lover, Shenandoah and NRA as mares. I also bought Chantilly, My Love and Funny Cut from Orange Valley Estates. The terrain was very hilly and not suitable for horses.

My objective at this time was to breed horses to race myself. In 1972, I received permission from Bob Mayall as manager of the racetrack to build a 17-stall barn, and office on the compound. That barn was the best kept barn at Caymanas Park. My brother, Harry was from inception until now the trainer at the stable. His son, Howard is also a trainer at the barn currently. My son, Andrew trained horses at the stable in the 1980s. Horses that I bred and raced myself were given Indian names.

In 1976, I then purchased the former Supreme Farm at Bushy Park, St. Catherine on the advice of the farm manager Bobby Hayes. It was owned by Ivor Hosang. The farm was on 14 acres of land. I acquired a further adjoining 6 acres, making it 20 acres in total. I named the farm Bombay Stud Farm. At the farm, I had A class mares; Polka Dotty, Glory's Mariposa, Chan Chan, Miss America, Paddy's Doll, Late Moon, Story Time, and Wrong Reason. Close Call was the first stallion that stood at the farm. I then imported Big Prince to stand as a stallion, as well as local top-class racer Reca. Reca won the Jamaica Derby, Governor's Cup, and the Gold Cup. I subsequently purchased him and won four races with him including the Guiness Mile and Mark Twain Trophy. At this farm, we produced 1989 1000 Guineas winner Lady Geeta, 1980 Governor's Cup winner Shady Grove, along with A class winners Tulsie Kumar, Lashanda's Devil and Lady Vasanti. Other useful performers were Lady Maharanee, Sir Henry Kumar and many others. At Bushy Park we held many Indian functions filled with good memories.

In 1990, I transitioned from being a hobby breeder to a commercial breeder by procuring the Family Farm in Grange, St. Catherine on 111 acres. The farm was owned by Bobby Clarke and his father-in-law Sydney Maragh. I had already sent six mares to be covered by the stallion Restless Thief, and boarded them there. Bobby Clarke notified me that the farm was to be sold, which led to me acquiring it. I also purchased most of the stock there, including the two stallions, Restless Thief and Joe Slew, and about fifteen mares including Music Belle, Glen Afric, Nicolina, Sky Train, and Babydun. I brought Big Prince along with the remaining mares from Bushy Park. I purchased many other mares both locally and imported from the United States. I imported Sir Lal Bahadur as a stallion followed by Holy Runner, Footloose, Legal Process and War Marshall.

At this farm we produced 2007 Superstakes winner, Major Mayer and 2008 Triple Crown winner Alsafra, who won the Derby, St. Leger, 1000 Guineas and also the Oaks. Other classic winners were Shady Grove (1980 Governor's Cup), Lady Geeta (1989 1000 Guineas), Lady Bangalore (1998 Oaks), Latonia (2004 1000 Guineas and Oaks), Run Papa Run (2004 St. Leger), Rum Talk (2007 2000 Guineas and St. Leger), Al Fouzia (2010 1000 Guineas), Niphal (2011 1000 Guineas), Big Man Boyu (2011 2000 Guineas), Lady Abhijita (2013 Oaks), and I Am Di One (2019 1000 Guineas). Governor's Cup winners were Run Papa Run in 2004, and It Is I in 2008. We also had success in Trinidad, breeding Flying Millie a multiple Grade-1 winner, and Legally Ready 2011 W.I. Bred 2yo Fillies Championship winner. We also raced Sir Rajah Raeby, Lady Bangalore, Sir Mohandas Baba, Sir Gobin Harrilal, Lady Baroda and Lady Jaipur in Trinidad. My trainers in Trinidad were Desmond Sagar and Neal Maharaj, and my agent was Rolf Bartolo.

I won the Champion Breeder Award 10 years. Of these 10 years, 8 were consecutive from 1997 to 2004, and then again in 2007 and 2008. In 1999, I won the most ever races as a breeder with 105 wins. In 1997, I received the None Such Award and in 2004 was inducted into the Jamaica Racing

Hall of Fame. For the first 50 years of horse racing at Caymanas Park, I was the All Time Leading Breeder by stakes earned. As a breeder, I have won over 1500 races.

The names I have given my fillies are Lady Abhijita, Lady Agra, Lady Ajiban, Lady Aleema, Lady Anandi, Lady Anarkali, Lady Arti, Lady Atwaree, Lady Bahin, Lady Bakul, Lady Ballari, Lady Bangadesh, Lady Bangalie, Lady Bangalore, Lady Bansari, Lady Baroda, Lady Basti, Lady Basanti, Lady Bastipur, Lady Chachi, Lady Chameli, Lady Chandra, Lady Chandrika, Lady Chatura, Lady Chiriya, Lady Danragie, Lady Devi, Lady Diwali, Lady Dularie, Lady Faizabad, Lady Gangadeo, Lady Gauri, Lady Geeta, Lady Geetadeo, Lady Gorakhpur, Lady Hyderabad, Lady Indira, Lady Jaanwar, Lady Jagranee, Lady Jagrati, Lady Jaipur, Lady Jameela, Lady Jamuna, Lady Jayshree, Lady Kaloutie, Lady Kamla, Lady Kampoor, Lady Kanchan, Lady Kumari, Lady Lachmin, Lady Latika, Lady Madras, Lady Maharanee, Lady Mala, Lady Maragin, Lady Nagara, Lady Nagin, Lady Najariya, Lady Najeeban, Lady Nanda, Lady Noorie, Lady Pakeezah, Lady Parbattie, Lady Phagwah, Lady Pooja, Lady Punjab, Lady Punjabi, Lady Radha, Lady Rajkumari, Lady Rakwalaay, Lady Ramkali, Lady Ramragie, Lady Rattapur, Lady Rukmini, Lady Rupamani, Lady Sabita, Lady Saburi, Lady Sapna, Lady Sattie, Lady Seeta, Lady Seetadeo, Lady Shabani, Lady Shalimar, Lady Shakeera, Lady Shanti, Lady Shareeda, Lady Sharmeela, Lady Sharvani, Lady Silsila, Lady Suhaagraat, Lady Suneeta, Lady Suraanee, Lady Suragie, Lady Tarkari, Lady Tulasi, Lady Vasanti, Lady Janakpur, Lady Pujarie, Lady Gobindia, Lady Sarsutta and Lady Seetarani. The colts are Tulsie Kumar, Sikhandar, Sir Abbas Mangal, Sir Ananda Baba, Sir Arjun Babu, Sir Badri Bansilal, Sir Banbihari, Sir Bhola Baba, Sir Chacha Baba, Sir Ganesh Baba, Sir Ganga Kumar, Sir GobinHarrilal, Sir Henry Kumar, Sir Jaadu Baba, Sir Jhunjhun Wala, Sir KedarRamlal, Sir Kishore Kumar, Sir Kisson Lal, Sir Krishna Baba, Sir Kunjabihari, Sir Mohandas Baba, Sir Mohan Gopal, Sir Muni Brijmohan, Sir Pardasie Baba, Sir Raja Kumar, Sir Rajah Raeby, Sir Rajesh Pattasar, Sir Rama Tulsidas, Sir Ramjas Jagdeo, Sir RamjasRamlal, Sir Ramnath Gupta, Sir Ravi Sankur, Sir Rohan Baba, Sir Rohanlal Baba, Sir Rohan Tulsidas, Sir Sadhu Baba, Sir Sastri Bahadur, Sir Shankar Dada, Sir Thakur Baba, Sir Vishnu Kumar, Sir Jagat Baba, Sir Ram Sundar, Sir Jeewan Babula, Sir Lal Beharie, Sir Ram Hari, Sir Jahaji Bhai, Sir Hajarie Baba, Sir RagbarBapi, Sir Ganga Jamuna, Sir Anil Tilakram, Sir Sunil Bhaijee and Sir Chowtie Lal.

Indo-Jamaican Racehorse Trainers

Troy Alexander	Rudolph Hardial	Aubrey Maragh	Barrington Rambally	Errol Subratie
John Amritt	Andrew Jaghai	Collin Maragh	BabuRamsingh	Gary Subratie
Phillip Amritt	Harry Jaghai	Shamir Maragh	Louis Richards	Cleveland Suckie
Steve Budhoo	Howard Jaghai	Alfred McIntosh	Derrick Roman	Henry Suckie
Wesley Charoo	LazelKwalsingh	Kenrick McIntosh	Cashbert Singh	Frederick Watson
Armstrong Chutkan	Clive Logan	Harry Parsard	Dalton Sirjue	Andy Williams
Hanif Darby	Mark Manasseh	Ian Parsard	Harry Sital	Luddy Williams

Indo-Jamaican Racehorse Jockeys

I. Adjmul John Amritt
GerryBaccas Sylvester Baccas

Douglas Badaloo
DelroyBeharie
Derrick Bisasor
Shaun Bridgmohan
Roderick DaCosta
Sammy Douthall
Wesley"Calaloo"Henry
Daniel Gazader
AlexanderGopie
N. Hepburn
Raphael Jagoo
BertranManchan
Collin Maragh
Reggie Maragh
Shamir Maragh
Vasell Najair
Lester Rambaran
Andre Ramgeet
Patrick Ramsay
Robert Ramsay
S. Rowe
Emmanuel Satal
LearieSeecharan
Vishnu Singh
Kenrick Sirjue
Cleveland Sukie
Marlon Sukie
Omar Walker*
Percival Williams*
Andre Worrie

A. Bailey
Alvin Bisasor
Jermaine Bridgmohan
Aaron Chatrie
James Douthall
Frankie Fraser
Wilmott Gajardah
Rayan Gazader
Winston Griffiths *
Harry Jaghai
Daniel Langott
Allen Maragh
Rajiv Maragh
Romero Ramsay Maragh
Tony Maragh
G. Narinesingh
Andrew Ramgeet*
Derrick Ramgeet
PaulRamsay
Alphonso Reid
M. Satchell
Gilbert Searchwell
Augustus Siddeo
Ian Sirjue
Clifford Stewart
Danush Sukie
H. Timol
GaryWilliams
Joseph Woodit

LADY PAKEEZAH

Lady Pakeezah (R. Parish) 50.5 is met by members of Bombay Stud Farm (owners) after victory in the 3 yo & upwards (Allowance) 1 mile on Saturday 26th ugust 2000. The 3 yo by restless Thief - Run Marisa Run, trained by H. Jaghai posted time Was 1:41:4.
Standing L-R: Howard Lyn, Rupert Maragh, Howard Jaghai, Henry W Jaghai O.D., J.P., John Khan, Frederick Watson, and Basil Murray

Sir Rajah Raeby a 3.y.o. Bay Colt by Restless Thief - Run Marisa Run (with jockey Richard Mitchell) is met by members of Bombay Stud Farm (owners) after victory in a 3.y.o. Restricted Allowance Event, after going 6 Furlongs in a time of 1:12.3 on Saturday the 27th of July 1996. He is bred by Henry W. Jaghai O.D., J.P. and trained by Harry Jaghai. Standing **L to R**: John Khan, Earl Guyah, Henry W. Jaghai O.D., J.P., Frankie Fraser, Dr. Junior Gallow, Annmarie Singh, and Shawn Williams.

Sir Mohan Gopaul a 2.y.o. Ch. Colt by Restless Thief – Lady Anandi (with jockey Andrew Ramgeet) is met by members of Bombay Stud Farm (owners) after victory in the Andrew H.B. Aguilar 8 Furlong race in a time of 1:41.2 on Wednesday 13th December 1995. He is bred by Henry W. Jaghai O.D., J.P. and trained by Wayne DaCosta. Standing **L to R**: Hanif Superchard singh, Vijay Thompson Henry W. Jaghai, O.D., J.P., Wayne DaCosta, and John Khan.

Sir Kishore Kumar a 3.y.o. Bay Gelding by Joe Slew – Music Belle (with jockey Andrew Ramgeet) is met by members of Bombay Stud Farm (owners) after victory in a 3.y.o. Maiden going 5 Furlongs Straight in a time of 1:00.3 on Saturday the 20th of November 1999. He is bred by Henry W. Jaghai O.D., J.P. and trained by Harry Jaghai. Standing **L to R**: Derrick Datadeen, Omar Dilmohammed, Barrington Simpson, Henry W. Jaghai O.D., J.P., Peter Singh, Howard Jaghai, Rupert Maragh, Orville Suckie, Basil Murray, Frederick Watson.

Sir Kisson Lal a 3.y.o. Ch. Colt by Restless Thief – Lady Rupamani (with jockey Allen Maragh) is met by members of Bombay Stud Farm (owners) after victory in a race run on June 17, 2000. He is bred by Henry W. Jaghai O.D., J.P. and trained by Collin Maragh. Standing **L to R**: Collin Maragh, Rajiv Maragh, Rajkamal Maragh, Wally Byroo, Groom, Henry W. Jaghai O.D., J.P., Patrick Jaghai, Wendy Maragh and Howard Lyn.

SIR RAMNATH GUPTA

Sir Ramnath Gupta a 3.y.o. Ch. Gelding by Restless Thief – Acetylene (with jockey LearieSeecharan) is met by members of Bombay Stud Farm (owners) after victory in the Hugh Levy Trophy going 6 ½ Furlongs in a time of 1:23.2 on Saturday, October 6, 1999. He is bred by Henry W. Jaghai O.D., J.P. and trained by Harry Jaghai. Standing **L to R**: Howard Jaghai, Henry W. Jaghai O.D., J.P., Cecil Singh, Frederick Watson, Rohan Basati and Patrick Jaghai.

SIR SASTRI BAHADUR

Sir Sastri Bahadur a 3.y.o. Bay Gelding by Sir Lal Bahadur – Lady Radhika (with jockey Andrew Ramgeet) is met by members of Bombay Stud Farm (owners) after victory in a 3.y.o. Maiden going 9 Furlongs and 25 Yards in a time of 2:00.2 on November 17, 1999. He is bred by Henry W. Jaghai O.D., J.P. and trained by Harry Jaghai. Standing **L to R**: Cecil Singh, Derrick Datadeen, Howard Jaghai, Henry W. Jaghai O.D., J.P., Peter Singh, Wayne Smith, Charmaine Seecharan, Patrick Jaghai, Basil Murray and Frederick Watson.

Sir Raja Kumar a 4.y.o. Bay Gelding by Element – Chan Chan (with jockey Everton Miller) is met by members of Bombay Stud Farm (owners) after victory in the Colin Melhado Cup D Handicap going 6 Furlongs in a time of 1:13.3 on Wednesday March 5, 1986. He is bred by Henry W. Jaghai O.D., J.P. and trained by Andrew Jaghai. Standing **L to R**: Joseph Maragh (holding Rajesh Jaghai), Lumsum, Rupert Maragh, and Henry W. Jaghai O.D., J.P.

Sir Gobin Harrilala 3.y.o. Bay Colt by Don't Blush - My Cheree (with jockey Charles Hussey) is met by members of Bombay Stud Farm (owners) after victory in a 3.y.o. Maiden going 5 Furlongs in a time of 1:02.2 on Saturday March 7, 1998. He is bred by Henry W. Jaghai O.D., J.P. and trained by Percival Hussey. Standing **L to R**: Patrick Jaghai, John Khan, Percival Hussey, Adolphus Arjun, Arthur Rhyman, Henry W. Jaghai O.D., J.P., Altimond Suckie and Aston Rhyman.

Sir Mohandas Baba a 3.y.o. Bay Colt by Sir Lal Bahadur – Lady Anandi (with jockey Nobel Abrego) is met by members of Bombay Stud Farm (owners) after victory in an 8-furlong race on Tuesday October 2, 1999 at Santa Rosa Park in Trinidad. He is bred by Henry W. Jaghai O.D., J.P. and trained by Neal Maharaj. Standing **L to R**: Rolf Bartolo and Bob Baychue.

Reca a 7.y.o Bay Gelding Dungaree - Royal Snob (with jockey Emilio Rodriguez) is met by members of Bombay Stud Farm (owners) after victory in the Mark Twain Trophy 8 Furlong race in a time of 1:37.4 on Saturday February 16, 1980. He is trained by Barrington Dawes. Standing **L to R**: Donald Makoo, Peter Jaghai, Henry W. Jaghai O.D., J.P, Patrick Jaghai, Andrew Jaghai, Donovan Phillips, Wally Byroo, Judy Phillips, Keith Nicholls and Sydney Ramdeen.

Sir Rajah Raeby a 3.y.o. Bay Colt by Restless Thief – Run Marisa Run (with jockey Allen Maragh) is met by members of Bombay Stud Farm (owners) after victory in the Jockey Club Stakes Gr. II going 7 Furlongs in a time of 1:25.0 on Saturday August 17, 1996. He is bred by Henry W. Jaghai O.D., J.P. and trained by Harry Jaghai. Standing **L to R**: John Khan, Earl Guyah, Henry W. Jaghai O.D., J.P., Patrick Jaghai, Shawn Williams and Frederick Watson.

Lady Dularie a 3.y.o. Chestnut Filly by Restless Thief – Lady Danragie (with jockey J. Bracho) is met by members of Bombay Stud Farm (owners) after victory in a 3.y.o. Maiden going 6 Furlongs in a time of 1:13.1 on Saturday November 15, 1997. She is bred by Henry W. Jaghai O.D., J.P. and trained by Percival Hussey. Standing **L to R**: John Khan, Wazeer Russell, Alphonso Latchman, Rupert Maragh, Patrick Jaghai, Rol Bartolo, Charmaine Seecharan, Percival Hussey, Henry W. Jaghai O.D., J.P., Dr. Vijayan and Bob Baychue.

Lady Shalimar a 3.y.o. Chestnut Filly by Restless Thief – Lady Rupamani (with jockey Valentino McBean) is met by members of Bombay Stud Farm (owners) after victory in a 3.y.o. Maiden going 7 Furlongs in a time of 1:29.4 on Wednesday July 25, 2001. She is bred by Henry W. Jaghai O.D., J.P. and trained by Harry Jaghai. Standing **L to R**: Howard Jaghai, Harry Jaghai, Hanif Jaghai, Herman Jaghai, Donald Suckie, Henry W. Jaghai O.D., J.P., Mitchie Suckie, Raju Maragh.

Lady Seeta a 4.y.o. Brown Filly by Hall of Reason – Len's Limit (with jockey Daniel Gazader) is met by members of Bombay Stud Farm (owners) after victory in a B1 Handicap 10 Furlong race in a time of 2:06.3 on Saturday May 3, 1986. She is trained by Andrew Jaghai. Standing **L to R**: Patrick Jaghai, Peter Jaghai, Andrew Jaghai, Henry W. Jaghai O.D., J.P., Rupert Maragh and Joseph Maragh.

Lady Jaipur a 3.y.o. Bay Filly by Joe Slew – Acetylene (with jockey Charles Hussey) is met by members of Bombay Stud Farm (owners) after victory in a 3.y.o. Maiden going 6 Furlongs in a time of 1:15.2 on Saturday May 9, 1998. She is bred by Henry W. Jaghai O.D., J.P. and trained by Wayne DaCosta. Standing **L to R**: Evon DePass, Winston Dixon, Alphonso Latchman, Henry W. Jaghai O.D., J.P., Rupert Maragh, Wally Byroo and Basil Murray.

Lady Suranee a 3.y.o. Bay Filly by Joe Slew – Lady Maharanee (with jockey Richard Mitchell) is met by members of Bombay Stud Farm (owners) after victory in a 3.y.o. Maiden going 6 ½ Furlongs in a time of 1:23.3 on Wednesday March 25, 1998. She is bred by Henry W. Jaghai and trained by Wayne DaCosta. Standing **L to R**: Winston Dixon, Vijay Thompson, Henry W. Jaghai O.D., J.P., Rupert Maragh, Wally Byroo, Evon DePass and trainer Wayne DaCosta.

Lady Shakeera a 3.y.o. Bay Filly by Restless Thief – R.D.'s Quick (with jockey Ameth Robles) is met by members of Bombay Stud Farm (owners) after victory in a 3.y.o. Maiden going 6 Furlongs in a time of 1:15.0 on Saturday August 30, 2003. She is bred by Henry W. Jaghai O.D., J.P. and trained by Howard Jaghai. Standing **L to R**: Howard Jaghai, Keith McConnell, Henry W. Jaghai O.D., J.P., Leon Sukoo, and John Khan.

Lady Aleema a 3.y.o. Chestnut Filly by Restless Thief – Lady Rupamani (with jockey Charles Hussey) is met by members of Bombay Stud Farm (owners) after victory in a 3.y.o. Maiden going 5 Furlongs Round in a time of 1:02.0 on Saturday July 6, 1996. She is bred by Henry W. Jaghai O.D., J.P. and trained by Percival Hussey. Standing **L to R**: Percival Hussey, Samuel Jackson, John Khan, Henry W. Jaghai O.D., J.P., Junior Gallow and John Brown.

Lady Agra a 3.y.o. Bay Filly by Joe Slew – Lady Anandi (with jockey Wesley Henry) is met by members of Bombay Stud Farm (owners) after victory in a 3.y.o. Maiden going 8 ½ Furlongs in a time of 1:51.4 on Monday October 17, 1998. She is bred by Henry W. Jaghai O.D., J.P. and trained by Robert Taylor. Standing **L to R**: Patrick Jaghai, Henry W. Jaghai O.D., J.P., Danny Martin, Rupert Maragh, Wally Byroo, Leonard and Robert Taylor.

Lady Bangalie a 3.y.o. Bay Filly by Sir Lal Bahadur – Lady Rupamani (with jockey Andrew Ramgeet) is met by members of Bombay Stud Farm (owners) after victory in a 3.y.o. Maiden going 6 ½ Furlongs in a time of 1:22.0 on Saturday June 5, 1999. She is bred by Henry W. Jaghai O.D., J.P. and trained by Harry Jaghai. Standing **L to R**: Winston Dixon, Henry W. Jaghai O.D., J.P., Rupert Maragh, John Khan, Patrick Jaghai, Rupert Holness and Frederick Watson.

Lady Bansari a 3.y.o. Chestnut Filly by Restless Thief – Two Notch Road (with jockey A. Thomas) is met by members of Bombay Stud Farm (owners) after victory in a 3.y.o. & upward Claiming race going 7 ½ Furlongs in a time of 1:32.3 on Saturday October 25, 1997. She is bred by Henry W. Jaghai O.D., J.P. and trained by Percival Hussey. Standing **L to R**: Henry W. Jaghai O.D., J.P., Patrick Jaghai, Rupert Maragh and Percival Hussey.

Lady Chameli a 3.y.o. Roan Filly by Restless Thief – R.D.'s Quick (with jockey Winston Griffiths) is met by members of Bombay Stud Farm after victory in a 3.y.o. Maiden going 5 Furlongs Straight in a time of 1:02.3 on Saturday June 30, 2001. She is bred by Henry W. Jaghai O.D., J.P. and trained by Tensang Chung. Standing **L to R**: Alphonso Latchman, Ganga Singh, Meghoo, Wally Byroo, Henry W. Jaghai O.D., J.P., Rupert Maragh and Patrick Jaghai.

Lady Basanti a 4.y.o. Chestnut Filly by Joe Slew – Lady Vasanti (with jockey VasselNajair) is met by members of Bombay Stud Farm (owners) after victory in a 4.y.o. Maiden going 5 ½ Furlongs in a time of 1:09.4 on Monday April 13, 1998. She is bred by Henry W. Jaghai O.D., J.P. and trained by Henry Harrison. Standing **L to R**: Alphonso Latchman, Ganga Singh, Henry W. Jaghai O.D., J.P., Winston Dixon, Rupert Maragh, Wally Byroo and Patrick Jaghai.

Lady Bakul a 3.y.o. Dark Bay Filly by Liver Stand – Classy Slew (with jockey Neville Stephenson) is met by members of Bombay Stud Farm (owners) after victory in a 3.y.o. Maiden going 7 Furlongs in a time of 1:29.4 on Wednesday December 26, 2001. She is bred by Henry W. Jaghai O.D., J.P. and trained by Harry Jaghai. Standing **L to R**: Derrick Datadeen, Barrington Simpson, Henry W. Jaghai O.D., J.P., Rupert Maragh, Michael Singh, Joseph Singh and Patrick Jaghai.

Let's Hope a 4.y.o. Dark Bay Filly by Rexson's Hope – Lori's Way (with jockey LearieSeecharan) is met by members of Bombay Stud Farm (owners) after victory in a 7 Furlongs 3.y.o. & upward Starter Handicap 1 & 2 event in a time of 1:24.2 on Wednesday April 16, 1997. Standing **L to R**: Harry Jaghai (trainer), Henry W. Jaghai O.D., J.P., Patrick Jaghai, Rupert Maragh, Charmaine Seecharan and Ali Bahadur.

Lady Rakwalaay a 4.y.o. Dark Bay Filly by Gold Alert - Kissable (with jockey DelroyBeharie) after a victory in a 8 Furlongs NB 4.y.o.& Upwards Restricted Allowance IV in a time of 1:41.1 on Saturday September 13, 2008. She is bred by Henry W. Jaghai O.D. J.P. and trained by Harry Jaghai. Standing **L to R**: Mohinder Byrosingh and groom.

LADY BANGALORE

Lady Bangalore(L. Seecharan) 47.0 is met by members of the Bombay Stud After victory in the 6 1/2 furlongs 'Henry McGrath Mem Cup' on Saturday, July 31st 1999. The 4 yo b.f. by Joe Slew out of Music Belle trained by Harry Jaghai, Won in a time of 1:20.0. Standing **L to R**: Frederick Watson, Winston Dixon, Howard Jaghai, Henry Jaghai, Mark McNaughton, Rupert Maragh, John Khan, Jim Roy and Basil Murray.

SIR THAKUR BABA

Sir Thakur Baba (W. Russell) is met by members of Bombay Stud Farm (owners) after victory in the 3 y.o. maiden 6 furlongs on Wednesday 5th July 2000. The ch c by Restless Thief - Lou B Lou, trained by Noel Ennevor, won in a time 1:16:4. Standing **L to R**: Noel Ennevor, Groom, Evon DePass, Henry Jaghai, Ram Ragbier, Sam Jaghai, Michael Singh

Lady Vasanti a 4.y.o. Chestnut Filly by Element - Polka Dotty (with jockey Trevor Simpson) after victory in a A2 class event going 6 furlongs in a time of 1:11.2 on Saturday March 25, 1989. She is bred by Henry Jaghai and trained by Harry Jaghai. Standing **L to R**: Adolphus Arjun, Harry Jaghai, Henry Jaghai, Donna Maragh and Henrietta Jadusingh.

Lady Kamla (R. Dacosta) 109 lbs is met by members of PELJAG Syndicate(owners)after victory in the B2 class 1 mile Rimsky Trophy on Wednesday September 9th, 1987. The 4 y.o. bay filly by Reca -Paddy's Dolltrained by Harry Jaghai. Posted time was 1:37:2 by 7 lengths

Lady Hyderabad a 3.y.o. Bay Filly by Sir Lal Bahadur - Papal Queen (with jockey Percival Williams) after victory in a 5 Furlong event in a time of 59.3 on Saturday June 29, 2002. She is bred by Henry Jaghai and trained by Howard Jaghai. Standing **L to R**: Stacy Bahadur, Tira Jaghai, Sasha Jaghai, Henry Jaghai O.D. J.P., Patrick Jaghai and Peter Jaghai.

Lady Gorakhpur a 4.y.o. Bay Filly by Footloose - Let's Hope (with jockey Aaron Chatrie) after victory in a 7 Furlong event in a time of 1:31.4 on April 14, 2010. She is bred by Henry Jaghai and trained by Harry Jaghai. Standing **L to R**: Harry Jaghai, Mohinder Byrosingh, Rajesh Jaghai, Myrtle Jaghai, Henry Jaghai and Patrick Jaghai.

Sir JhunjhunWala a 3.y.o. Chestnut Gelding by Rising Moon - Niphal (with jockey Anthony Thomas) after victory in a5 Furlongs St. NB 3.y.o. Maidena time of 1:00.3 on Saturday May 12, 2018. He is bred by Henry W. Jaghai O.D. J.P. and trained by Howard Jaghai. Standing **L to R**: Coorie Grant, Michael Pottinger, Morris Powell, Raheim Baccas, Matthew Williams, Howard Jaghai, Earl Williams, Matthew Jaghai and Michael Singh.

Sir Arjun Babu a 3.y.o. Bay Gelding by Legal Process - Lady Abhijita (with jockey Christopher Mamdeen) after victory in a 8 Furlong event in a time of 1:42.0 on Sunday June 30, 2019. He is bred by Henry Jaghai and trained by Howard Jaghai. Standing **L to R**: Tiffany Jaghai, Adam Jaghai, Henry Jaghai, Howard Jaghai, Mark Williams, Shari Williams, Andrea Williams and Matthew Williams.

Lady Suneeta (R. Parish) 52.5 is met by its owners, Bombay Std Farm (owners) after victory in the 4 yo & upwards (maiden) 7 1/2 furlongs (st) on Saturday 1st April, 2000. The 4 yo.ch.f. by Sir Lal Bahadur - Lady Jagranee, bred by Henry W Jaghai OD, JP, andtrained by H. Jaghai posted time was 1:38:3.

From L-R Henry W Jaghai, Fredrick Watson, Howard Jaghai, Rupert Maragh, Wally Byroo and John Kahn.

Lady Tulasie (Chris Green) 52.0 is met by its owners, Bombay Stud Farm after victory in the 4 yo & upwards (maiden) 9 furlongs & 25 yards on Saturday 14th April, 2001. The 4 yo. Ch. F. by Schism - Papal Qeen, bred by Henry Jaghai OD, JP, and trained by M. Powell, posted time was 2:05:4. Standing from **L to R**: Rupert Maragh, Ganga Singh, Henry W Jaghai OD, JP, groom, Morris Powell and Patrick Jaghai

Raheim Baccas receiving the Jamaica Racehorse Trainers Association Trophy from Monica Edwards following the win by Sir Jhunjhun Wala on Saturday July 14, 2018.

Andrea Jaghai-Williams collects the winning breeder trophy for I Am Di One after winning the Jamaica 1000 Guineas.

Mr. Danny Melville (L) presents the 1997 None Such Award to Mr. Henry W. Jaghai O.D.J.P. Owner/Breeder of Bombay Stud Farm

Mr. Phillip Feanny (L) presents the 1997 Champion Breeders Award to Mr. Henry W. Jaghai O.D.J.P. and his son Andrew Jaghai

Dream Marie (R. Mitchell) a 2.y.o. grey filly by Graydar - Lin Marie by Curlin after victory at Gulfstream Park West, Florida on November 20, 2019, going 7 Furlongs in 1:25.07. She is owned by Miracle's International Trading and trained by Matthew J. Williams, grandson of Henry Jaghai. **From L-R** Fernando, Everton Bennett, Mark Williams (Miracle's International Trading), Spencer McDonald and Matthew Williams (Miracle's International Trading).

Areyoutalkingtome (Richard Mitchell - Jockey) a 5.y.o. chestnut gelding by Tapizar – Senza Paura by Fly Till Dawn after victory at Gulfstream Park West, Florida on November 24, 2019, going 7 Furlongs in 1:25.79. He is owned by Miracle's International Trading and trained by Matthew J. Williams (extreme right). **From L-R:** Jean, Peter Jaghai, Patrick Jaghai, Tiffany Jaghai, Tony Jaghai, Andrea Jaghai Williams, the Mitchells, Spencer McDonald (groom -back) and Mark Williams (Miracle's International Trading).

Lady Rattapur (ridden by Dane Nelson) a 4.y.o. Bay Filly by Miracle Man - Lady Jagrati after victory in a 4YO Maiden going 7 Furlongs in 1:29.2 on Sunday October 4, 2020. She is owned by Bombay Stud Farm, bred by Henry W. Jaghai O.D. J.P. and trained by Rowan Mathie. Standing L to R: Ali Bahadur, Barry Goljar and Rowan Mathie

Excellence in horseracing plaque awarded to Henry Jaghai OD., JP, on September 2019.

He won the Breeder's Championship for 10 years

CRICKET, LOVELY CRICKET

Pastimes

I loved-cricket. I had started playing school boy cricket when I was ten years old. This passion has remained with me throughout my life. In 1954, I formed the All Indian Cricket Team, assuming the roles of financier, manager and captain for a few years. The team competed in many local competitions and won several trophies-the most prestigious being the Rankin C up.

In 1973, accompanied by a large contingent of family and friends as supporters, the team toured Trinidad and Guyana, where we won most of our matches. It was a good occasion where sporting, cultural and social activities merged to make the tour an unforgettable experience.

Group photograph of 1973 all Indian Balraam Cup Champion cricket team, which toured Trinidad and Guyana. Henry W. Jaghai was team manager and player. Standing (L-R): Carlton Lawla, William Mitchell, Henry W. Jaghai, Maurice Rambana, Kenneth Beepat, and KeithSingh. Sitting (L-R): Robert Maragh, Adolphus Arjun, Danny Lewis-Captain, Lynval Rhyman, Aston Rhyman, and AliBahadur.

L-R Dr Cheddie Jaggan, President of Guyana. Dr Jaggan and Dr Balwant Singh, Myrtle Jaghai, Henry Jaghai

During his 1973 Trinidad and Guyana cricket tour with the Balraam Championship team, Henry W. Jaghai met Dr Cheddie Jaggan, President of Guyana. Dr Jaggan and Dr Balwant Singh were particularly helpful in accommodating the team at the Ghandi Youth Organisation Center in Georgeton, Guyana.

In August 1973, my wife Myrtle and I, along with friends, went to Guyana, where we visited the homes of famous West Indian cricketers Rohan Kanhai and Alvin Kalicharan, in Port Morant in Berbice. The cricketers were away on tour, but we met with their families.

From left to right: Betty Hussman, Myrtle Jaghai, Ivan Suckie, Henry Jaghai, Pearl Hussman

Henry W. Jaghai and wife Myrtle at the Taj Mahal Agra, India during their 1987 visit to the motherland. The famed Taj Mahal is one of the Seven Wonders of the World.

Myrtle Jaghai (left) with friends Cynthia, Ezekiel Williams And Jocelyn Williams during their Guyana visit.

(L-R) Henry and his wife Myrtle (back row) Leslie Gareave, Lillian Thompson, Gladys Richards (front row)

The Hamilton Cup Champions of 1944, an all-Indian cricket team

In 1944, the All Indian Cricket Club won the Hamilton Cup. The team consisted of Capt. Bertie Smith, Vice-captain Munesar, Baby Latchman, George Pagu, John Barker, C. Jullur, Wilfred Dean, Charles Harry, Solomon Lal, Baggabaga Maragh, and Cecil Allan.

In 1949, the All Indian Recreation cricket team entered the Junior Cup competition. The team consisted of Austin Jadusingh, CaltapJadusingh, Willie Budhoo, Mannie Budhoo, Daniel Mykoo, Solomon Lal, Fredrick Lal, Luluman Maragh, Samuel Harry, Arnold Abdully, Ernest Bulli, Adolphus Lal, and David Ramdeen.

In 1952, Arthur Sardarsingh entered the Carib Cup competition with most of the players from the 1949 team along with two additional players, Joe Maragh and Robert Maragh. This team was successful and emerged winners of the Carib Cup. Most of the players from this team eventually migrated to England.

In 1953, Samuel Singh formed the Indian Youth Cricket Team with many young players. This cricket club started at the home of Singh at 167 Spanish Town Road, St Andrew. The club secretary was Ralph "Littleman" Binda and members of this new club were Aston Arjun, Adolphus Arjun, Henry W. Jaghai, Oscar Singh, Bal- am Hardiall, Staggy Hardiall, Moses Watson, Ruffus Ramsay, Hugh Roy Damalie, David Ramdeen, Cecil Barker, Jack Thompson, Finger Thompson, Melvin Dama- lie, and Sucksingh Badrambally. This group of players played many curry goat and friendly matches.

In 1955 and 1958, this group of players entered the Hamilton Cup competition.
Other players that joined the team were Dudus Williams, Harry Maragh, Sydney Maragh, Alvin Maragh, Baby Rhyman, Aston Rhyman, Raymond Mahabir, Leonard Chambers, Keith Singh, Colin Hinds, Donald Maragh, Alfred Bahadur, JoeMaragh, Robert Maragh, Roy Banasee, and Morris Rambana.

All Indian Cricket Team – 1961 Rankin Cup Champions

All Indian Cricket Team-1960RankinCupChampions.
Standing (L-R): Altimon Suckie, Henry W. Jaghai, Aston Rhyman, Joseph Maragh, Ganesh Maragh, Baby Rhyman, George Lallo.
Sitting (L-R): Dudus Williams, Raymond Mahabir, Adolphus Arjun (Captain), Munesar Maragh - Manager, Wilfred Suckie, and Lynval Rhyman

In 1959-1960 Munesar Maragh became manager for the All Indian Cricket Team. Regular meetings were held at his home at Spanish Town Road in St Andrew. The All Indian team entered the Rankin Cup competition in 1960. Before matches were played, the team members would gather at the manager's home and he would conduct puja prayers before each game. The team was successful and won the Rankin Cupthat year.

The players consisted of the manager, Munesar Maragh, Adolphus Arjun, the captain, Raymond Mahabir, Dudus Williams, Wilfred Suckie, Arthur Rhyman, George Lallo, Baby Rhyman, Danesh Maragh, Joe Maragh, Aston Rhyman, Henry W. Jaghai and Altimond Suckie.

Masterton Cup Champions, late 1961

All Indian Cricket Team Masterton Cup Winners 1960.
Back Row (L-R): Henry W. Jaghai, Adolphus Arjun, George Laloo, Altimond Suckie, Joseph Maragh, Baby Rhyman.
Front Row Sitting (L-R): Ganesh Maragh, Aston Ryhman, Dudus Williams, Rama Maragh-Captain, Lynval Rhyman, Raymond Mahabier

Again, in 1960, the team entered the Masterton cricket competition, under the leadership of Captain Rama Maragh and won. That year the team had two back-to-back wins. After 1960, members of the team went to play for different teams, resulting in a fragmentation of the team.

Masterton Cup Champions, 1965

All Indian Cricket Team-1965 Masterton Cup Champions.
Standing (L-R): Dada Maragh, Altimond Suckie, Adolphus Arjun, Joseph Maragh, and Tulsie Bally singh- Manager.
Sitting (L-R): Carlton Lawla, Abdul, Lynval Rhyman, Keith Singh-Captain, Henry W. Jaghai, Aston Rhyman, Bingo Singh

In 1965, Henry W. Jaghai decided to put another all-Indian cricket team together, and entered the Masterton Cup cricket competition. He appointed Ezeikel Ballysingh as manager and Keith Singh as captain, other members included Ivan Suckie, Dada Maragh, Altimond Suckie, Adolphus Arjun, Joe Maragh, Carlton Lawla, Aston Abdul, Arthur Rhyman, Aston Rhyman, Vishnu Bingosingh and Kenneth Beepat.

1968 Rankin Cup Champions - Jaghai's Garage Limited Cricket Team

Jaghai's Garage Limited Cricket Team-1968 Rankin Cup Champions.
Front Row (L-R): Adolphus Arjun, Lynval Rhyman, Leonard Chambers, Henry W. Jaghai-Captain, Robert Maragh, Alvin Thompson Maragh.
Back Row (L-R): Morris Rambana, Collin Hinds, Less Brown, Aston Ryhman, Victor Hunter, Kenneth Beepat, Sam Morgan, Bobby Mignott

In 1968, Henry W. Jaghai became manager and captain of a new team, Jaghai Garage Cricket Team and he entered them in the Rankin Cup cricket competition. The members of the team included Leonard Chambers – vice-captain, Colin Hinds, Morris Rambana, Adolphus Arjun, Arthur Rhyman, Aston Rhyman, Alvin Thompson Maragh, Bobby Mignott, Kenneth Beepat, Sam Morgan, Laga Reid, Rex Suckoo, Terry Roman, and Robert Maragh. This team became successful and won the Rankin Cup that year.

1970 Balraam Trophy Champions – Indian Youth Cricket Club

Balraam Trophy Champions for the Year 1969/70. Seated (L-R): J. Harry, O. Bhalai – Manager, G. Harry-Captain, N. Maragh-President, E. Pandohie, D. Harry.
Standing (L-R): L. Maragh, V. Budram, T. Guyah, J. Rhyman, G. Maragh, N. Alexander, R. McDonald, A. Persaud, and J. Roberts

In 1969, Balraam Maragh donated a trophy, the Balraam Trophy for Indian players. The teams that entered this competition were the Indian Youth Cricket Club from the two miles area; the East Indian Cricket Team led by Ezeikel Ballysingh; Sudine Eleven from the Red Hills area, led by Albert and Daddy Sudine; the Clarendon Indians from Vere, Clarendon, led by Albert Gidarisingh and SDM led by Rama Maragh; All Indian Junior Team managed by Henry W. Jaghai and led by Danny Lewis.

In 1970, the winners of the first Balraam Trophy went to Indian Youth Cricket Club, Manager Arjun Bhalai, and Captain Glen Harry. The president of this club was Neville Maragh. The players included E. Pandohie, Danny Harry, J. Harry, Lloyd Maragh, V. Budram, Tyrell Guyah, Glen Maragh, J. Rhyman, N. Alexander, R. McDonald, A. Persaud, and J. Roberts.

1973 Balraam Cup Champions – All Indian Cricket Team

In 1973 the All Indian Junior Cricket Team managed by Henry W. Jaghai, with Captain Danny Lewis won the competition. The players included Carlton Lawla, William Mitchell, Morris Rambana, Kenneth Beepat, Keith Singh, Robert Maragh, Adolphus Arjun, Arthur Rhyman, Aston Rhyman, and Ali Bahadur. The 1973 Balraam Cup winners led by Captain Robert Maragh and Vice-captain Adolphus Arjun. Other players included Wilfred Suckie, Krishna Deonarine and a contingency of about thirty supporters who traveled to Trinidad to play two friendly matches. The team won one and lost one. They continued onto Guyana where they were scheduled to compete in friendly matches, but this was can- celled due to rain.

1983 Caribbean Cup Champions – All Indian Cricket Club

1983 CARIB CUP CHAMPIONS ALL INDIAN CRICKET CLUB
BACK ROW - STANDING, L-R: EARL CHETRAM, DONOVAN NACTI, JOSEPH MARAGH, NOEL HARPAUL, ANDREW GREENWOOD, RAJU MARAGH, ANDREW JAGHAI, DERRICK MARDIO, PATRICK JAGHAI
FRONT ROW - SITTING, L-R: PAUL HARPAUL, HUGH MARAGH, HENRY JAGHAI O.D.J.P.(MANAGER), MARK WILLIAMS(CAPTAIN), DANNY CAYMAN, HERBERT MITTOO, KENNETH BEEPAT

In 1983 there was another all-Indian cricket club, under the management of Henry W. Jaghai and led by Captain Mark Williams. The players included Earl Chetram, Donovan Nacti, Joseph Maragh, Noel Harpaul, Andrew Greenwood, Raju Maragh, Andrew Jaghai, Derrick Mardio, Patrick Jaghai, Paul Harpaul, Hugh Maragh, Danny Cayman, Herbert Mittoo and Kenneth Beepat.

1985 Gleaner KO Champions – All Indian Cricket Club

Gleaner 1985 K.O Champions-All Indian Cricket Club.
Standing (L-R): Harry Persaud-Manager, Peter Mykoo, Derrick Mardio, Earl Chetram, Henry Cayman, and Noel Harpaul.
Sitting (L-R): Donovan Nacti, Paul Harpaul - Vice Captain, Hugh Maragh - Captain, Danny Cayman, Herbie Mittoo, Ronald McDonald

In 1985, the All Indian Cricket Club led by Manager Harry Persaud and Captain Hugh Maragh entered and won the Gleaner K.O Championship. The other players included Peter Mykoo, Derrick Mardio, Earl Chetram, Henry Cayman, Noel Harpaul, Donovan Nacti, Paul Harpaul, Danny Cayman, Herbie Mittoo and Ronald McDonald.

CRICKET TOUR TO GUYANA, 1973

L-R Jeewan Chowtie, Authur Ryman, Adolphus Arjun, Tater, Bob Maragh, Keith Singh,

Dun Williams

1991 Rothman Trophy Champions – All Indian Cricket Club

1991 Rothman's Trophy Winner - All Indian Cricket Club
Back Row - Standing left to right
Hebert Mittoo, Donavon Nacti, Anthony Martin, Noel Harpaul, Andrew Greenwood, Paul Harpual, Andrew Jaghai, Derrick Mardio, Patrick Jaghai
Front Row - Sitting left to right
Mark Foote, Henry Jaghai, OD JP Manager, Mark Williams Captain, Danny Cayman, Kenneth Beepat

The All Indian Cricket Club was again successful in 1991 when they entered and won the Rothman Trophy. They were led by Manager Henry W. Jaghai OD., JP, and Captain Mark Williams. The players included Herbert Mittoo, Donavan Nacti, Anthony Martin, Noel Harpaul, Andrew Greenwood, Paul Harpaul, Andrew Jaghai, Derrick Mardio, Patrick Jaghai, Mark Foote, Danny Cayman and Kenneth Beepat.

S.D.M. Cricket Team, by Wilbert Tallo, JP

The S.D.M. Cricket Team was founded in 1966 and was Balraam Cup Champion in 1974. The executive committee comprised: Rama Maragh – president, Loran Bachan– treasurer, Samuel Bachan– secretary, Babsey Maragh – club member, Neddie Newman – club member.

The team players were: Rupert Amjurey Alfred Bahadur Ali Bahadur SunnyBahadur Samuel Bachan– captain Ronald Gidarisingh, Author Latchman, CarltonLawla, DaneshMaragh Kenneth Mittoo Noel Rambally Winston Ramsay Elizah Shaw, Ganga Singh – vice-captain Donald Suckie, Wilbert Tallo George Vernal, Herbert Vernal- wicket keeper

Standing L to R: Deodat Maragh (manager), Derick Mardio, Danny Cayman, Donnavon Nacti, Joseph Maragh and Raju Maragh
Sitting L to R: Andrew Jaghai, Paul Harpaul, Adolphus Arjun, Henry Jaghai J.P.(captain), Alvin Thompson and William Mitchell

INDO-CULTURAL CONTRIBUTION

My Aaji, Nani and Nana inspired me so much with their culture that it became an integral part of my life. To this day, I still eat my roti and dhal, listen to my Indian music and attend cultural get together to hear the musicians play and watch the dancers move rhythmically in their colourful costumes.

My passion for the preservation and propagation of the Indian culture in Jamaica has been far-reaching and very tangibly demonstrated. I was instrumental in giving and getting financial support to build Jamaica's first ever Hindu temple – The Sanatan Dharma Mandir in 1976. In 1984, I donated my premises at 10 Henderson Avenue to the Prema Sastsangh to house its temple as well as its medical clinic. In 1978 I, along with other East Indians formed The Indo-Jamaican Cultural Society, which was committed to the promotion, propagation and preservation of East Indian culture in Jamaica. The society was instrumental in organizing the 150th celebration and re-enactment of the landing of the first set of East Indians in Jamaica. 9Between 1978 and 1990, I hosted the grand Phagwah and Diwali festivals on my premises, at Bombay Stud Farm in Bushy Park, St. Catherine. I promoted numerous stage shows featuring

Indian dancers, musicians, and singers from Jamaica, Trinidad and Guyana. In the early 1990's, I spearheaded two cultural tours hosted in Trinidad, and sponsored by UNESCO.

Spectators watch as dancers enjoy the music at Bombay Stud Farm

Dancers enjoying the music

Audience at Bushy Park

In April 1994, I traveled to Cunupia, Trinidad to take part in the wedding of my Rakhi sister, Polly Sookraj. I performed the duties of the elder brother of the bride during the ceremony.

Polly's wedding

My fervour for the Hindu culture led me to produce eight LPs of traditional Indian folk music of the Caribbean, utilizing local talents as well as performers from Canada, Guyana, India, Trinidad, and the United Kingdom. In my ongoing quest to preserve the culture of my forefathers, I decided to record all information in print - a medium that could be passed down to future generations. I commissioned the services of researchers to write a book starting with the historical journey of the East Indian indentured labourers and how they integrated to become part of the cultural, economic, political, and social fabric of Jamaica. The book, Home Away from Home: 150 Years of Indian Presence in Jamaica, was launched in 1999.

On Monday, October 15, 2007, I was invested by the Jamaican Government with the insignia of the Order of Distinction for my contribution to the development of East Indian culture in Jamaica.

Despite having retired and now living in Florida, I still try to promote the culture as much as I can. I am readily available to give information to enquiring minds and to share my many resources (cultural books and music records) with others in the Indo-Caribbean Diaspora. I was recognized by Jayadevi Arts Inc., an organization committed to the rejuvenation of Indo-Caribbean cultural and artistic life in the United States. I received an award from them on Saturday, January 25, 2014 at the Walter C. Young Performing Arts Centre, Pembroke Pines, Florida for my contribution to Indo-Caribbean culture.

Henry W. Jaghai O.D. J.P.- Producer *Ram Ragbier- Assistant Producer*

As a child growing up, I was enamored with the Indian folk songs that my fore parents brought from India. My grandmother, Jaitun was a talented singer of these folk songs. This further piqued my interest in them.

In the 1980's, I produced eight volumes of "Indian Folk Songs of the Caribbean." I commissioned Ramlal Malgie to write three songs of the journey from India to Jamaica. The first of which was "Palisa does Ohrni Jahaaj," the second was "Jamaica Pardesi Chale" performed by Berverly Pancham, and the third was "Blundell Toe Peheli Jahaaj" performed by Petronia Dean.

The rehearsals for these songs were done at Malgie's house. The Malgie family was most gracious in hosting and welcoming us. I would like to thank all the singers and musicians that contributed to this project.

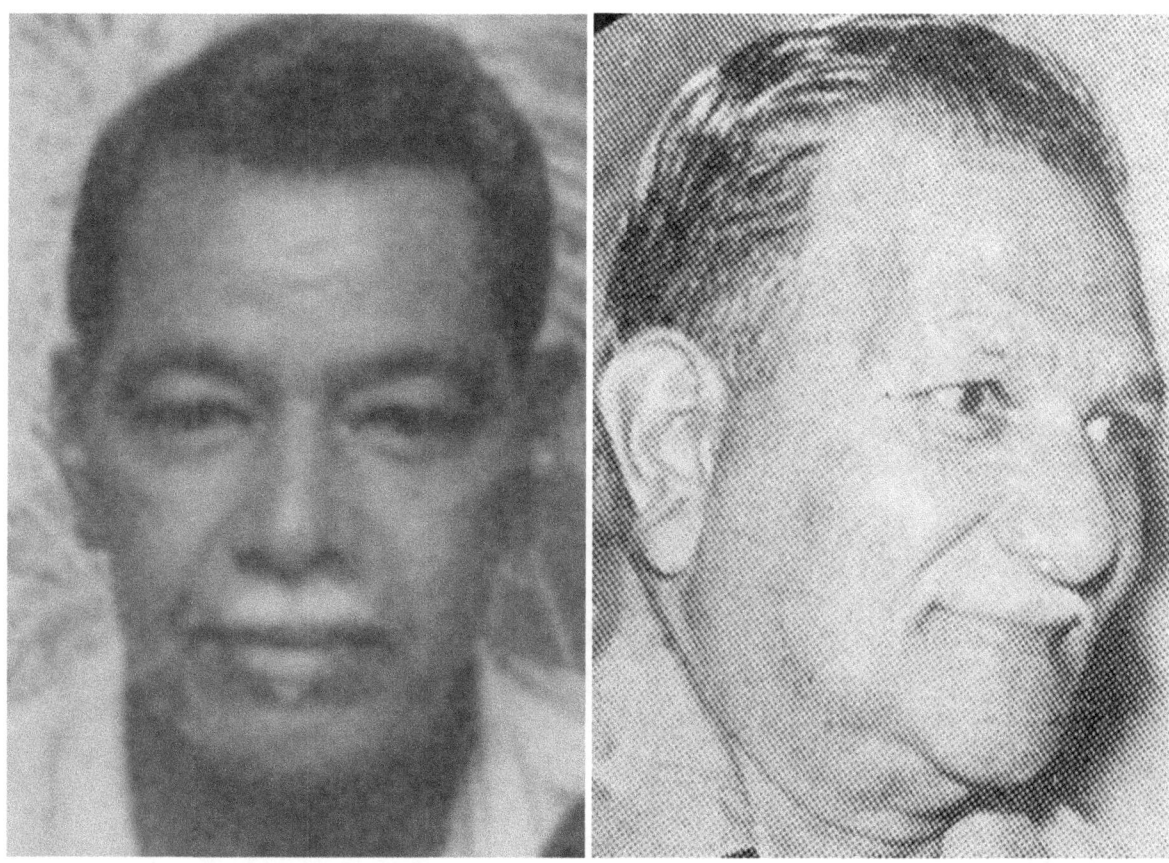

Ramlal Malgie   Graham Dookhie

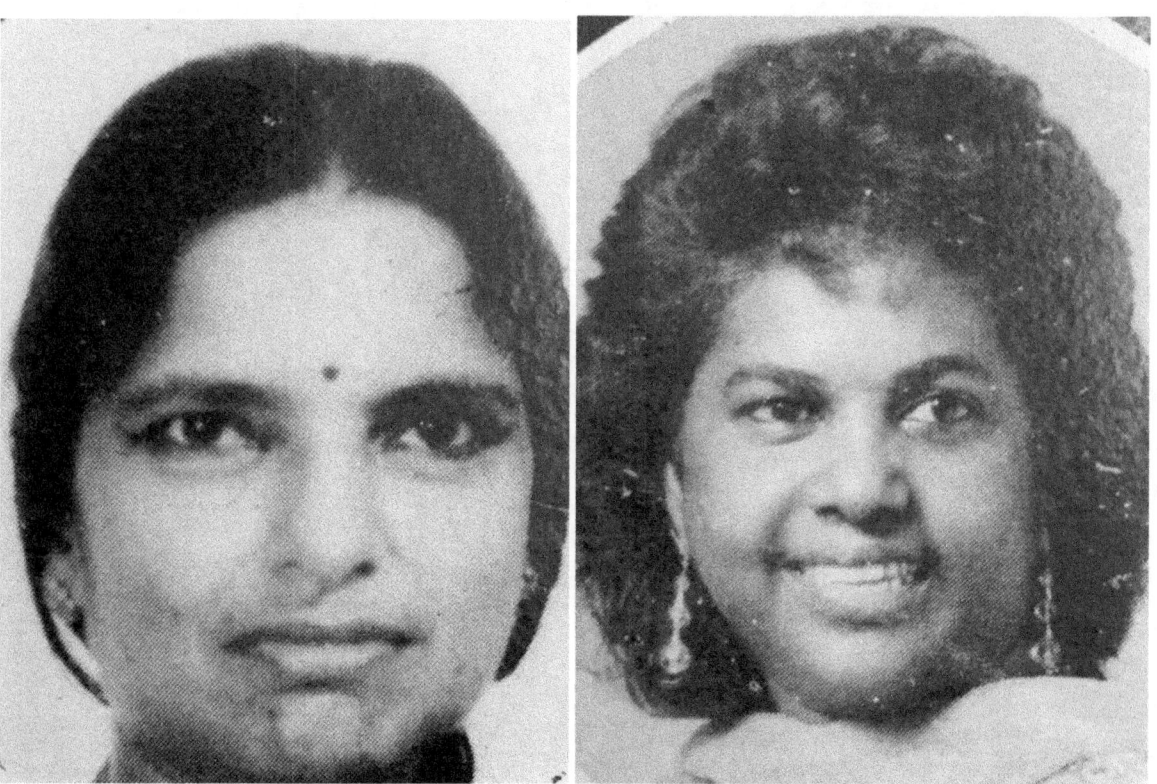

Dr. K. Kamala   Beverly Pancham Rampersaud

Polly SookrajRajdaye Sookraj

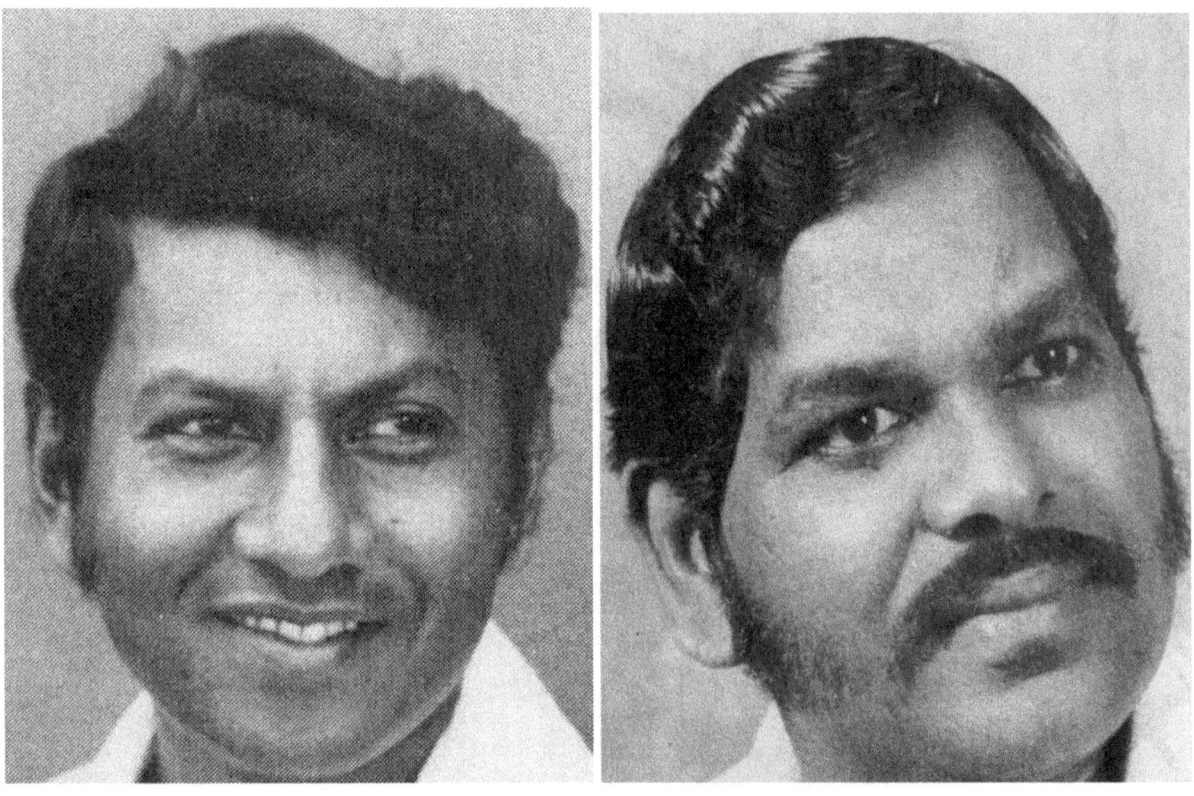

Jeewan ChowtieSagar Sookraj

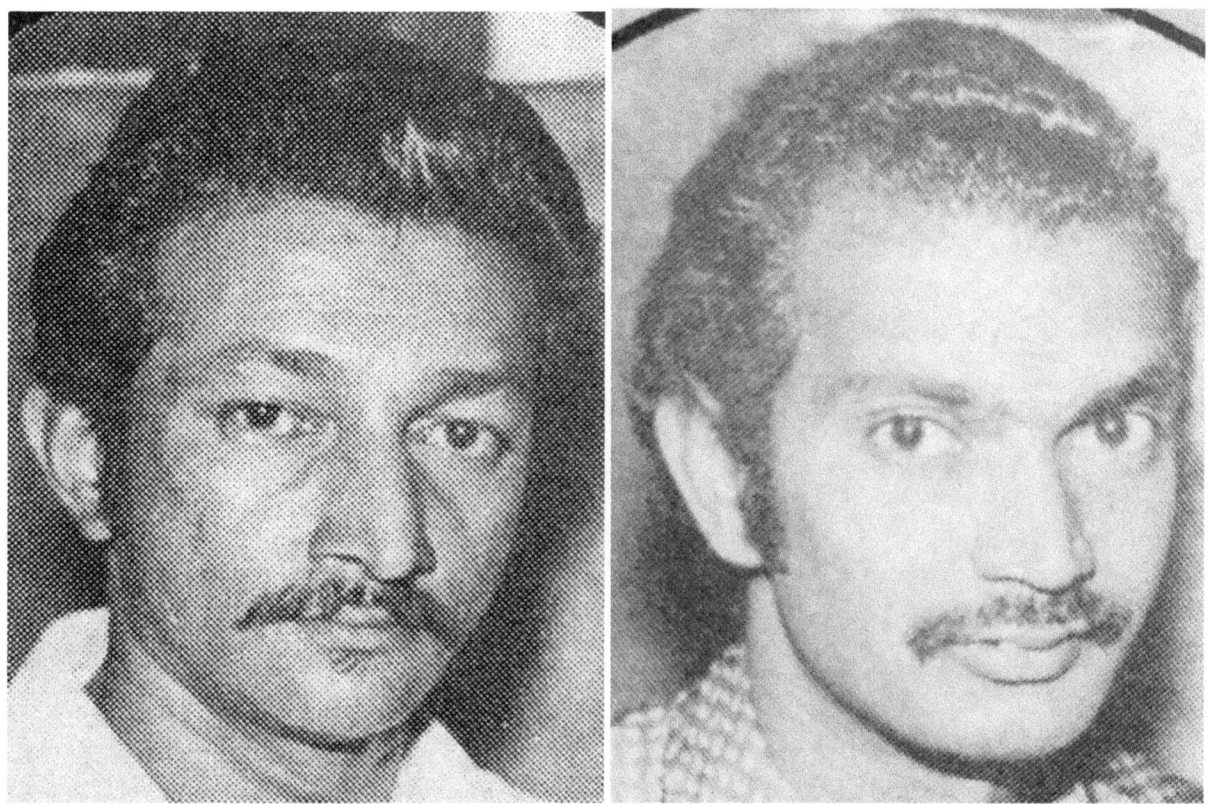

Gangaram Tolan

Dr. Winston Tolan

Thaddeus Bessi

Samuel Abdul

Azim Beharrie   Dr. Ashraf Beharrie

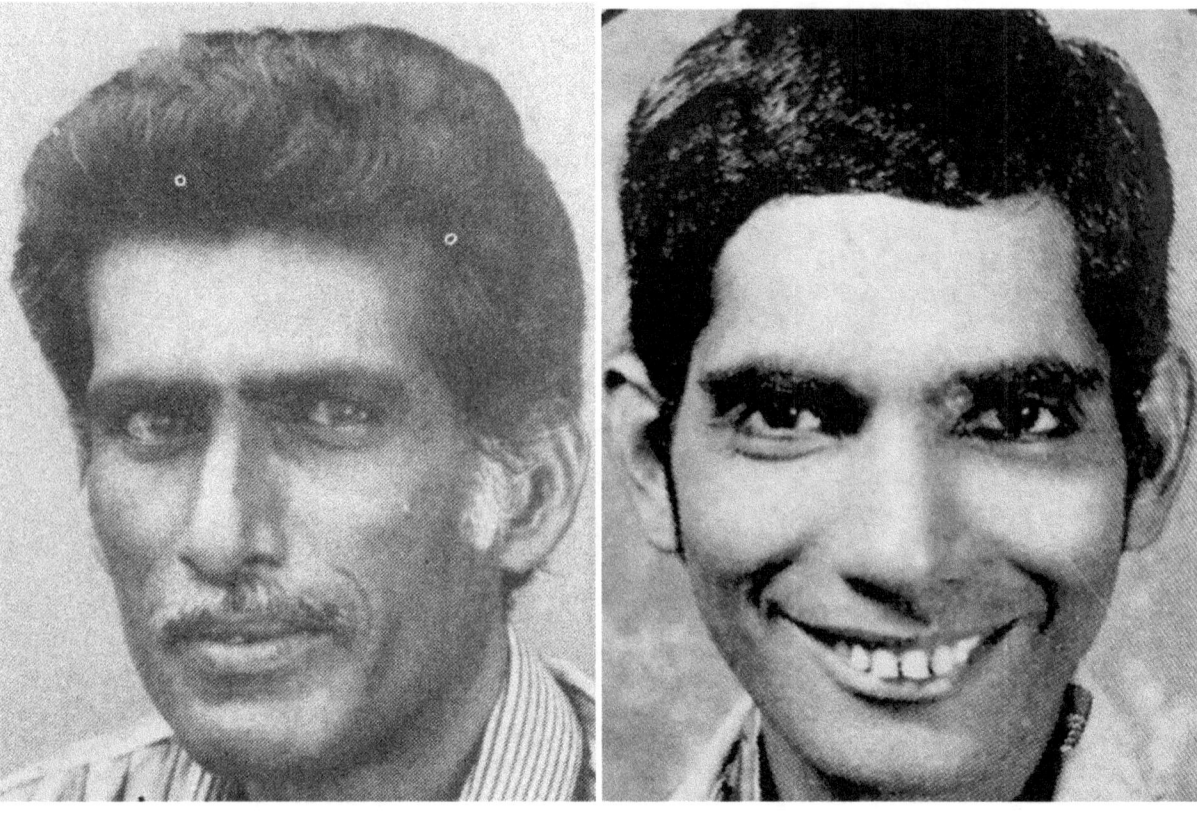

Wally ByroIndarpaul   Beharry

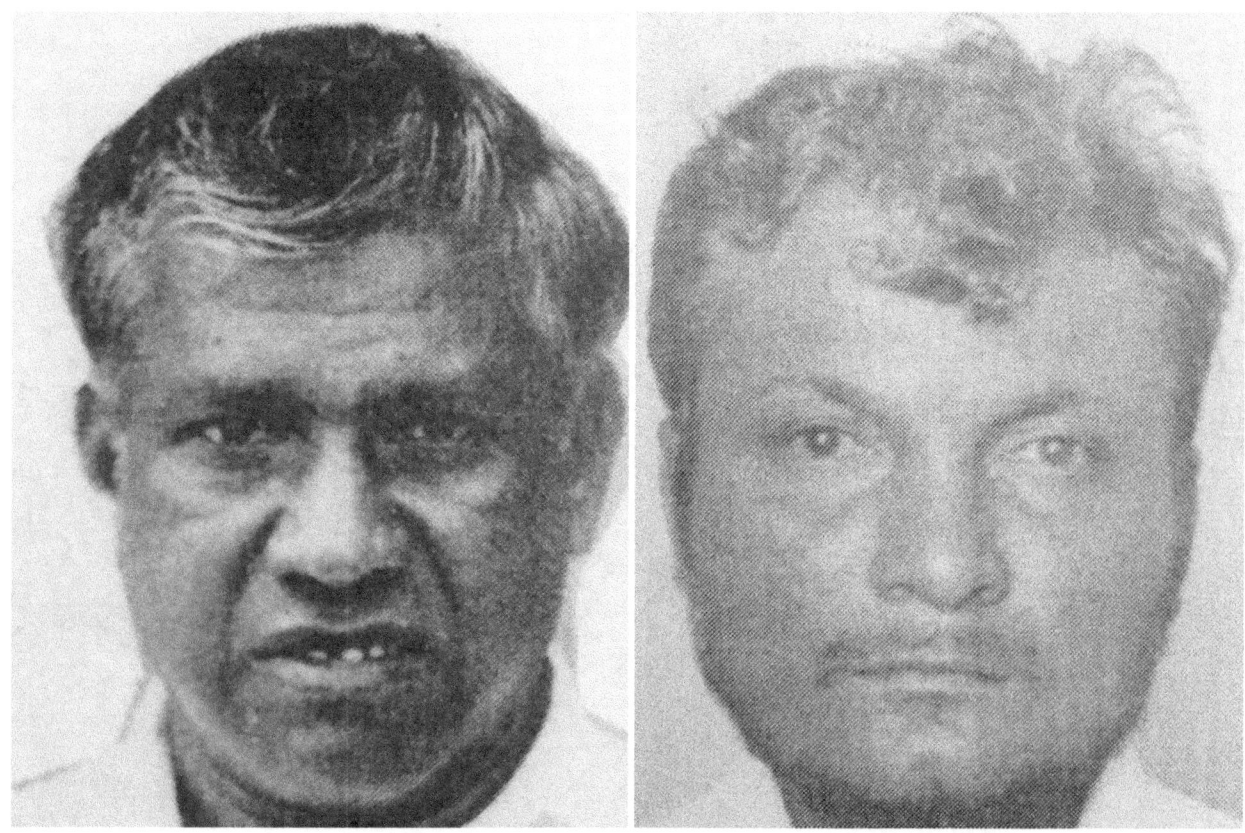

Sagun Beepot

Donald Buddha

Johnny Mykoo

Petronia Dean

Jeremiah Campbell   *Denyse Baboolal*

Jeremiah Campbell and Denyse Baboolal through their radio program, WAVS Indian Talent Sangeet on WAVS 1170 AM in South Florida, regularly play the songs of Indian Folk Songs of the Caribbean. On Sunday, January 7, 2018, WAVS Indian Talent Sangeet dedicated an entire program to the album, bringing the production to a new generation, more than thirty years after its release.

Jeremiah was born in the parish of St. Elizabeth and grew up in Big Lane, Central Village, St. Catherine, a once vibrant Indian community. He inherited his love of the Indian culture from his mother. Jeremiah is a good friend of the Malgie family. He is a radio personality at WAVS 1170 AM.

Denyse is from Trinidad and currently runs an Indian cultural group, Jaya Devi Arts Inc. in South Florida. Jaya Devi Arts promotes Indo-Caribbean culture within the Diaspora residing in South Florida. Denyse and her group performs at numerous locations, including Jamaica.

Members of the Indian Talent Merrymaker Band which worked on the production of the Indian Folk Songs of the Caribbean series.

From Left to Right: Dr. Junior Moses Gallow, Joe Allen, Dr. Ashraf Beharrie, Roger Gallow, Errol Gallow, Michael Gallow, Bobby Maragh. At Front is Krishna Deonarine.

EXEMPLARY COMMUNITY SERVICE

As a Justice of the Peace for twenty-five years, I was awarded the prestigious Golden Scale Award in 2002 by the Lay Magistrates Association for being the most outstanding Justice of the Peace in the county of Surrey.

Justices of the Peace at Bombay Farm. From Left to Right: Roy Beckford, Carlton Stephen, Dorothy Findlayson, Rainford Harding, Carl Estick, Henry Jaghai, Wilbert Tallo, Kenton Morgan, Wilbert Elliston, Arthur McNeish. At Front: Elvena Reittie, Noreen Charlton, Merline Heholt, Clarice Campbell, Norman Heholt

St. Thomas Aquinas Classmates Reunion at Bombay Farm. At Front from Left to Right: Ronald Bryan, Harry Jaghai, Sunny Brown, Mrs. Alvin Brewster, Alvin Brewster, Brewster, John Russell, Gifford Morris, Cherry Montgomery. At Back: Ivan Montgomery, Leslie Smith, Oswald Green, Basil Murray, Henry Jaghai, Buster.

FAMILY LIFE

Myrtle and I have been thankful for all of life's mercies. We especially feel contented and confident that we have laid a solid foundation for our children, five of whom are married and have their own families. We find happiness in our grandchildren, Alicia, Stacy, Rajesh, Tira, Shari, Sasha, Alex, Adam, Tiffany and Matthew, and our great grandchildren Alani, Miya, Dominic and Ari.

Pardes Book Launch

In 2015, I released Pardes: Stories Through The Eyes of a Pardesi's Grandson inspired by my grandparents Jaghai and Autaria. The publication featured the stories of the journey made by my grandparents and other East Indian indentured immigrants to Jamaica and the subsequent achievements of their descendants. It also depicts the cultural and religious influences they brought to Jamaica.

In September 2015, I held a launch for the book, in Miramar, Florida to celebrate and promote its release. The launch was well attended, and the program consisted of Indian cultural performances. Many of those featured in the book were present.

Pardes book launch at St. Bartholomew Hall, Miramar, Florida

Attendees at launch

The Jaghai Family

Standing L to R: Mark Williams, Patrick Jaghai, Andrea Jaghai-Williams, Joy Jaghai, Rajesh Jaghai, Adam Jaghai, Myrtle Jaghai, Henry Jaghai, Matthew Williams, Andrew Jaghai, Barbara Jaghai-Bahadur, Sasha Jaghai, Stacy Bahadur, Peter Jaghai, Ali Bahadur, Marcia Jaghai, Miya DeLisser

At Front: Dr. Alicia Bahadur, Tira Jaghai, Tiffany Jaghai, Alani Milan, Charmaine Jaghai

L-R: Barbara Jaghai-Bahadur, Alani Milan, Dr. Alicia Bahadur, Myrtle Jaghai, Stacy Bahadur, Henry Jaghai O.D. J.P., Ali Bahadur

L-R: Rajesh Jaghai, Myrtle Jaghai, Henry Jaghai O.D. J.P., Patrick Jaghai, Joy Maragh-Jaghai

L-R: Tira Jaghai, Miya Delisser, Adam Jaghai, Andrew Jaghai, Laura Persaud, Marcia Baccas-Jaghai, Alex Jaghai

L-R: Mark Williams, Andrea Jaghai-Williams, Myrtle Jaghai, Henry Jaghai O.D. J.P., Matthew Williams

L-R: Sasha Jaghai, Tiffany Jaghai, Myrtle Jaghai, Henry Jaghai O.D. J.P., Charmaine Francis-Jaghai, Peter Jaghai

L-R: Tiffany Jaghai, Sasha Jaghai, Tira Jaghai, Stacy Bahadur, Dr. Alicia Bahadur

L-R: John Khan, Crista Sirjue, Doreen Sirjue, Jean Khan, Myrtle Jaghai, Andrew Jaghai, Henry Jaghai O.D. J.P., Barbara Khan, Ingrid Persaud, Keith Sardarsingh

L-R: Myrtle Jaghai, Andrea Jaghai-Williams, Crista Sirjue, Henrietta Jadusingh, Doreen Sirjue, Jean Khan, Donna Maragh, Ingrid Persaud, Barbara Jaghai-Bahadur, Barbara Khan

L-R: Connie Kadoo, Irene Arjun-Henry, Blossom, Silvia Deans, Myrtle Jaghai, Rosetta Arjun-Singh, Henrietta Jadusingh, Jayla, Karen Chevannes, Alvarene Arjun, Donna Maragh

L-R: Crista Sirjue, Henry Jaghai, Rajesh Jaghai, Hazel Maragh, Myrtle Jaghai, Terry Maragh, Andre Maragh

L-R: Marcel Chevannes, Rajiv Chevannes, Karen Chevannes, Donna Maragh, Henrietta Jadusingh, Joseph Maragh

From L-R: Mark Williams, Monica Campbell, Shari Mendel, Julian & Ari Mendel, Myrtle & Henry Jaghai

Dax Reid

Dax Reid and Jamindians of South Florida performing at the launch

Dax Reid was born in Vere, Clarendon to parents Roydel and Rosetta Reid. He was the third of seven children. He attended Vere Technical High School, C.A.S.T. and V.T.D.I., studying Mechanical Engineering. Reid worked as a high school teacher for 21 years. Upon migrating to the USA he worked at Air Jamaica for 10 years and for the Broward County Aviation Department for the past 5 years, being based at the Fort Lauderdale Hollywood International Airport. He learned to dance from Azim Beharrie's first record. He danced for the Indian Merry Makers Band, the Johnny Mykoo Band, and the Indian Band of Clarendon. Reid served on the committee to celebrate the first Indian Arrival Day festivities on May 10, 1995. He prepared and read the script of the history of the arrival, and did a frock dance. He performed a Nachania dance at the launch of Pardes in September 2015 to great acclaim.

I would like to sincerely thank the Jamindians of South Florida band, vocalists and all performers at the Pardes book launch.

Dax Reid, Krishna Budhoo, Henry Jaghai, Suckmin Ali, Glen Maragh

Henry Jaghai, Rose, Juliette/HUsband, Sam, Barry

Ali and Barbara Bahadur

Ali Husain Bahadur *Barbara Bahadur*

Ali Husaine Bahadur was born on April 9, 1949 at East Avenue, Greenwich Farm to parents Alladeen Bahadur and Miriam Bahadur. His siblings are Huimad (Sonny), Lovina, Patricia, Lateka, Alfred and Donald. The family relocated to Windsor Road in Spanish Town.

Ali attended St. Catherine Primary School, then went to Barracks All Age School. In 1966, he moved to Kingston to live with his uncle and aunt, Ernest and Hussaine Husman. There he learned the trade of tyre vulcanizing. His expertise in the field led him to be a co-owner and manager for A & A Tyre and Vulcanizing Company Limited.

Ali was a member of the All Indian cricket team that won the Balram Trophy in 1973. He also toured with the All Indian team in 1973 to Trinidad and Guyana. He is a member of Domtar Cricket Club. He is also an avid racehorse fan.

He married Barbara Jaghai, a registered nurse in December 1979. The union produced two daughters, Alicia, a medical doctor, and Stacy Ann, a registered nurse. Ali is the proud grandfather of Alani and Dominic Milan.

Barbara Jaghai was born on September 4, 1958 to parents Henry and Myrtle Jaghai. Her siblings are Patrick, Andrew, Andrea, Peter and Paul. Barbara attended Wolmer's Prep School then, Wolmer's Girls' School for her secondary education. She attended nursing school at the University of the West Indies, Mona.

After graduating from nursing school, Barbara worked as a school nurse at Wolmers Prep, her Alma Mater . She volunteered her services at Prema Clinic run by Dr. Hame Persaud at 10 Henderson Avenue. A few years after, she migrated to the United States. Her first job there was in Texas. After that she went to Florida and currently works at Memorial Manor in Miramar, Florida.

Barbara was a stellar hockey player and represented her school.

Dr. Alicia Bahadur, Dominic Milan, Stacy Bahadur R.N., Alani Milan

John Hill Suckie and wife Bhagwantie

John Hill Suckie, known as Hagaroo was born to parents Suckie and his wife Harkey who left their homeland Uttar Pradesh, India in February 1903. They boarded the passenger ship SS Dahomey, which sailed from Calcutta (Kolkata), en route to Jamaica. They landed in Portland, Jamaica in April 1903. Suckie and his wife were recruited to work on the Vinery Estate in Portland, on a five- year indentureship work programme.

Up on completion of the contract, they remained in Jamaica and started a new life. While working on the estate, Harkey gave birth to her first child in 1905, Gurcharan, commonly called Hagaroo (my wife's father).

Hagaroo, was registered in the name of the estate owner, John Hill, and consequently became known as John Hill. His siblings included John, George, Benjamin, Taga, and Louisa.

Hagaroo married Bhagwantie (Minnie) Sirichand in an arranged marriage as teenagers while living in St. Mary.

Bhagwantie's parents came from Bombay, India on April 8, 1903. Her father, Sirichand and her mother, arrived in Jamaica on the ship SS Dahomey that sailed from the Port of Calcutta (Kolkata). They were recruited to work at Fort Stewart Estate in St Mary, owned by Wilmot Westmoreland.

Sirichand went to Cuba in the hopes of securing economic prosperity, leaving his wife and two of Minnie's siblings George and Alice in Jamaica. After a year Minnie's mother became frustrated and went back to India with her two other children. She encouraged Minnie to go to India as well, but Minnie chose to stay with her new husband and his family in Jamaica.

Suckie and Harkey relocated their family to Sam Brown Pen in Whitehall, St. Andrew to seek a more secure future.

The union of Hagaroo and Minnie produced eleven children (my wife and her siblings): Alfred, Rosetta, Louisa, Joseph, Henrietta, Katherine, Elizabeth, Ivan, Myrtle (my wife), Enid and Parceram.

Hagaroo and Minnie leased seven acres of land situated at the bottom of 23 Mannings Hill Road, known as Lindsay Pen. The property adjoined his parents own at Sam Brown Pen. They built a wattle and daub house, made of bamboo and cow dung mixed with clay. To provide for themselves and their children, they planted peas, tobacco and tomatoes while utilizing the rainy season to water their crops.

Sirichand returned to Jamaica and learned his wife and two youngest children went back to India. While seeking employment at Grays Inn Estate in St. Mary, Sirichand met Bafatan and together they had a son Sankar who was born on the estate in 1924. Subsequently, Sirichand formed a relationship with Margaret Hill known as Maya, who was married and had children before but her husband had died. Sirichand and Maya had a daughter together, Icilda known as Auntie Dad. Sirichand purchased thirteen acres of land on Job Lane in Spanish Town, St. Catherine. He divided the land equally between his two daughters Minnie and Icilda. The area consisted of a vibrant Indian community where rice farming was supported by an irrigation system.

During dry times, farming was difficult at Lindsay Pen so Hagaroo brought most of his children to Job Lane on the weekends to help cultivate the rice crop, while he worked on the land for most of the season.

At Lindsay Pen, on the weekends Minnie would bring her produce of peas, tobacco and tomatoes to sell at Coronation Market in Kingston. She used the money earned to purchase groceries to sustain her family for the week. Hagaroo and Minnie also had cows that they milked and gave Hagaroo's brother John to sell the milk. Hagaroo also owned two steers that he would use to plough his own land and would also be hired to plough the land of others.

Mr. Lindsay gave Hagaroo and Minnie notice to vacate the land at Lindsay Pen after many years living there, as it was sold for development. They then purchased a quarter acre of land at 5 Plum Lane, Kingston 8.

Most of their children migrated to England, some to United States and the rest remained in Jamaica. Ivan was the first to migrate to England in 1955 paving the way for his other siblings. Parceram was the first to migrate to the United States followed by Alfred and his family, and Myrtle and her family.

Wedding of Catherine (Hagaroo and Minnie's daughter) From Left to Right: Herbert Maragh (son-in-law) Elizabeth Sukie (daughter and wife of Herbert) Daisy Sulie (daughter-in-law), James Anderson (son-in-law), Juggie Sukie (daughter), Baba Juggan (son-in-law, married to Catherine), Catherine Sukie (daughter), Pung (son), Ivan Sukie (son)

Everal "Baba" Juggan and Catherine Suckie Juggan

Everal Juggan, also known as Baba, was born on 25th February 1930 in St Mary, Jamaica. He was the second eldest of seven children born to parents Samuel and Catherine Juggan. His siblings were Martha, Edna, Dolly, Herbert, Stanley and Icy. He attended Elliott School situated at the top of a hill in St Mary, Jamaica.

To help his parents and siblings, Everal left school at the age of 14 to perform rural farming duties. He gained employment at the Experiment Farm also known as Orange River. His job was doing lining and contouring of the land, until the Farm was acquired by Morris Cargill, a prominent land owner in St. Mary.

He went to England on the 23rd October 1957 and started working on the 24th October 1957 with the company Bradley Crook in Park Royal. At the age of 87 years he is still with the company despite changing hands several times. It is now called Hanama Storage. Baba frequently visits his family home in Jamaica.

In 1958 Everal met Jane Catherine in Park Royal. Catherine, whose parents Hagaroo and Minnie, who were also from St. Mary, was born on the 22nd April 1929 in Sam Brown Pen in St. Andrew. She attended Swallowfield School located on Mannings Hill Road. After leaving school she was the primary specialized chef for her family. Her siblings were Alfred, Rosetta, Louisa, Joseph, Henrietta, Elizabeth, Ivan, Myrtle, Enid and Parceram known as Mitchie. She migrated to England in 1958 and worked at Aaron Wesley, then at St. Mary's Hospital in London. On the 8th August 1959, Everal and Catherine got married. They raised three children Peter, Paul and Priscilla, and lived at Chevening Road in Kensal Rise.

Everal and Catherine were very accommodating to Henry Jaghai and his workers, when they visited England on business trips.

Everal and Jane have three grandchildren and one great grand-daughter. Their twin grandsons are Aaron and Joshua from Paul, and grand-daughter, Keisha who is studying Level 3 Business/Marketing and has her own clothing business, from Priscilla, a civil servant. Their great grand-daughter Isabella is the daughter of Joshua.

Peter Paul Priscilla

Joshua and Isabella Aaron Keisha

Hagaroo's and Minnie's Grandchildren and Great Grandchildren

Phyllis Hill Sukie-Bijou

Phyllis Hill Sukie-Bijou was born in 1947 to parents Alfred Hill Sukie of Sam Brown Pen, St. Andrew and Maggie Puranda of Jabbie Gullie in Norbrook, St. Andrew. Her siblings are Winston, Roosevelt, Theresa, Hewitt, Venmarie, Aston, Althia, and Horett. They lived at 53 White Hall Avenue and in 1962 moved to Red Hills Road.

Phyllis attended Swallowfield All Age from 1953-1962 and the Jackie Swaby School of Business in 1979. She received certifications from the Jackie Swaby School of Business and Leonard DeCordova Seminars.

Phyllis worked at LDC Lighthouse in Kingston as a Branch Manager from 1979-1983, as a supervisor for Leonard DeCordova Ltd. from 1984-1991, and then as a sales associate at American Jewelry Company from 1991-1999. Upon migrating to the United States in 1999, she gained employment at J. C. Penney as a sales associate until 2013, after which she worked part-time at T.J. Maxx.

Phyllis married Lester Bijou, of St. Thomas in 1966. They had 3 children Douglas, Richard and Susan. Both boys went to Jamaica College, and Susan attended Queens and Immaculate High Schools. Susan spent a year at the University of the West Indies Mona, and then transferred to Barry University where she graduated as a nurse. She worked at Parkway hospital and Memorial West. Susan then studied to become a pharmacist at Nova Southeastern University and now works at Memorial West Hospital. Richard operates a trucking business in Jamaica. Unfortunately, Lester passed on in 1984, and Douglas died in 1987.

Back: Phyllis, Theresa, Venmarie, Hewitt, Winston, Aston
Front: Maggie, Alfred, Horett

L-R: Lester, Phyliss, Susan, Richard, Douglas

Faith Maragh

I'm Faith Maragh (Fay) I'm the daughter of Elizabeth Suckie Maragh (Lizzy) and Herbert (Butty) Maragh I'm the oldest of 7 Children I was born in Mary Brown Corner, St. Andrew on March 19, 1951. My siblings are Herman, Junior, Christine, Tony, Derben, and Michael. I spend many Happy Day's with my beloved Grandparents Minnie and Aggroo Suckie Hill who lived on Plum Lane off Whitehall Avenue. As the years went by my Daddy decided to migrate to England in 1958. We all attended Swallowfield Elementary.

In October 1961, my Parents decided it time for me to join them in London England. My Auntie Myrtle and Uncle Sonny took care of my Immigration Papers. They saw me off at Palisados Airport Kingston for my flight to Gatwick England. My parents were living in Fernhead Road Paddington N.W.9. I attended St. Luke Primary School at the top of Fernhead Road 10 minutes from our home I was there for short time my parents move to another Flat 38 Chippenham Road Paddington, after awhile my parents decided to move to a larger house, so we move to 165 Fordwych Road Cricklewood N.W.2. After awhile my parents decided it's time their 4 younger childrens should join us I was so excited our family would be together as one big happy family.

It's time for me to think my future Career that I would like to pursue I sat with my daddy to discuss this, my mummy stay out of this cause she knew I really wanted to do Modeling but my daddy never hear of this. I said to my daddy I'm going to tell you what job I like he nod is head, I would like to join to the "Woman Royal Air Force" my daddy "No" why not daddy? you'll have go to War and they will shoot you down, ok what about working for Air Lines as a Air Hostess " No the Plane will crash" ok well daddy there's a Hairdressing course and it's for 2 Years at Chiswick Polytechnic, is reply " well this sound good" started college it's going well I entered quite a few Hairdressing Competition and did very well.

After my 2 years ended I was offered a Job working on a cruise line, low and behold my daddy said "No No" but why daddy? "the Ship can Sink" I said daddy what would you like me to do he said "I want you to be a Secretary and work in a Office" Anyways after finish College I work as a Hairdresser in a busy Salon in Kilburn High Road but I still wanted do my Modeling but I would never disrespect my daddy. I met my husband through family my daddy met him and gave 3rd Degree, daddy was cool so was my intended husband you may have read about my now Ex-husband from Westmoreland In my uncle's book Parades, when my Daddy Aunts and Uncles visited the family many years ago.

After getting married I started working for a Fashion House doing Modeling I was enjoying my work I was give the opportunity to go to Paris to do the Catwalk but I was expecting my first baby. I have Pursue many jobs after having my first daughter, I was the first Pinup Girl for the New West Indian World Medical Optical Nurse went into Medical Nursing which I'm qualified as a LPN. The Good Lord as BLESS me with 8 Children, Andrea Donna, Natasha, Samantha, Denise and Marvin Davis (twins). I have 6 Grandchildren 4 Boys 2 Girls, Conrad Jr and Ocean Glaze; Aja Glaze; Semiia Pierre; Tarai and Sanai Edgehill. I know my daddy is looking down on me smiling because I'm working in an Office.

Faye and her eight children Faye, Andrea (cousin), Christine (sister)

Bennett Family

There are many outstanding Indians who have contributed to their communities in various ways. I would like to tell you about one humble family which did their part to make their local community, and by extension, our island, a more pleasant place to live.

Mr Harold Bennett hailed from Annotto Bay, St Mary. He was a goat trader, travelling the length and breadth of the island buying goats to sell at McCook's Pen. He made many friends on his treks, and was fond of telling tales of his adventures. His father, Benjamin, a worker at the Grey's Inn Plantation, helped him to meet a suitable match in Belfield, St Mary in the Matthew's family. Her name was Lewine, but was called Bee because she was always busy.

 After getting married in the late 1940's, they moved to Kingston, living with other Indians at Payne Land. They later acquired land at Goffe Terrace where they started their family. As the family multiplied, Mr Bennett knew that he could no longer travel and so he did a course in bartending and became employed in the hotel industry, where he worked for many decades. He won a number of prizes for his cocktails and mixed drinks in competitions. Poppa is proud that he appeared (as a bartender) in Dr No, a James Bond movie. Mr Bennett was an industrious man and had to work extremely hard to adequately provide for his growing family.

Aunty Bee, as Mrs Bennett was called, wanted to help her husband, but he was adamant that his wife would not work in any of the numerous factories situated around Spanish Town Road. Mrs Bennett started growing calalloo and other vegetables, which she would sell to the local community. She would, however, give away ackee, limes, soursop because her philosophy was: if it grows naturally without cost, it is a sin to profit from it.

It is during this time, in the 1960's that she started making our famous marsala. Every one of her children had to become involved in the making of this labour intensive spice: parching, milling, mixing, packaging and marketing. This gourmet delight has satisfied palates all over the world, including British royalty.

Our family had strong and loyal political views. They were unashamedly JLP, when political views were not as violent or all-consuming as it has been in past decades. As Indians, they loved Tevares because they felt he understood their plight and trusted him to address them.

This love of community made Harold and Lewine's children pursue vocations and professions that reflect this. Accounting (Owen), nursing, (Rachel and Annett), business (Melvin) and education (Magurite), were just some of the occupations of the family.

We must never forget the late Courtney's contribution to Indian music, being the first bass guitar player to play in a band of its kind. Melvin was instrumental in helping the poor in our community by convincing the church and politicians to build houses, help with school supplies and fees, providing food as well as seeking to train young people to run their own businesses.

Our family has always been involved in Dharma. When we were small, although we went to the Catholic Church in the mornings, we had to go to SDM (Sanata Dharma Mandir) in the afternoons. Mr Bennett believed that his children should become acquainted with Hinduism and our culture. We met at Cling Cling Avenue and was taught by MrCaloo. Years later, Prema Satsangh had one of its first meetings at our house and the whole fun of fellowship began. Phagwah celebrations were one of the highlights of the year. Hame Persaud was the leader, and along with Lewis Sipaul, Owen Badaloo, Winston and Rohan Toland and family, Daddy Ram and Phillip Graham, Cherry and the Sobah family, we had a wonderful time exploring our culture. Of course over time many were added to our numbers.

One of the main events that is memorable to me was the stage show that we performed in. Mr Jaghai's home on Rosalee Avenue was the destination for us three girls to rehearse. Jewan Chowte was the organiser of that show and he did an excellent job. Annett and I were given a chance to dance, sing and I performed a monologue that I had written. Rachel designed the costumes, which were used again for performing at the Kingston Centenary at the National Stadium. Going to Clarendon, St Mary and performing on the stage at Regal Theatre was a wonderful experience. Our parents were so proud.

The boys in the family were not to be outdone by the Bennett sisters. Melvin, Owen and Courtney along with others from the community saw a need for activities to occupy our young people. They formed The Turban Youth Club. Although on the face of it this club engaged in domino and cricket competitions, the ethos of professionalism went much deeper and the youth saw their potential. Young people were exposed to formal meetings, accountability, fun, achievements and comradery.

13 Goffee Terrace was the community hub for so many. Mrs Bennett was always the matriarch, overseeing the well-being of visitors, feeding them and giving advice. When people think about our family, it is with the memory of acceptance, full stomachs and comfort. May our children and our children's children continue this tradition.

Melvin Bennett

Being the sixth child in a family of seven is not always easy in the 1960's. The Bennett family were never laid back and expected much from their children. Melvin was a leader of mischief for the three last boys: Owen, Melvin and Courtney (now deceased).

Harold Bennett had to work at nights, so the children had to keep quiet while he slept in the afternoons. Mud was one of the medium they used to play in. They made televisions, which were the new thing in those days. There were only a few in the community, and the Bennett household had not yet acquired a set in 1965. Melvin remembered fashioning and shaping them from mud, then putting glass over the front after putting comic strip pictures to make them realistic. They even included tiny knobs to simulate on/off switches and antennae for bright pictures. Ironically, they also played 'shopkeeper' where they would have sand, dirt, rotten breadfruit (for butter) and old tins and bottles as goods. At other times, they indulged in games of 'cowboys and Indians' or 'police and thieves'.

There is fond memory of all the brothers and sisters helping in some way to build the back room of the house at Goffee Terrace; Melvin became interested in DIY at an early age and helped his parents to repair and build many things. He helped to extend the family home by adding three bedrooms, bathroom and store room, while training amateur builders, who later helped him to repair the temple. It is a point of interest that he built his own house consisting of two bedrooms, luxury bathroom, living room and veranda, above his extended business.

After leaving DuPont Primary school, he went to Penwood Secondary, then on to St. Andrew Technical to do a course in Carpentry and Building. He returned to Penwood at the request of the Principal to help to teach the students in Grades 7-9 Woodwork (Youth Service). Later, he was invited to sit on the Board of Governors where he proposed some changes for improving the school. He was also a member of DuPont Primary School Board and the West Central Kingston Trust Fund.

In February, 1983 he was asked by the legendary Johnny Mykoo to join the Raja Sarangi Group as his personal assistant, treasurer and promoter. In only one year, they achieved the greatest success any traditional Indian band could achieve. They played at different venues fifty four (54) times, including five (5) major stage shows. They bought the first Indian band to visit Westmoreland in Grange Hill. As a result of this success, they were able to replace old equipment with new and purchased t - shirts emblazoned with the name of Johnny Mykoo, to identify us as a proper band.

In June of 1984, the discussion of an Indian club started, but did not materialise immediately. When Kamla Tolan asked him to start Turban Youth Club, it was really needed. He was in charge for fifteen (15) consecutive years; 7 times he was elected president and 5 years as director. The nickname 'Gadhafi' was given to him because of his strict style of leadership. This style had to be enforced because there were some 'loose cannons' whose only objective was to bring distention among our members. Although cricket and dominoes were the sports played competitively, there were many other youth development programmes that were entered into. There was a need for re development in the community because of the violence and chaos they had gone through during the 1980 election campaign, so the club became more than just a sports club. The club encouraged skills training. Melvin remembers sending members of the club to Sully's and Shaw's garage to be trained in mechanics, Stedman's Welding Shop and Olive's Beauty Shop to be trained in Hair and Beauty. Some have established successful businesses both in Jamaica and other foreign countries because of the training, ethos and discipline of this club. Members of the club volunteered to help children with their school work and Courtney taught subjects at CXC level.

After Hurricane Gilbert in 1988, many people lost their homes so Melvin and members of the Turban Youth Club helped to house 62 people of one week, and then helped them to get back on their feet. The club was also concerned about the pollution caused by the smoke from fires at the Riverton City dump, so they wrote letters as early as 1984 to the then Minister of Environment, Mr Ronald Ervin, complaining about smoke and odour exuding from the dump.

Melvin was concerned about the state of the Indian Temple on Hagley Park Road. It had not been in operation for nearly 17 years. He started to negotiate with Mr. D. 'Gums' Maragh. They started Satsang with the help of some friends at 11 Goffee Terrace. The Indians in the community were thirsty for mandir, and over 50 became members in only three months. This convinced Mr Maragh of the need for a permanent place for worship and cultural fellowship, and so the clean-up and repairs to the Temple was given the go ahead on May 3rd, 1995. It took 8 long months of meetings and hard work, but by January 1996, the Sanatan Dharma Mandir was open for worship and cultural community activities. Melvin was president of the committee for 5 years before migrating to Florida.

While at a meeting of the West Central Kingston Trust Fund, Melvin and MP Hon. A. J. Nicholson discussed the importance of the development of housing and easier access to land for the poor in Jamaica. Three months after that, Operation Pride was introduced. During this time, he decided to go into politics and ran for a seat in Cockburn Pen. He lost, but continued working in the community for another two years as caretaker. Melvin was a member of the church council of St. Pius X for 10 years. He negotiated with Food for the Poor and Father Burchell (now the Arch Bishop of Cornwall County) to redevelop the Bellrock community by building 128 X2 bedroom houses for the poor, whose houses were falling apart. In addition to this, he was also a part of the committee which set up medical, optical and dental clinics to benefit the wider community. Melvin also negotiated to rebuild and repair Saint Steven's and Trinitarian Basic Schools.

In all this time, Melvin was a businessman who operated a grocery business. He started his shop with only $750, but as an entrepreneur, saw opportunities to gain customers while helping the poor of the community. The people were going Downtown, Kingston looking for cheaper goods, so he started the concept of wholesale shopping for the poor. The shop was a great success and had to rapidly expand and employ more staff. At one-point Melvin was in charge of 14 members of staff and had the most modern cash register and electronic scale, the first in the local area.

Melvin Bennett has 3 children: Shakera, Indra and Daneash, 3 grandchildren to date, is divorced and living in Fort Lauderdale, Florida and is now working as a seafood manager at Publix.

Sogun Beepat

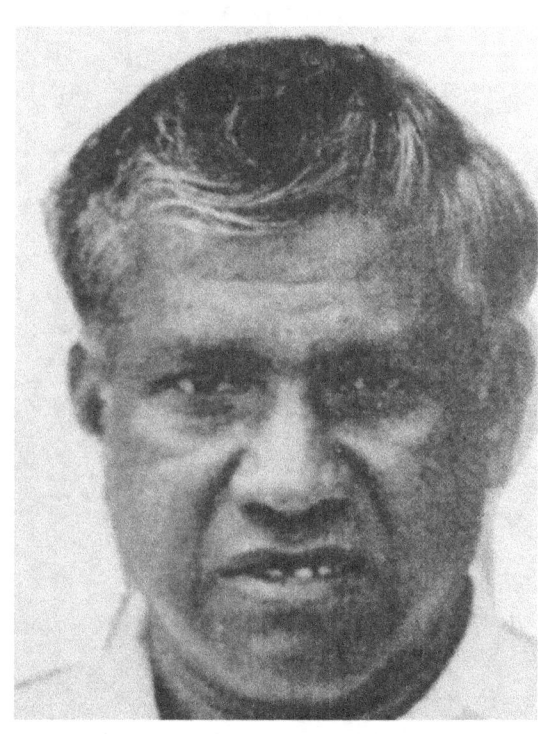

Rambahal "Sugun" Beepot was born on 31St January 1933 and lived at 124 Spanish Town Road Grantham Pen near the Majestic Thaetre. His mother Elizabeth "Dantali" Beepot was from St Mary his father Dindial Beepot from Maypen Clarendon was a carpenter. Sugun has been singing local Indian traditional folk songs from as early as 1948 and his rendition of traditional Indian folk songs draws strong appeal and support from both young and old alike.

Sugun attended the Greenwich Farm school in Kingston Jamaica and by 15 years old was involved in fishing and farming and started working at Woods Product near Captain Morgan in four miles making foodbox for food transportation and export.

His interest in traditional Indian folk music was fueled by

his uncle Hardial Beepot, a singer and a drum and fiddle (sarangie) player who was taught by his mother Sugun's Agie (grandmother) and he along with Dookie and Baran played at Indian functions all over the island especially in Clarendon, Portland, St. Mary, and at Norman Browns home at four miles Penwood Road especially at Hosay events celebration that Norman would keep in lieu of a serious injury he received from the horns of one of his bull cows where they would play the Tassa, a small loud drum that was played with two flexible sticks and a large Yabba Drum made from mackerel barrel and supported around their necks with a strong rope and played in a procession as they carried the beautifully decorated Mosque shaped tomb known as the Tadjah to the beach and discard it in the sea with the purpose of drowning the sickness. Later on during subsequent trips to Jamaica from England he would sing at venues like Red Head's Bar at Solitair Road with the Raja Sarangi Group which was led by Johnny Mykoo and sons Phillip and Treavor, and musicians Francis Baccas, Courtney Bannett, Bobby Maragh.

He recorded his first two wedding songs for Mr. Henry Jaghai OD JP on the "Indian Folk Songs of The Caribbean" album in 1988 titled "Aila WehRanga Bhawan Me" and "Joban Ochari"

Sugun and his wife Dorris Beepot (Miss Grassy daughter) along with his adopted sons Ronald, Satcha and Kimraj Jackson migrated from Jamaica to England in 1958 initially to London and then moved to Birmingham. He has four sisters Jugia, Evelyn, Mavis and Rosie along with three brothers Raphael, Lothan, and Suielal.

Indian Folk Artistes and Musicians.
Back Row (L-R): Wally Byroo, Thaddeus Bessie, Samuel Abdul, Ramlal Malgie, Sugun Beepat, John Khan.
Front (L-R): Polly Sookraj, Jody Doodnath, Henry W. Jaghai, Sagar Sookraj, Petrona Deans

Thaddeus Bessi

Thaddeus was born on March 31, 1948 to parents Bessie and Agatha Jaggon. He attended Hayes All-Age School in Clarendon. He worked as a successful motorcycle mechanic. He was married to Joy Bessi. They have four children; Christine, a nurse in Canada, Andrea, Indarpaul, director of a heavy-duty equipment company in Jamaica, and Simone. Thaddeus started singing at age 18. He recorded songs on the Indian Folk Songs of the Caribbean L.P. produced by Henry Jaghai. Thaddeus was the best singer in Clarendon of Indian Folk Songs, and was known as the "crowd pleaser." He also recorded his own CD with 8 heart rendering melodies. Thaddeus traveled to perform in Trinidad at various stage shows with other Jamaican artistes. He was well received by the Trinidadian crowd. This tour was under the patronage of Henry Jaghai.

His songs included: Suba Bharnee Na Jai, Baiya Moray, Ramchandra, Siya Maanalay, Waha Gore Tu, Rame Rame Ratan, Suba Barni, Sugana Rama.

Thaddeus was one of the main singers at the Bushy Park stage shows. He was on of the singers for the dancing contests. He was an integral part of the 150 Celebration of Indian arrival in Jamaica. He won the singing contest in Hayes, Clarendon his home town. His prize was fifteen thousand Jamaican dollars. He was well respected in the Clarendon area.

Cislyn Marie Brown

Born in Belfield, St. Mary on July 16 19 44, to Parent Moses and Sarah Ouditt, she moved to Kingston when she was 6 years old with her sister Lethie. Her family was humble and hard working people, who taught her to work for what she need. Both grand Parents from both sides the Ramdans and the Ouditt came from India as indentured laborers.

In Kingston she attended Cockburn Pen and Seaward All age school, then move on to Winsor High school. She did not complete high School as her parent could not afford it and she went on to learn dress making and fashion designing with Madam Nina Pile.

In the 1970s her family left Jamaica because of the political violence but she stayed at her Lothian Ave home located in the volatile waterhouse community along the borderline of the two major political constituencies, it was at this time she start taking care of other children whose parent had left them because of the violence, she took in about 8 boys and sometimes their parent would visit them. She was involved in youth club and other activity to keep herself occupied. She then met Mrs. Coleen Yap, wife of MP Ferdinand Yap who ask her to assist in the political work in the area. She did not think of the dangers involved in the political work, she only thought of the needs of the community. Both women had a lot of respect for each other as they worked in service of the community; Mrs. Yap became the first Mayor for Kingston and St Andrew from West Central Saint Andrew and was a great source of pride and inspiration. She ran in the local Government Election in 1991 and lost, but continues to work for Jamaica Labor Party.

Cislyn worked at several different kind of jobs firstly as a manager for a restaurant and operated a canteen at the New Yorker shirt factory for seven years. After her family left Jamaica she started her own Security Training School called the Delta Security Training School and after a few years of operation was employed by the Vanguard Group of companies as a security trainer, a job she maintained even while serving as a councilor, she was ordained as a Justice Of The Peace in 2003.

After the passing of Mr. Yap she was ask by MP Derrick Smith to do the enumeration and with his guidance and help from other members of the party they had several caretakers coming to the constituency. While most didn't believe they could win they left the constituency. Mr. Andrew Holness who was the youngest to come and offer themselves for service, had developed a very strong team by then. Mr. Andrew Holness became our MP in 1998 and she won the Local Government Election for the Olympic Garden Division by over 1600 votes and served the division for 3 terms totaling almost 14 years.

During those years they had youth clubs, Golden age club, food programs to assist the elderly with food packages and Back to school assistance for families with financial difficulties, she had friends who she could call on to assist with paying school Fee for several students and also kept a annual Christmas dinner for the elderly. She was the only Indian Councilor at the KSAC until Answerd Ramcharan won his Division.

She feels very proud to have had the pleasure of working with 3 Prime Ministers; Hon. Edward Seaga, Hon. Bruce Golding and Hon. Andrew Holness who is also the current MP.
She is the mother of 6 children 3 girls and 3 boys Dianne, Michelle, Selena, Andrew, Rupert Jr and Maurice.

Wally Byroo

Albert Wally Byroo, was born March 17, 1940, to father, Alfred Byroo of Westmoreland, and mother, Violet Byroo of Seafort, Saint Thomas. When he lost his father at an early age, he and his mother went to live with her family [in Seafort, Saint Thomas for approximately 1 year; before later settling down with her in Kingston. He is the eldest of 3 children. His 2 sisters are Dorothy and Merclyn.

Wally attended 'Halfway Tree Elementary School'. At the age of 15, he enrolled at 'Prendigas Engineering Works', on Spainsh Town Road, to learn the trade to become a machinist. However, he decided to leave the training after 6 months, following an altercation between himself and another apprentice of the program. He then decided to take up the trade of barbering instead. His career began at 'Khani's Barber Shop'. He later transferred to 'Samuel Narainsingh Barber'; and then finally settled down at 'Daniel Rainbow Barber's', where he spent approximately 5 years.

In 1958, he met a young lady, by the name of Amy Thomas; who hailed from Stand Pipe Lane in Saint Andrew. In time, they married and started growing their own family. The couple had 3 children, 2 boys and 1 girl. Their son, George Kishnan, was born in the year 1960. They welcomed their daughter, Christine Bishon Byroo, into the world a few years later in 1965. Their last son, Rohan Mark Byroo, followed in 1968. His 2 grandchildren are Calif Byroo and Warren Crabble.

Wally developed a love of music and his singing talent from his Indian grandfather, Dose Byroo, who came from India as an indentured laborer; as well as his mother, who was also a talented singer of Indian cultural music.

He was a member of the Indian 'Merrimaker Band' and performed annually at the state show, [for 12 years] from 1978-1990 at 'Bombay Farm'. He also participated in the re-enactment of the 150th year arrival of Indians to Jamaica. During the 1980s, his friend, Henry Jaghai, was actively involved in the promotion of Hindu culture in Jamaica. This was done through stage shows held all over the island. Because of his incredible talent as an Indian folk singer, he became a popular and favorite entertainer at these functions. They traveled together, performing, all over the island. As part of the promotion, a delegation was put together. Henry was the stage manager for the Jamaican delegation set to visit 'Saint Augustin University' in Trinidad, and paved the way for Wally to visit to perform [his Indian folk songs] with the group there in Trinidad.

His growing celebrity status then landed him a music deal, with which he performed and recorded eight folk songs, on an Indian folk song album, which Henry produced. The songs are: 'Bin Gokula', 'Ghari Na Day Maharaj', 'Janakpur', 'RadheShyam', 'BigareRassiya', 'Pardessia', 'Lachkainna', and 'Sakhiya Ana'. Also a frequent visitor of 'Caymanas Park', Wally was photographed on many occasions leading in winning horses for the 'Bushy Park Stud Farm' in St Catherine. Wally was frequently asked to perform at many Indian events and celebrations throughout the island.

Mohinder Byrosingh

Mohinder Byrosingh is a third generation son of Indian descendants that arrived in Jamaica in 1845. He was born in Central Village, Spanish Town in the parish of St. Catherine. Mohinder stems from a linage of musicians on both sides of his family.

He is a devoted Hindu, his many talents includes playing the Dantaal, the Dholak and also singing the traditional Jamaican Indian Folk Songs.

In 2014 he was presented with the Hall Of Honor Award in Florida for his dedication and contribution towards Indian culture and Hindu religion.

He has performed at various events including Mandir, Puja's,

Wakes (nine nights) and other Indian functions. Mohinder participated in Indian Arrival Day in Jamaica and also participated in Trinidad Indian Arrival Celebration in Florida. He attends several Mandir's in America highlighting the Jamaican Indian Culture and folk music.

Mohinder's mission is to showcase the Indian culture that his ancestors brought from India to Jamaica so many years ago and to communicate to the world that Sanathna Dharma is alive in Jamaica today.

Derrick Denniser

Derrick Creswell "Shastry" Denniser was born on the 14Th September 1952 at 7 ½ East Road in Trench Town Kingston 12. His mother Margaret Sepaul was from St Mary was born on May 4Th 1918 she worked with the local Government for a while and died January 7Th 2002. His father Walter Denniser was born on August 25Th 1925 was a mechanic who worked with the KSAC and then started doing Haulage with his truck, he died August 9Th 2008. Derrick has on his mother's side two brothers Aubrey and Alva now living in Miami, and on his dad's side Derrick has sisters Annette, Susan, Michelle and Doreen and brother Michael.

Derrick attended the St Albans Primary school in Denham Town and passed the common entrance examination to attend Kingston College in 1965. He was affectionately called "Shastri" one day in class at KC while he was feeling sick and coincidentally unbeknown to him was the same day the Prime Minister of India Lal Bahadur "Shastri" Shrivastav (2 October 1904 - 11 January 1966) the third Prime Minister of the Republic of India and a significant figure in the Indian independence movement died, and his teacher asked him if it was because of the death of the PM that caused him to be ill prompting his classmate to tease him about it and the name has stuck with him since then. He is also a graduate of the College Of Arts Science and Technology (CAST) Now known the University of Technology (UTECH).

Derrick's link with Boys Town spans beyond his generation as not only that his home was behind the Boys Town property but his grandfather Charles Denniser would plant calaloo beds on portions of unused lands belonging to Boys Town during the time and with the permission of the Boys Town founder and Methodist minister Father Hugh Sherlock. His interest in football was aroused as a youth being the youngest among his brothers he had the duty of rounding up the families goats in the evening that grazed and mowed the adjoining Boys Town football field and it was while he was over there that he started playing football with friends like Herbert Gordon, Lacelles Shaw, Devon Lewis, Carl Brown, Victor Hunter, Archie Reid, Stuart Pinnock and Les Brown.

He earned the alias name "Coolie Pele" from spectator's conversation while playing a league match at Boys Town when he was playing a game at about age fifteen while he was told that spectator asked in jest, if he was the famous Pele they all were hearing about and someone commented that Pele was black player from Brazil to which the spectator asserted in an endearing way that this must be our Coolie Pele by the way he mastered the football.

Derrick's football career started at the Junior Level in 1969 with the Boys Champion team minor league under 17 and most outstanding player Award, at the high school level he was part of the 1970 Kingston College Manning and Walker Cup Champions and the 1971 All Manning and All School team. His Club and Business House League ran from 1968 to 1976 with highlight includes, KASAFA Division 2 Champions Boys Town, Division 1 Champions, 1971 KASAFA All Stars, Business House Division One Champions Desnoes & Geddes, 1973 Major Leagues Champions Boys Town, 1974 Triple Champions ALPART, Allen Shield Kaiser Cup St. Elizabeth F.A. Parish Champions, 1976 Major League Champions Boys Town.

1970: Manning and Walker Cup. *Rear:* Claude Bruff, Mario McClennon, Milton Evering, Patrick Vernon, Trevor Campbell. *Middle:* Robert Smith, Delton Dawkins, Winston Brown, Derrick Dennicer, Howard Bell (captain). *Front:* Donovan Haynes (goalkeeper).

At the national Level he represented Jamaica between 1971 and 1975 as part of the National Senior team for matches in the Pan American games in Jamaica, Colombia, Bermuda, Curacao, Guyana, New York, and Mexico

Derrick was no ordinary midfield linkman player who would normally function as a creator of openings and a provider of key balls for his forwards but his skillful agility and athleticism allowed him to score about 30 Walker and Manning Cup goals for Kingston College between 1968 and 1971 and over 40 goals for Boys Town for over seven years between 1969 and 1976

Among Derrick's most memorable moments in his football career was a 1969 Header against Franklyn Town Minor League at Emmet park that boys won, a 1970 manning cup match playing for KC against JC and scoring the equalizer and the go ahead goal after JC had scored first and his team eventually won 4-1, a 1972 header that he scored against Santos in a Major League final where he was awarded the most outstanding player award, also in 1974 scoring a goal against Guyana in Guyana during a friendly match that Jamaica lost 2-1

The elegant Derrick Denniser in Jamaica's first encounter in Guyana, November 1973

Major Surgery from injury on his right knee in 1975 at Lukes Hospital in New York curtailed his playing career. He however has been doing football analysis and sports commentator assignments at major football matches for Radio Jamaica (RJR) since 1992 till present and have an employment history since his football day with major companies such as Desnoes & Geddes, Antillean Sports, In Sports, Alpart, Xerox, Institute of Sports.

Derrick Dennicer receiving 2017 Bell Zadie Masters Awards for outstanding contribution to the development of Football in Jamaica as former National Player and Admin by the founder of the Masters & Celebrities foundation Clive Campbell and member Ian Wilkinson QC

Derrick is married to Nelly Johnson and has two children Nicholas and Nicola and a grandson David Shastri Denniser by way of Nicholas, although now retired from work Derrick does sales for Qual Care.

By Roy Amritt Sweetland, July 22, 2018

Richard Francis

Richard Francis, Lovey Dayal, Ashutosh Diljun

Guru Brahma, Guru Vishnu, Guru Devo Maheshwara. Guru Sakshat, Param Brahma, Tasmai Shree Guravay Namah. A true Guru is God personified. He is Brahma who creates the fire of Divine love and knowledge in the heart. He is Vishnu the one that grows and preserves that fire of Divine love and knowledge. He is Maheshwara by following his teachings he purifies the heart by destroying ignorance, all types of Karma, all Sufferings, ends the cycle of life and death. He then bestows God Realization and Divine love, the soul meets God and is eternally blissful, contented and peaceful with God in his divine abode.

My name is Richard Francis- Damodar is the name received from my Gurudev Jagad Guru Shree Kripaluji Maharaj, whom I am forever indebted. Through his Divine teachings-Tattva Gyan, he has revealed the answers to the three main questions of every human being. Who am I, What is my purpose and how to achieve it. I have learnt the best way to satisfy one's debt to our parents, ancestors, fellow mankind, animals the earth etc. It is through his grace that led me to India for my spiritual upliftment. His JKP Charitable Foundation operates three hospitals totally free to the poor people in India, schools for poor village girls from elementary to postgraduate totally free and numerous charitable programs. JKP also operates four major Ashrams, along with four historic temples Bhakti Mandir, Prem Mandir and Kirti Mandir in India and Radha Rani Temple at Radha Madhav Dham in Austin, Texas USA. It is through these trips that I became a part of this book.

I was born 1960 in Kingston, Jamaica fifth of nine children to my most loving and dedicated parents Adassa and Samuel Francis. I pay special love and tribute to my mother who brought up single handedly nine young children after our father passed away at an early age. I am unable to fathom her love and dedication as we grew up to become responsible adults with families of our own. The Lord has entrusted me with two loving sons Richard Rajiv and Marc. I attended Balmagie Primary School, Kingston College and the University Of The West Indies. Through God's grace, supported by my mother, brothers Cecil and Allan, my uncle and aunt Lloyd and Zola Guyah whose home my business started. Later partnered with Richard Bansie and with resources of my then spouse Lorna we operated and expanded the business Cecil Tyres and Accessories for over two decades. I am very grateful to many persons who helped during the tenure of this business. I presently work with the largest automotive retail service business in the USA for over fourteen years in Florida where I have settled.

Maternal grandparents were Jemima and Thomas Guyah from Linstead and finally settled in Brunswick Avenue, Spanish Town, Jamaica. They had operated successfully trucking, sawmill hardware and farming businesses with their children following their footsteps as business owners. They have many notable grand and great grandchildren mentioned in previous book Pardes. Paternal grandparents Rajpati and John Mattai settled at Pelican Parade, Kingston, Jamaica. They operated a trucking business with their sons following same. Their son Roy and his daughter Meena were avid singers in the Jamaican Hindu cultural arena. Grandsons Ravi and Ramesh Mattai, Gregory, Mark and Roberto Clay owns and operates tractor trailers in USA.

In January 2016 on my trip to India Mr. Henry Jaghai arranged with his advocate Mr. Ashutosh Diljan whom along with his brother Arvinda and fellow retired advocate Lovey Dayal took me to Ratapur and Bahadurpur villages. It was a very nostalgic and unforgettable trip. The villagers made me feel like a Raja- King. I am humbled by their warm, sincere welcoming love. I am now a part of their villages. Mr. Jaghai has privileged me to help him with his ongoing charitable programs. My sincere thanks and appreciation to the Diljan family, Lovey Dayal and wife Doctor Kalpana Srivastava for their loving accommodation. I applaud Shree Henry William Jaghai, OD, JP for his lifelong contribution to the Emigrated Indians along with their descendants. Through his books he has paid a great tribute to all the ancestors of Indian descendants to Jamaica. We all are blessed as part of the history and fiber of Jamaica. His personal quest in finding his origins in India represents all of us. We are indebted to him.

L-R Lovey Dayal, Ashutosh, Manju Diljun, Richard Francis, Avnindra and Anju Diljun in back

L-R Lovey Dayal, Richard Francis, Kalpana Srivastana, Deepak Mishra

L to R: Charmaine Francis-Jaghai, Errol Francis, Henry Jaghai, Myrtle Jaghai, Allan Francis, Cecil Francis, Barrington Francis

The Gallow Family

The Gallow family are fourth generation descendants of India, most likely from the state of Uttar Pradesh, where most Indian descents are from in Jamaica. We are of Muslim descent.

The name Gallow is not the original surname of our forefathers. This was the first name of our paternal grandfather who was born in Jamaica. His father, our great grandfather (paternal) was Hasalat Maya, who was born in India and came to Jamaica as an indentured labourer. He settled in Greys Inn, St. Mary. When he came on the ship, only one name was recorded.

His son's first name was Gallow (our grandfather). However, this was due to a misspelling of his original name as he was not literate and he was not registered officially. Upon necessary registration, he gave his first name and subsequently was registered as Gallow. Of interest, his son's name (our father), Moses Gallow, was spelled differently as well as some of our relatives. Consequently, all descendants inherited the name Gallow. They all settled in Grey's Inn, St. Mary. Our grandfather had two sisters who settled in Portland, Jamaica. He is deceased.

My paternal grandfather's wife, Halagi Mohammed, was also born in Jamaica from parents of indentured labourers from India. Her father's name was Lal Mohammed. She was of Muslim descent and was from Lionel Town, Clarendon. The graves of her parents, indentured labourers from India, still exist in the family yard in Lionel Town. Interestingly, fourth generation great grandchildren, often sat on these very graves, under the cool shade of a Tamarind tree eating tamarinds. All descendants from her side inherited the surname Mohammed. She is now deceased.

Our paternal grandfather, affectionately called "Daddyman" and grandmother, called "Mum" (Halagi Gallow nee Mohammed), had five children, three sons and two daughter. One son is deceased. Our father, the eldest son, is Moses Gallow (born June 22, 1936, age 80 years), currently resides in Seivright Gardens, Kingston, Jamaica with his wife Myrtle Gallow nee Ameir (born August 8, 1938, age 78 years).

Our maternal grandparents resided in Mona, Jamaica. They were also of Muslim descent. Our maternal grandfather was Ali Ameir who died very young in his 40's. All his descendants have the surname Ameir.

Our parents, Moses and Myrtle Gallow have five sons.

The first son is Dr. Patrick Anthony Gallow, who is a medical doctor with his own Practice, currently resides in Kingston Jamaica. He has two children with his wife Sheila Nee Pancham (the Pancham family is a renowned Indian family from Jamaica). His daughter, Dr. Kamilah Shadha, is also a Medical Doctor, working at the University Hospital of the West Indies, Jamaica. The son is Sadiq Anthony, who is currently in University pursuing his degree in Electrical Engineering.

The second son is Jeffery Garth Gallow who also resides in Kingston, Jamaica. He works with the Jamaica Civil Aviation Authority as an Aeronautical Information Services supervisor. He is married to Yvonne nee Mykoo, who is professionally employed and the daughter of the famous Indian folk (Bhojpuri) singer, Johnny Mykoo (deceased). They have two children. The son,

Tahir Asif, married to Marja nee Morrison, is a College graduate with a Bachelor's degree in Business Administration, majoring in Finance, and currently employed as a banker. The daughter, Sherizah Karimah, also has her Bachelor's Degree in Business Administration, majoring in Marketing and currently employed with the Jamaica Civil Aviation Authority as an Air Traffic Controller.

The third son is Errol Courtney Gallow, who has been residing in Tampa, Florida, USA since 1989 and employed with Federal Express (courier company). He is married to Christine nee Francis (the Francis family is also a renowned Indian family from Jamaica). He has two children, his son Salim Errol, is a College graduate with a professional degree in Media Arts and Animation. His daughter is Nadia Christine, currently in college majoring in Psychology. Both were born in Tampa, Florida, USA.

The fourth son is Roger Heron Gallow. He is married to Debbie Kamla nee Ramballie (another renowned Indian family from Jamaica, currently residing in Canada). They resided for many years in Canada before recently relocating in Miami, Florida, USA. Roger has his Bachelor's Degree in Science and is currently employed in the Pharmaceutical Industry as an Analytical Research Scientist. They have two daughters, the eldest is Candice Hasinah Maragh (married to Rajkamal Maragh) is currently employed in Finance and Sheridan Aaliyah, recently enrolled as a college student to pursue a degree in criminology.

The last son is Dr. Moses Junior Gallow (Jr). He currently resides in the Cayman Islands, employed as a doctor at the Cayman Islands Hospital. His daughter, Amirah Faridah, is currently completing her International Bachelorette diploma, with the ambition of being a Medical Doctor.

Roger Gallow and Dr. Moses Junior Gallow were members of the Indian Talent Merrymakers band of Kingston, Jamaica. Roger played the bass guitar and Moses Junior played the rhythm guitar. The Indian Talent Merrymakers band is a renowned Indian orchestra and pioneers of modern Indian music in Jamaica, originated since 1965.

Mr. Moses Gallow (our father) was the manager of this band. His younger brother, Michael Gallow is a talented dholak and tabla player. He was a member of the band and a very active member of the Jamaican Indian Diaspora and very dedicated to Indian culture and music. Michael has excelled academically and graduated from College with the highest honors in Engineering. He was employed by the Daily Gleaner as an Engineer for 28 years after which he migrated to Tampa, Florida, USA with his wife Janet nee Singh (another prominent Jamaican Indian family) and his two daughters, Shanti and Sharda.

This has been a synopsis of the Gallow family, of Kingston, Jamaica.

Author: Dr. Moses Junior Gallow

From Left to Right- Jamina, Herbert Maragh, Moses Gallow, Tatty, Myrtle Jaghai, Jagat Maragh, Audrey Carvalho, Astil Jadusingh, Myrtle Gallow, Myrtle Jadusingh. At front from Left to Right- Lydia, Violet, Henry Jaghai, Laddy Nathan and Ramu Graham. Photo taken on a visit to Little London, Westmoreland.

Cecil Suckram Gibbore

Cecil Suckram Gibbore was born in Belfield Penn, St. Mary, Jamaica on February 17, 1933. He was the youngest child of Jibodh and Pulcora, immigrants from India. Jibodh had been born in the village of Oonchgaon in Sultanpur district, and he migrated to Jamaica in 1913. Cecil's siblings are William, Mary, James, and John. Cecil attended Bromley All Age School in St. Mary. He subsequently worked as both an independent farmer and as a security guard with the Ministry of Education at Bromley All Age School. Cecil was involved in a variety of Indian cultural activities in Jamaica. He played both the dholak and the sarangi. He also performed as a singer and a dancer.

Cecil married Zelpha Adina Hanam, who came from Belvedere, Portland. She was the granddaughter of immigrants from India. Cecil and Zelpha have nine children: Joyce, Cynthia, David, Rowan, June, Janet, Jenieve, Janeen, and Janeh. Joyce works as a Registered Nurse in Toronto, Canada. Cynthia and Janeen work as Registered Nurses in the United States, in Florida and Connecticut, respectively. The other children currently still reside in Jamaica and work in Kingston. David works in installation in the signage industry. June and Janet work as accountants. Rowan and Jenieve work in the Information Technology field. Janeh works as an administrator for the Ministry of National Security in Jamaica. Cecil and Zelpha also have fifteen grandchildren: Mikhail, Janelle, Yanick, Rashaan, Joel, Rasheed, Danielle, Gabrielle, Kishawn, Rajon, Rishka, Raniah, Rasha, Rashmi and Alexandria.

Mr. Gibbore and his family were kind to Mr. Henry Jaghai, whom they accommodated as a house guest. Both Mr. Gibbore and Mr. Jaghai used to tour St. Mary on their bicycles.

Donald Goluab

Donald Golaub is the first of fourteen children seven girls and seven boys, to parents Sabreau (Lillian) and Sylvester Golaub. Born January 2nd, 1945 in Westmoreland of a very humble beginning. To make ends meet he started working at age fourteen yet earned his degree in Management Studies at the University Of The West Indies. His wife of forty three years Maureen achieved her Masters Degree at UWI also. He has five children, three daughters, two earned Masters Degrees, CPA and youngest doing premed studies, son earned Pharmacy Diploma.

Donald worked in the lab at The West Indies Sugar Company and Sales and Marketing Department of Goodyear Jamaica Limited. In 1991 was major step he resorted to the almighty Lord in whom he has unwavering faith, he started his own company Mr. Tyre Jamaica Limited. With his devoted wife and their hard work the business skyrocketed. He was feature in many articles notably Rags to Riches in a major magazine.

Donald served as President of the Indo Jamaica Cultural Society. He is generous, philanthropic and always giving back. A few of his charitable programs were the Elsie Beaman Children's Home, Eltham Community Basic School, Bridgeport Infant School. He had sponsored many sports programs including Senior Basketball competition and Phil Palmer Lawn Tennis Tournament. He is also a Justice Of The Peace and was conferred the Governor General Achievement Award. Donald is presently retired.

Franklyn Jaghroo

Franklyn Jaghroo was born on March 13, 1955 in Mitchell Town, Clarendon to Nathaniel Sr and Hyacinth Jaghroo. My parents had six children. I am the eldest. My parents are now deceased. My father was an electrician at Monymusk Sugar Factory. My dad's parents were Jhagroo Chutkan and Florence Dookie. My paternal great grandparents were Chutkan and Bachnie. They came from Calcutta India in the 1800 's. They live on several Sugar cane farms in Vere Clarendon. Bachnie died at Banks in 1956. Bachnie and her husband Chutkan had twelve children. Their children were born on different Sugar Estates I knew two of my grandfather's siblings Arthur who lived in Banks. He died in 1980's and Ethel Chutkan died in Nov 2014 in Portland Cottage. I have one daughter named Ariel.

My mother's parents were Charles "Cyril" Scott and Henrietta Ramlal Cyril's parents were James and Jane Scott from Trinityville, St Thomas. Jane's parents were John and Sarah Shubrati. The name Scott was actually "LIAKAT" from India. Henrietta's parents were Alice and Jagval Ramlal. Alice my great grandma was born in Lionel Town in 1890. She died March 1995 in Lionel Town. Alice's parents came from India. Her mother had two sisters from India also. One married a Jagessar in Race Course. The other married the Bassier in Mitchell Town.

My parents lived in Salt River Clarendon. I attended Watsonton Primary. I attended Glenmuir High School 1967- 1972. We migrated to New York in 1973. I attended Bronx Community College, and Pratt Institute where I earned a B.E. in Chemical Engineering. I worked at Union Carbide, in Tarrytown, N.Y. I did a M.S. in Science Education at City College of NY. I taught Mathematics and Chemistry in NYC, High School for 31 years. I retired in June 2014. I have been an Adjunct Professor at Bronx Community College (CUNY)-Chemistry Dept from 1992 to the present. I enjoy visiting Jamaica. I do so at least twice a year.

I have made connections with other Jagaroo's in Westmoreland, St Mary, Siloah, St Elizabeth and Kingston. Mr Noel Earl Alexander Jhagroo O.D. (1997) was president of the Jamaica Montreal Association. He lived in England and played club cricket. During the late 1950's - 1960's. He has been honored for his philanthropic work by the government of Jamaica and the provincial government of Quebec. He founded the Jamaica Day Festival in 1983, which is still popular and active today. Steve Jagaroo from Petersfield, Westmoreland is a NYC police officer.

Violet Johnson and Tomlinson Sweetland

Miss Violet "Miss Vie" Johnson was born on May 16Th 1928 in Harmony Hall St. Mary Miss Vie dad an indentured laborer (Dada) Ramjawan William Johnson who arrived in Jamaica at 19 Years old in 1871 and mother Victoria Johnson Moved to Ramble then to Bottom Albany St Mary. As a child she would take two days off from school to assist her father in pay bill as part of his work as a Busha on an estate where he served after his indentureship tenure ended.

Her dad later took her mom (Vickie) Victoria, one dining table and a black wooden bed in a donkey cart to start life in place called Cockburn Pen known for its numerous cow pens and settlement for many other Indian indentured laborers of the replacement post British slave system. Her shop and home was situated at the end of a dirt track that started from Three Miles Hagley Park Rd. and ended at her shop and continued as a foot pass to places now know as waterhouse and tower hill.

A very self reliant and independent person who rode her ladies wheel bicycle to work at Gores making cigars and later as a seamstress for Azan stores down town Kingston where she called the "Big Tree" in parade. She would also spend time helping the Rampassards in their downtown grocery store and learning what was to become her future and main source of income for her family.

When she was expecting her first child Patricia she made the decision to stop working and start working for herself and proudly proclaimed that she started her business with four shillings and sixpence, a one faced scale, a scoop, a red handle bread knife and shop that was fashioned out of discarded wooden box boards that she purchased downtown and arranged to be transported for use to her Cockburn pen home by a handcart man. From this humble start selling fried fish, pickled red herring, and fried dumplings in a little glass case she continue to grow and expand the business to take care of her family and also took responsibility for her two sisters children as well.

Originally the business she established at 50 Olympic Way with seed money from her first shop and a loan from her grandfather and was the very first dance space in the community called the Bamboo Lawn which was an unpaved dirt floor dance space bordered by bamboo fencing she established in the early fifties with sound systems such as the Four Aces Sound System, and live mento and reggae band such as the monkey man mento band, Albert Griffiths and the Gladiators Band, Douse's Black Seed and the Stepping Stones band, and had to get electricity all the way from Spanish town road to keep her first dance.

She was a deeply committed community person and the first in her community to receive utilities such as Electricity, Water, and Land line telephone service, and had to collect names from other people in the neighborhood to petition the utility companies to start supplying service to other people in the community.

Shallimar, the new name of the business was actually given to her by a customer who saw it in a news paper comic strip and later found that it had a Indian roots as a spiritual place and operated her grocery store, bar and entertainment business with integrity that was befitting of the name as she transformed the business from its humble tiny wooden shop to bricks and later to concrete blocks and steel, and is still part of a complex of shops of restaurant, wholesale, bar, and other shops.

Miss Vie met Tomlinson Sweetland a flamboyant free spirited person who worked in the housing department and the union yielded four children Patricia Figueroa, Marcia Francis, Roy Sweetland and Pauline Hislop, she later met Irvin Fearon who worked at the United Motors company and had three children, Paul & Don Fearon Christine Pollard. A very modern and stylish country girl who was always a supporter of the weak and the underdog, and was the first to travel overseas in her family and planted the early seeds of migration trend for her eldest daughter Patricia in NY and all have followed in that trend since. She survived various setbacks through her life including hold ups, break-ins, extortion attempts, storms, Hurricane, personal loss and tragedies and always remained wiser and positive about the future for her family and country.

Ramlal and Sara Malgie

Ramlal Malgie, wife Sara and their children Milton, Linton and Judith

Ramlal Malgie was born on July 6, 1916 in West Retreat, Portland, Jamaica. He is the first of five children born to proud parents Malgie and Gaurya. Ramlal's parents were born in India. His father Malgie came from Rai Bareily, while his mother came from Basti in the state of Uttar Pradash, India. His parents came to Jamaica on April 13, 1903 aboard the SS Dahomey. They came to Jamaica as indentured labourers, and worked at Vinery Estate, in Portland. Working together at the estate, they developed a relationship, which blossomed into their marriage.

The birth of Ramlal was followed by his sister Dhanraji, and three younger brothers, Kalap Nath, Baij Nath and Ramaisser. After a few years, the family relocated to Mona, St. Andrew, where they worked and eventually started their own cattle rearing business.

Growing up, Ramlal attended the Providence Elementary School, while learning the cattle trade from his father. He learned to read, write, and speak the Hindi language from the community leaders, at the same time showing a great interest in the Indian customs and traditions. He learned to play several Indian musical instruments and sang Indian folk songs and semi classical music, from his father. Being fluent in Hindi, Ramlal started composing and performing his own songs, and dances at many Indian functions.

Living in Mona, he met and became good friends with Seenayee (Abraham Jaghai), his neighbour. They would often travel to school together, hopping on the tramcar en route to Providence School, about two miles down the road. Seenayee had mastered the skill of hopping the tramcar and he would teach Ramlal his tricks. This childhood prank of hopping tramcars, gave Ramlal the nickname "Skipper."

In 1934, Ramlal got married to his childhood sweetheart, Sara. He also started his own cattle rearing business, to support his growing family, which consisted of three children, two sons and a daughter. After about five years, Ramlal moved his family to Ward Lane off Whitehall Avenue. His rich Indian heritage and fluency in Hindi, led him to establish an Indian school to preserve the culture and traditions of the Indian culture. Here, he taught the Hindi songs and traditional dances to the children born to indentured labourers in Jamaica. He was very prominent in the Indian community and would often be requested to serve as master of ceremonies at Indian functions, festivities, and traditional Indian weddings. In 1954, he officiated at the wedding of Henry and Myrtle Jaghai.

In 1988, Ramlal was invited by Henry W. Jaghai to compose and perform three of his Indian songs, which were recorded on the fourth volume of the music album Indian Folk Songs of the Caribbean. Mr. Jaghai also brought Ramlal to perform in Trinidad. Ramlal started out from a humble beginning, but his wealth of knowledge of the Indian culture, history of Jamaica, his fluency in Hindi, his versatility in playing various musical instruments, his musical talent of composing, directing and singing of Indian folk and semi-classical songs will be remembered for a very long time. He will be remembered as a pioneer in preserving and promoting Indian culture in Jamaica.

Olive Maragh, PhD. J.P.

Olive M. Bujham-Maragh is the 4th of 13 children born to George and Hilda Bujham in the Food Basket parish of St. Elizabeth, Jamaica W. I. Her siblings are Michael, Victoria, Amy, Harry, James, Sheila, Edna, Paul, Peter, Helen, Richard, Carlena. George worked as a millwright and Hilda produced cane tops at the Holland Estate in St. Elizabeth. She attended Primary and High School there and later moved on to the University of Technology, Jamaica, (UTech), the University of the West Indies (UWI), Mona and Northern Caribbean University (NCU) in Mandeville where she pursued a Teachers' Diploma and B.Ed. degree at UTech, an M.Ed. degree at UWI and a Ph.D at NCU, respectively. Prior to her employment at the Ministry of Education in 1996, she worked at several schools including Lacovia, Mannings and St. Catherine High.

Although now retired from the Ministry of Education as an Assistant Chief Education Officer in the Technical Vocational and Media Services Units, Dr. Maragh continues to serve as Chief Examiner for CXC, an External Examiner for the Joint Board of Teacher Education (JBTE), UTech and the Mico University College, as well as an Inspector with the National Education Inspectorate (NEI) where she inspects Primary and High schools mainly in Kingston and St. Andrew and adjoining parishes.

She is still very active at the Villmore S.D.A. Church in Spanish Town, serving as an ordained Elder and Education Sponsor, among other positions. She conducts an Education class at the church every Sunday evening to assist persons, children and adults alike, to acquire literacy and numeracy skills.

Dr. Maragh is very supportive of her immediate family, her two daughters, Sashana and Kamala who are graduate teachers at the Secondary and Kindergarten level respectively, and her son Ramesh, an Executive Chef in Kingston. She is very fond of her two grandsons, Ramesh Maragh Jr, two years old and Rajesh Ramsamugh who is six years old. Her late husband, Tulsidas Joe Maragh, son of Pandit Ramadar Maragh, who are both deceased in 2001 and 2013 respectively, has played a pivotal role in her life. Dr. Maragh is blessed to have joined the Maragh's family who she describes as humble, altruistic, loving, caring and sincere.

Over the years, Dr. Maragh maintains a close relationship with her brothers and sisters, ten of whom are alive. She lost two sisters namely Amy and Annie in 2003 and 2010 respectively. Her parents, Hilda and George Bujham passed away in 1984 and 1998 respectively. The passing of these very close relatives, along with others, has been one of the darkest periods in her life. Her six brothers, Michael, Harry, James, Paul, Peter and Richard are engaged in farming and entrepreneurial activities, while her 4 sisters, Victoria, Edna, Helen and Carlena are employed as nurses and business personnel.

Dr. Maragh is an avid reader, she loves to cook and attend to her flowers, counsel and surf the internet. She is a people-person and loves to attend Indian cultural events. She lives by the mantra: 'Make a difference, by daring to be different'.

Olive at front, centre with siblings from left: Michael, Victoria, Amy, Harry, James and Sheila. At back from left: Carlena, Richard, Helen, Peter, Paul, Edna (partially hidden).

Ramesh Maragh/Maharaj

I was born in Kinston, Jamaica in 1964 to the parents of Pandit Rama Maragh and his wife Lucille. Two years later our family grew with the addition of my sister Andrea. At the age of six, my parents made the decision to migrate to the United States of America and more specifically to New York City. Although I left there at a young age, I still hold on to very fond memories of time in Jamaica.

My parents who started their American lives with not very much monetarily worked hard and with my mom's fiscal discipline, after a few years, saved enough to purchase a six-family apartment building in Brooklyn, New York. In addition to a first-floor apartment, my parents made a stairway access and converted the basement to add to our living space. This would remain our home for the next seven years.

My major recollection of these times was the weekend gatherings with family and friends. This was where my love for singing was developed. Our Sunday church was also an important aspect to my life. In 1980 my father, after another cold winter, said, "No more cold for him" and that summer moved the family, yet again, this time, with my new born brother Rajesh, we relocated to Miami Florida.

Here in Miami, I would graduate High School in 1982; I would meet the love of my life Hemi "Kamini" Latchman in 1983, join the US Air Force in 1986 and would marry Kamini a year later. Our first child, Keera was born in October 1990. In December of 1990, in support of Desert Storm/ Desert Shield, I was given orders and deployed to Saudi Arabia. Leaving my family, my wife and my newborn daughter was maybe the hardest thing I had to do. I returned home in April and a couple of months later I was honorably discharged from the US Air Force. In 1993,

I attained an Associate's Degree specializing in electronics. After school, I returned to my military specialty of Inventory Management, a field which I have continued employment to the present day of this writing. In 1994, my second daughter Daya was born. My son, Shashi was born in 1997. Five years later we would be blessed with my youngest child Tulsi.

My father who passed away in 2009, was a great influence in preserving our religion, customs and traditions of our ancestors to his children and grandchildren alike. Our daily lives continue with us practicing his teachings, as well as, the teachings of the spiritual leaders that he brought into our lives.

My two favorite hobbies are singing and writing. I began writing since I was fifteen years old. In 2017, a lifelong dream of mine became closer to reality when I signed a contract to publish my first book. I also have a commitment to publish two more works in the not so far future.

At a dead end, your life may seem.
Continue to aspire and chase your dreams.
Avoid regrets and go with the flow.
If you don't try, you surly will never know.

WE SHOULD NEVER FORGET

Ramesh Maragh

Once upon a time during British rule.
Our ancestors left their motherland, looking for life's renewal.
How difficult it must have been leaving family and friends.
With their departure knowing, they may never see them again.
With courage and determination that was as strong as stone.
They traveled the world with their futures unknown.
As indentured servants they migrated to different lands.
Working the fields with fortitude and the strength of their hands.
Credit them for holding on to their religion, customs and traditions.
Many a times going against social pressure and very difficult conditions.
Always remember our ancestors and their many sacrifice
Doing it for their future generations, so we may live a better life.
No matter where we are today we should never forget.
It all started with our ancestor's
decisions, work and sweat.

Wendy Maragh

A prominent member of the Indo-Jamaican cultural society at an early age Wendy was a product of proud parents Donald & Shirley Maragh. Together her parents had seven children, six girls and one boy. Wendy was born into a loving and fun filled home where her dad Donald ensured that the Indian culture was part of their daily life filled with the food, music and prayer.

Born in Washington Gardens in 1968 her parents moved a year later to Cockburn Pen, which was highly populated with Indians. It was here in Cockburn pen that her dad Donald reconnected and moved next door to his best friend Johnny Mykoo. In 1977, Johnny decided to revamp the Raja Sarangie group. Donald entrusted his three younger children Rose, Andrea & Wendy who was nine at the time under Johnny's mentorship to be part of the band. Rose got training in doing the Indian folk dancing while Andrea and Wendy became part of the four girls used as back up vocalist for Johnny. The other two were Petrona Dean and Christine Mykoo. The subsequent years were filled with practicing after school and traveling with the band on weekends to social and cultural events across the island.

In 1978, Wendy was successful in her first attempt at the Common Entrance exam and went to her school of choice Immaculate Conception High. In 1984 at age 16, she graduated with eight distinction awards in combined GCE and CXC exams at the time. That same year she auditioned with a group of girls for a coveted spot to represent Jamaica in Trinidad as part of an Indian cultural visit sponsored by Henry Jaghai. Wendy was selected and went with Johnny Mykoo, Henry Jaghai and several prominent members of the Indian community. There she performed a traditional Indian Jamaican dance at a cultural show held in Trinidad. The performance was enlightening to the Trinidadians present who expressed that they were not aware that there was an Indian population in Jamaica. During the early years, Wendy also contributed as a backup vocalist on Johnny Mykoo's album as well as an album sponsored by Henry Jaghai featuring several Indian artists across the Caribbean.

After High School Wendy pursued an undergraduate study in Computer Science at the University of the West Indies. She had her first major job at National Commercial Bank in 1988. In 1996, Wendy switched careers to being an Operations Manager overseeing six locations for a tire company. There she stayed until she migrated with her husband and two children in 1999 to Florida.

Since being in Florida, she has been successful both personally and professionally. She held several positions as an Account Executive, Human Resources Manager and currently is an Implementation Consultant with a Leading Software company in Chicago. Wendy is married to Jockey/Trainer Allen Maragh and has two children together Rajkamal and Crystal Maragh & daughter in law Candice Maragh nee Gallow. Wendy & Allen actively participates and supports Indian cultural shows in Florida and Jamaica whenever they can.

Ronald McDonald

Ronald McDonald Sr was born on July 30, 1946 in St Andrew, Jamaica. His parents were Albert and Bertina McDonald. Ronald was the eldest of 3 sons for his parents. His siblings are Harold (Papa) McDonald and Damon McDonald.

Ronald, known to some as Sax or Doctor, attended Coburn Garden Primary School in St Andrew. Ronald worked for the Kingston and St. Andrew Corporation (KSAC) and as a delivery man for Facey Commodity.

Ronald also played cricket. He was an all-around player. He played for the All Indian Cricket Club, Indian Youth Cricket Club and many more clubs. He was an effective pace bowler who maintained a smile both on and off the field. He played against the senior All Indian Cricket team, led by Henry Jaghai on multiple occasions, performing at a high standard each game.

Ronald married Isabella (Emily) Guyah in 1976. Isabella was the daughter of Samuel (Tat) and Louisa (Mother Lou) Guyah. She is the youngest of 15 siblings, 10 sisters and 5 brothers. Isabella attended Spanish Town Primary School in St. Catherine, Jamaica. Emily owned and operated a restaurant in Spanish Town.

Ronald and Emily lived in Kingston when they were married, they then relocated to Spanish Town. They are blessed with 3 children and 2 grandchildren.

Their first born was Marilyn McDonald (died 1983) attended Hagley Park Prep school in Kingston. The second born was Ronald Jr. (Raj) who was born in 1980 in St Andrew. The third was Marlon who was born in 1981 in Spanish Town. Both Raj and Marlon attended Spanish Town Primary School and Jonathan Grant High School in Spanish Town, Jamaica. They then graduated from Clearwater High School in Clearwater, Florida.

Raj studied engineering at DeVry University in Atlanta, Georgia. He met his wife, Abby Ginter, while living in Atlanta. Raj and Abby then relocated to Minneapolis, Minnesota where they currently are raising their 2 children, Layla and Dylan McDonald.

Marlon attended Johnson & Wales University in Miami, Florida for his undergraduate degree. He then got his MBA from the University of South Florida in St Petersburg, Florida.

Ronald and Emily currently call Clearwater Florida home. While they are far away from their birth home, they still manage to keep their Indian culture alive their home and community.

Johnny Mykoo

Johnny Mykoo was born in Bachan Pen (Spanish Town Road), Kingston, Jamaica in February 9, 1941. He was born to parents Alice and Ram-Bali Mykoo, who had five sons and five daughters. His parents were devoted Hindus and Johnny grew up inspired by their religious values. His siblings are Darlin, Uline, Claris (Daughter), Elizabeth, Mavis, Olive, Rosetta, Samuel (Son Son), Albert (Buchun), Iris, Glora, Ronald and Mertilla. As a child, he was often seen participating in Hindu rituals such as pujas and often joked about his delight of blowing the conch shell during the aarti ceremony. He was also the local "trainee" nachania dancer. During the Indian festival of "Hosay," he was also seen playing sword fighting in the celebrations. Johnny went on to learn the trade of professional barbering and moved to the United Kingdom (UK) in 1964 where he opened his first barber and record shop in Leeds.

He was married to Pearlina Mykoo (nee Baccas) and they had seven children - Yvonne, Philip, Trevor, Christine, Richard, Jason, and Steve. While living in the right atmosphere in the UK, he had a dream from a Sadhu (an old Hindu sage) to return to Jamaica to make Indian music. He returned to Jamaica in 1969 where his dream eventually became a reality when he founded the Raja Sarangie Group in 1974.

On a Friday evening at his residence at 65 Cockburn Avenue, Kingston 11, he would entertain with his Raja Sarangie band where people could also buy Indian food and drinks. For over ten years, he was a regular participant in Mr. Henry Jaghai's stage shows at Bushy Park Farm in St. Catherine. He was one of the main singers for the dance contests, as his energetic songs provided the right atmosphere for the dancers. During the UNESCO cultural trip in Trinidad, in 1980, his sterling performance attracted over 50 fans of all ages to seek his autograph at the near-campus accommodation where he was staying.

Sadly, in 1981 his wife passed away. Years after, he re-married to Salema Williams and had another son, Surrug. Johnny's grand children are Yvonne's children; Tahir and Sherizah Gallow, Phillip's son Kiran, Trevor's children; Priya and Rishi, Christine's children; Gemma Fenlon, Zara Fenlon, and a son, Richard's children Sanjine and Suraj, Jason's son Malik, Steve's daughter Monesha and Surrug's daughter Chandini.

The songs he performed on Henry Jaghai's LPs Indian Folk Songs of the Caribbean were Krishna Ko Sang, Bol Baba Ho, Paradesiya Balam Tor, Bansi Bajay, Raja Janakji Angane, Panchi Akela, Raja Toray, Tumahi Anokha and Bhola Baba.

Members of the Indo-Jamaican contingent to UNESCO's Conference on East Indians in the Caribbean, Trinidad, 1980.

Back Row L-R: Ram Ragbeir who celebrated his 90th birthday on August 29, Herbert Maragh, Henry Jaghai, Peter Jaghai, Myrtle Jaghai, Matthew Purai, Rupert Maragh, Johnny Mykoo, Sona Singh, Raju Maragh.
Front Row L-R: Six trinidadian fans

Icilda Pandohie

Icilda Pandohie (Auntie Dad) was born to parents Sirichand from Basti in India and Margaret Hill from Portland at Long Lane, Banana Walk District. At six years old, she was sent to the Wortley Home School. By age 14, she left school and married in Hindu tradition to Theophilus Pandohie, born in St. James on June 12, 1926. He died in 1975 when he was 50 years old. He was an employee of KSAC. Before having her first child at age 16, Icilda sold callaloo, and other green vegetables in the market.

She went through much hardship and struggle for many years to single-handedly raise ten children: Adolphus, Herbert, Beatrice, Richard, Herman, Robert, Errol, Elsie, Pamela, and Delcetia.

At age 30 after the birth of her last child in 1959, she got a job to work at Metal Box situated on Spanish Town Road. She remained in this job until 1987. During this time, she moved in to her own home at Hunts Bay Lane near her work place. The ophilus worked at KSAC and unfortunately died at age 50.

Icilda spent a lot of time with brothers Sankar, Joseph, William and sisters Bagwantie (Minnie), Elizabeth, and Dudie. Her children, grandchildren, and great-grandchildren are great comfort to her as she has lived to see them become professionals and doing well for themselves.

Icilda celebrates her 90th birthday on August 5th with her children, grand children and great grand children.

From Left to Right: Elsie, Delcita, Icilda (Aunty Dad) Beatrice and Kamala. Son Errol is in the background.

Robert and Miriam Pancham

Robert Beharrie Pancham was born on April 10, 1919 in Kilancholy, St. Mary, Jamaica. His parents, who were from the district of Faizabad in the village of Karaundi, India, immigrated to Jamaica on June 02, 1905 on the ship 'SS' Indus as part of the Indentureship program. They had five children, all sons. As a young boy, it was a tradition for Robert's parents to have daily morning pujas and it was his responsibility to distribute prasad in his neighborhood before going to school.

On March 02, 1947, Robert married Miriam (Blanche) Henry, daughter of William and Rosetta Henry. Miriam was born on May 22, 1925 in Bog Walk, St. Catherine and had nine siblings. They moved to Kingston and settled in Cockburn Gardens where they started their family. The union produced seven children: Lucilda, the late Gretchen (Fay), Jasmine (Beverly), Ferdinand, Sheila, Marva (Fern) and Indra. Following in his family's lineage Robert became a successful barber and operated a barber shop in downtown Kingston for many years. He enjoyed cutting hair so much that he even had a barber chair at home where his friends and neighbours came to get a haircut on the weekends. This was his way of giving back to the community. Miriam worked at The Jamaica Packaging Industries Limited until her retirement.

Robert and Miriam instilled strong family values in their children and encouraged them to become involved in the community. The family was very active in the Indian community and as members of the Sanatan Dharma Mandir, they participated in satsang every Sunday, celebrated Hindu festivals, as well as many fundraising events for the temple where Miriam, Beverly and Indra sang, and Sheila, Fern and Indra danced. Meetings, Christmas treats, dance and skit rehearsals, were often held at the Pancham's residence. Lucille, Fay and Beverly were members of SDM's Saki Samaj club where Hindi classes were held.

Miriam loved to write her own music and sang these original songs at family birthdays and weddings. On August 6, 1977 Robert passed away unexpectedly at 58 years old and Miriam had to raise her younger children alone. Through her commitment and dedication to her family she still ensured that they received a good education to secure their future. In 1985, she was the recipient of The Good Citizen Award issued by the Municipality of Kingston and St. Andrew and the Model Family Award for Exemplary Family Life, issued by 'Harmony in the Homes' Movement. Miriam passed away on May 11, 1998 at 72 years old.

Robert and Miriam were blessed with 13 grandchildren: Neesha Graham, Tashna Newman, Ghanesh, the late Prakash, and Rishi Maragh, Fazia and Faraz Ward, Sadiq and Dr. Kamilah Gallow, Sunil and ZianaPancham, Anil and Asha Dalling. Eight great-grandchildren: Roshan, Sajiv and Shivani Graham, Vishal and Sajni Maragh, Sanjay, Kajal and Nilesh Maragh. Ghanesh is only one of a few Indo-Jamaicans that still performs the Nachaniya dance which is a popular folk dance from the city of Lucknow in the state of Uttar Pradesh. The family continues to carry on the legacy of Robert and Miriam.

L-R: Indra, Fern, Sheila, Ferdie, Beverly, Fay, Lucille

Front Row: Fern, Sheila, Indra (on chair) Ferdie
Back Row: Lucilda, Fay, Robert, Miriam, Beverly

Ramesh Pershad Singh

Ramesh Pershad Singh was born in Kingston, Jamaica to Roy and Pamela Pershad Singh in August of 1972. He was the third child in a family of four, Rohan, Arlene and Mukesh.

Ramesh attended Monymusk Preparatory in Clarendon and passed his Common Entrance to Clarendon College.

Ramesh with his parents and siblings migrated to Florida in 1984 where he attended North Miami Senior high.

From childhood, Ramesh was fond of the automotive field being exposed and grew up in an automotive/diesel repair shop with his father in Clarendon. Much of what he knows is a result of his fundamental auto training from his father.

While in high school, Ramesh enrolled in auto mechanic classes for 3 years. Ramesh entered statewide competitions for auto mechanic and won 1st place in his school subsequently earning him a scholarship from Toyota for the T-TEN(Toyota Technical Education Network) training program. He also went to Broward Community College.

After graduating from T-TEN, Ramesh worked with Toyota for 9 years as a certified automotive technician and service advisor. He then went on to work for Porsche, BMW, Lamborghini, VW and Honda where he held various positions from Service Manager, Service Director, Parts and Service Director and Fixed Operations Director. In addition to being on the Advisory Board for various technical schools, Ramesh was also the president for BMW Parts and Service Club for Central and Northern Florida. Ramesh recently attended NCM Institute in Kansas where he completed his training in General Management for automotive dealerships.

Ramesh went to Lucknow, India in 2000 to study at the feet of Professor Sudhir Varma in the field of music and tabla. During his time in India, Ramesh visited many cities and had the great opportunity of staying in the palace of Maharaja Sawai Bhawani Singh in Jaipur, meeting the children of the Maharaja and dining with them. On his second day in India, his guru Sudhir Varma instructed him to attend and play dholak for the Chief Minister's wife and friends of Uttar Pradesh Mr. Rajnath Singh. Rajnath Singh is currently the Home Minister of India.

Ramesh returned to the United States and soon after wed Jolene Maragh daughter of Harry and Angela Maragh of Kingston, Jamaica. Ramesh has 3 children Amir, Anjani and Pavan. He currently lives with his family in Wesley Chapel, Florida where with his wife Jolene own and operate a preschool Discovery Point.

Ramesh has developed a love for the film industry/acting and has appeared in the film Stratosphere and short film Djjinn Joint. In addition, he is currently working on a feature film

Kohinoor, it is a movie about the diamond that was stolen from India and currently in the Tower of London. His dream is to see the Kohinoor diamond return to India.

Ramesh is passionate about Hinduism & Indian music. He attended Satsangh service in Race Course at Simeon Jagasar's home where his foundation of Bhajans and Hinduism began. His mother Pamela was a member and secretary of the Sai Darbar Satsangh Group. Dancing, playing dholak & tabla is a passion for him as well; He loves to discuss music language of tabla with anyone that understands the North Indian Classical Music.

George and Miriam Ragbar

George Ragbar was born on July 10, 1926 to parents Ragbar and Madeline Bagwandeen. He attended Enfield School in St. Mary. While growing up, he learned the trade of his father and worked alongside him, cultivating the land and selling the produce.

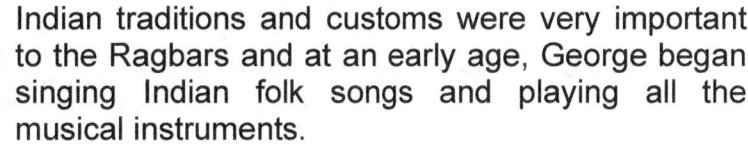

Indian traditions and customs were very important to the Ragbars and at an early age, George began singing Indian folk songs and playing all the musical instruments.

On July 2, 1944, George got married to Miriam Barrowsin from Epsom District, St. Mary. Her life was defined by hard work, running her grocery store and caring for her husband and children. In humility and quiet dignity she upheld her Indian culture and traditions. Her home was always open to the elderly and those who were in need. She derived comfort and a sense of belonging when she played the drums and participate in Indian folk songs sing along.

They worked extremely hard to make a living. They produced a large family of eight offspring. Carlton was the eldest, followed by Sylvia, Clive, Ivy, Evis (Evrol), Cecil, Raphael, and Avis.

Avis, Carllton, Evrol and Sylvia live in Canada and Ivy lives in Texas. Clive works with the Parish Council in Portland and Cecil operates a gas station in Rosend, St. Mary.

Raphael is a farmer in Whitehall District, Portland.

George continues to live in St. Mary. He has twenty-four grandchildren and 42 great grandchildren.

George's 90th Birthday on July 10, 2016

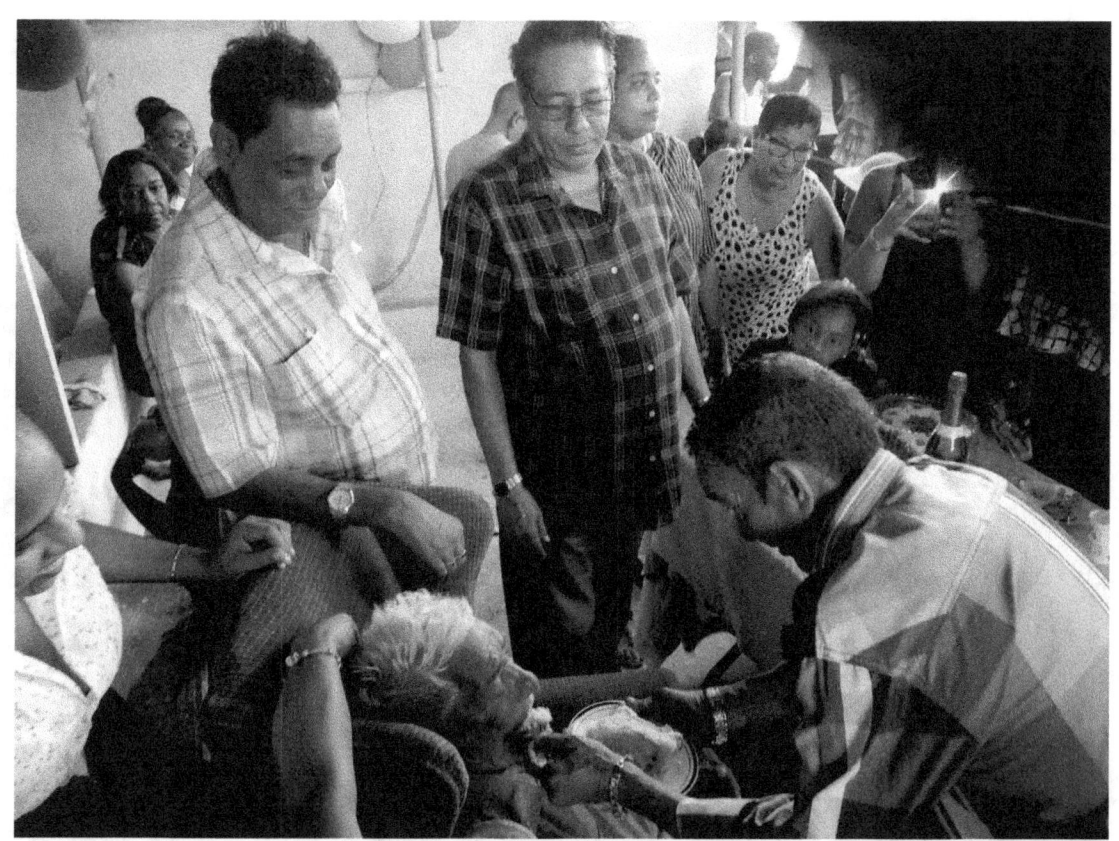

Ramharaz and Ethlyn Ragbeir

Sir Florizel Glasspole and Lady Glasspole presenting Ram and Ethlyn Ragbeir the 1983 National Model Family Award.

Ramharaz Raghubir was born on August 29, 1928 at 48 Spanish Town Road, Kingston, Jamaica. He was born to parents Raghubir and Balwante, both of whom came from Gorakhpur, Basti, Uttar Pradesh, India as indentured labourers in 1907 on the ship S.S. Mutlach II. They were recruited to Orange Hill Estate in St. Mary owned by Sir John Pringle. Ram's siblings included one brother and three sisters.

Ram attended Ebenezer Elementary School. Upon leaving school at the age of 15, he learned the machinist trade at Henriques Kingston Industrial Engineering Works situated at Darling Street. A change in ownership of the company led to a name change to Caribbean Casting LTD., Ram continued to work there for 63 years. Ram celebrated his 90th birthday on August 29.

In 1952, Ram wed Ethlyn Baccas, who was born in 1931 in Grays Inn, Annotto Bay, St. Mary to parents Ishmael and Slety Baccas. Her siblings are Srantis, Stanley, Hilda, Evelyn, Norma and Pearl. Ishmael and Slety migrated to Kingston, and there Ethlyn attended St. Alban School located in Denham Town. After leaving school, she became a dress designer. Ram and Ethlyn's marriage produced eight children Merciline, Rosalin, Barrington, Michael, Raymond, Donald, Joy and Miranda.

Harold Ramcharan

Harold Ramcharan was born on September 24, 1955. He is the great-grandson of Ramcharan, who emigrated from the Allahabad district of northern India to St. Mary, Jamaica in the year 1900. Harold's grandfather, Isaac was born in St. Mary and married Balkeshia, later known as Louisa, who had emigrated from India in 1913 from the Gorakhpur district. Their firstborn son, Alexander, would marry Ivey Puddie and go on to have seven children: Hyacinth, Harold, Jennifer, Winston, Rachael, David, and Caston.

Growing up in St. Mary, Jamaica, Harold would attend Water Valley All Age School, then both the College of Arts Science and Technology and the College of Business Studies. He is currently employed as an accountant.

In 1988, Harold married Cynthia Gibbore. She is the granddaughter of Jibodh, who emigrated from the Sultanpur district to Jamaica in 1913. She was born to Cecil Suckram Gibbore and Zelpha Gibbore on February 5, 1963. Her siblings include Joyce, David, Rowan, June, Janet, Jenieve, Janeen, and Janéh. She graduated from St. Mary High School, before completing a Nursing degree at Miami-Dade College. Currently, she works as a Registered Nurse.

After immigrating to the US in the 1980s, Harold and Cynthia had two children: Mikhail and Janelle. Mikhail was born in Miami, Florida on October 3, 1988. He received his high school diploma at College Academy at Broward College. He earned a Bachelor of Arts in Religious Studies from University of Central Florida, a Bachelor of Accounting from Florida International University, and a Master of Accounting from Florida Atlantic University. He is currently employed as an accountant.

Janelle was born in Ft. Lauderdale, Florida on October 17, 1994. She also graduated from College Academy at Broward College. Afterward, she earned a Bachelor of Science in Biology from Florida International University. She is currently attending Nova Southeastern University College of Osteopathic Medicine and plans to become a physician.

Cecil Ramsamugh (Snr) and Family

Cecil Ramsamugh (Sr.) was born on February 16, 1950 in Slipe, St. Elizabeth, Jamaica to proud parents Jacob and Edith Ramsamugh. Cecil Ramsamugh (Sr.) is the sixth of eight children. His siblings are Ruby, Clinton, Anderson (deceased), Eva, Lola, Levi and Lloyd. Cecil Ramsamugh (Sr.) was an accountant with the St. Elizabeth Parish Council. Cecil is very mathematically inclined. He could find the sum of numbers without the use of the calculator. He left the Parish Council in 1987 and is presently an accomplished beef cattle farmer. He married Ruby Dajue on August 23, 1972.

Ruby Ramsamugh was born on August 1, 1956 in Alley, Clarendon, Jamaica. Her siblings are Mavis, Ivan, Novellete, Michael, Alvile, Stedman (deceased), Cordella (deceased), Beverly, Sandra, and Ralston. Ruby Ramsamugh moved to St. Elizabeth when she was three years old and resided in Middlesex, St. Elizabeth. Ruby operated an Indian restaurant and club named Aquarius in Santa Cruz. Her restaurant was very popular for the scrumptious and mouthwatering dishes, especially the curried goat and roti. These dishes attracted many dignitaries from other parishes. They were blessed with two handsome sons, Cecil (Jr.) and Omar respectively.

Cecil Ramsamugh (Jr.) is a trained Graduate from the University of the West Indies. He is currently a teacher of Mathematics at The Black River High School since the year 2000. He is also a successful businessman. He is married to Kamala Maragh. His wife is presently pursuing her Masters Degree at the Northern Caribbean University in Reading and Language Arts Education. Their union produced a son named Rajesh Tulsidas Ramsamugh.

Omar Ramsamugh is a successful businessman and a farmer. He is married to Tanya Ebanks. Their union produced three children. They are Sunil, Rihanna and Surav Ramsamugh respectively.

Cecil (Sr.) and Ruby Ramsamughare active participants in their community and have carried on their traditions of the Indian culture to their grandchildren.

Cecil Ramsamugh JR

Born to Cecil and Ruby Ramsamugh who are both Jamaican Indians, Cecil Ramsamugh (Jr) grew up in Santa Cruz where he attended Santa Cruz Preparatory and later Munro College. He was former head boy of Santa Prep School in 1985 and Head Prefect of Munro College in 1992.

He completed his Diploma studies at the University of Technology, Jamaica, specialising in Business with an emphasis on Marketing and later at the University of the West Indies a first degree in the Bachelor of Education with an emphasis in Mathematics. He is a trained graduate and has been in the classroom for over 17 years teaching Mathematics to the CXC level.

He is married to Kamala Maragh second child of Dr. Olive Maragh and Mr. Tulsidas "Joe "Maragh. Kamala is also a trained graduate with a first degree in Early Childhood. She has been in the classroom for over 11 years.

As a Mathematics teacher Mr. Ramsamugh has worked with the Ministry of Education as a former Mathematics coach with responsibility for three high schools, namely Lacovia, Maggotty and Lewisville High schools. He has also worked as Mathematics coordinator of an intra-parish M&M Mathematics competition on behalf of Black River High school for 14 years, where the High school was placed in the top three (3) position for twelve (12) of those years.

Cecil Ramsamugh is also a businessman who operates a Transportation company along with his wife Kamala. The union of Cecil and Kamala has produced a son, Rajesh.

Alvin Singh

Alvin Ramrod Singh (Chun-Chun) was born in 1935 to Ragnaught Singh and Ethlyn Mohan. They lived off Spanish Town Road in Kingston, Alvin had three brothers; David and Samuel were older and George was the youngest.

Alvin's father, Ragnaught was a renowned dancer in the Indian community while his maternal uncles Galgal and Baby were renowned for their drumming skills. Some of Alvin's fondest memories as a young boy growing up was attending various Indian functions in Kingston and other parishes, enjoying the music and dance while connecting with friends. Alvin has maintained some his friendships developed during these early years, namely, Henry Jaghai, classmate at Ebenizer and Rama Maragh, classmate at St. Albans.

In 1957 Alvin married the love of his life Gloria Harry, the daughter of Frederick (Pudun) and Lucilda Harry. Gloria was the eldest of eleven children, Vincent, Joseph, Daniel, Glenroy, Joyce, Donavan, Solomon Verona, Sharon and Fredeman. They also grew up off Spanish Town Road then the family moved to Oakland Ave off Waltham Park Road.

Alvin and Gloria also moved to Oakland and brought up their six wonderful children, Superchard (Anief), Sandra, Yasmin, Beverley, Sonia and Reta there. Both parents worked hard to provide for their children, Alvin worked at the Kingston Wharf and Stacote Paints for a number of years while Gloria worked as a dressmaker at Handal Garment Factory. In 1970

Alvin began working at Jamaica Packaging Industries Limited until he retired early in 1997 after suffering from a stroke. Gloria stayed at home full-time after the birth of their fourth child, however, she continued dressmaking to the delight of her family and friends.

The family shared many wonderful memories and developed a strong bond of family and friendship while living at Oakland. Friends living within and outside of Kingston often meet there on the weekends to hang out or take a trip to Hellshire Beach and making a pot of soup on the shore. Alvin loves playing dominoes and has participated in many tournaments including some hosted at Oakland. Cricket was another family favorite, especially when some of Gloria's brothers are part of the team.

The year 2000 was very significant in the lives of the Singh Family; Alvin and Gloria migrated to Miami, Florida and their children, Superchard and his sisters started a family business, Bhajan-Singh Company Limited/Rainbow Paint Centre. They sold only household paints and supplies but over the years have expanded into select hardware items also. In Miami, Alvin spends his time tending his lawn and numerous fruit trees, including a Jamaican Otaheiti apple. He enjoys sharing the fruits with neighbors, family and friends whom he hangs out with ever so often. Gloria now spends her time doing embroidery and like all her daughters enjoys a deep faith in Jesus Christ, serving others in need and always ready to show hospitality to family and friends that visit. Alvin and Gloria agree that as time passes, they treasure more and more the time spent with any or all of their eleven grandchildren.

Ragnaught Singh

Ganga Singh

Ganga Pershad Singh was born on May 10, 1947 in Kingston Jamaica. He was born to parents Khun Khun and Etwari Singh. Khun Khun his father was born in India and at the age of 12, he and his mother an indentured laborer came to Jamaica. At this age Khun Khun was able to read Sanskrit (extinct language of India). Ganga's mother was born in the parish of St. Thomas in Jamaica. The couple came to Kingston to seek a better life for their family.

Ganga was the fifth of eight children born to the Singh's. His siblings are Doris, Clarice, Deloris, Jamwant, Mahadeow, Chuman and Kisson Singh. Ganga attended Coburn Pen Primary School and Kingston Technical High School. He continued his education at the St. Andrew Technical High School in the evenings. At the end of his schooling he was successful at the 1st and

2nd year ULCI Examination in Mechanical Engineering. During his tenure at these schools he joined the apprenticeship programmed and started working at Kelly's Engineering Works Limited and Masterton Jamaica Limited. At the end of his five years apprenticeship period he received a certificate from England stating that he had successfully completed his apprenticeship. At this time he was recommended to C.A.S.T now UTech to further his education in his field. Due to financial constraints he was not able to pursue the course. He then moved on to the Jamaica Ice Company in the capacity of a machinist. He soon moved on to Jamaica Packaging industry and then again to Colgate Palmolive Jamaica Limited. After some years he started his own business.

Ganga had also worked at the Deluxe Theatre where he aligned his regular shift work to a part time job as a projectionist. It is famous for putting on Indian film shows. He enjoyed this job immensely, more so when he starred his own show after meeting his lead actress Cherry Bisnaught. It was love at first sight. They got married; the union produced 3 lovely children. Seeta, Raami, Lally and four grandchildren namely Shemar, Sanjeev, Rajesh and Ariana.

Ganga a born Hindu whose father read the Ramayan in the evenings to Ganga and his siblings, never found it difficult to gravitate towards the encouragement of Doctor Hame Persaud O.D. The doctor encouraged him to get active and get involved in his Indian culture and religion. At age 18 Ganga started making frequent visits to Satsang where he develop a deep love and passion for the religion and culture. He was also actively involved in the youth organization which consisted of sporting events and was captain and vice president of the SDM cricket team. Some of Ganga's teammates include the likes of Freddy, Ally and Danny Bahadur, Winston Ramsey, Donald Suckie, Herbert Vernal, Arthur Latchman, Sam and Larry Bachan, Noel and Roy Rambally, Lisha Shaw, Wilbert Tallow and Andurie (Macka). Within this time period he was the opening batsman for the cricket team. Ganga also had a great passion for horseracing. He would visit the racetrack namely Caymanas Park in Jamaica with much regularity and was a great friend to many horsemen from various walks of life and was very close to the legendary Mr. Henry Jaghai where he would spend a lot of time with him in his private box and watched the races.

L to R: Ganga, Lally, Raami, Cherry, Seeta

Sukhdevi Singh

Sukhdevi "Sukhi." Singh, Born October 14th, 1960 from Hindu parents, at Co-Burn Gardens, Kingston, Jamaica. She was raised by her grandmother Atwari Singh lovingly called (Etwari) and her grandfather Khun Khun Singh since birth.

Both grandparents were immigrants from India who were born in a small village called Baral Ganch and immigrate to Jamaica in the early year of 1912. Sukhi lived with her grandparents for 10 years, then resided with her aunt and uncle, Mr. & Mrs. Wilfred & Clarice Calu, at 16 Cling Cling Ave. Kingston 11. Jamaica, WI. The Calu's were ardent Hindus, and practice this religion both spiritually and culturally to its fullest and spoke both English and Hindi fluently while residing in the home of her aunt and uncle, Sukhi would sing bhajans as she does her daily chores. She was that little girl, who would start the dance on the dance floor whenever there was a family party at home. This interest in her dancing and singing was noticed by Mr. Calu who was impressed by her talent and potential she was gifted with. After much deliberation and thought, he decided that he wanted her to start participating in the Indian functions that was held. She could use these talents in a constructive way to do her part in keeping the culture alive.

The Calu's took her to Sanatan Dharma Mandir (SDM) which is located at 114 Hagley Park Road, on Sundays where Satsang Was held. In addition she also started to practice singing and dancing with the Indian Talent Merry-Makers, one of Jamaica's top Indian bands. Sukhi started to perform in live concerts since she was 12 years old. She did her first live performance at SDM Mandir before it was completely built. She joined with other excellent singers and dancers, such as Sheila &Fern Pancham, Indra Pancham, Sweetie Cobb, Annette & Grace Jackson, Barbara & Valerie Durga-Singh, Valda Williams, Marine Sukoo and Carrol Singh. Among others male participants were, Patrick, Roger & Errol Gallow, Devon Singh & Carlos Ramsey, among other male performers. As the years went by everyone who participated, gave their all and did their best. It was a lot of work, but also very enjoyable which is held precious in everyone's hearts. There is a much memory of satsang being held at the Calu's & the Pancham's homes, before the Mandir was available for holding prayers.! GREAT TIMES.!! It was a wonderful feeling to use her time in helping to maintain this uplifting, inspiring and knowledgeable organization. She has had the privilege of attaining peace of mind, good health and knowing some great history of Hinduism. So, she continued to do as much as she could, to give her all.

The years are going by, and new developments are taking place. Another of her endeavor was to join with the well-known Krishna Deonarine, in hosting the program, "Indian Talent on Parade." This program was aired live on the national radio on RJR. On Sundays. Sukhi spoke on many different Exotic Indian cuisine, in this way many could hear and share this delicacy. Her love and happiness for the uplifting and strength, led her to, "Club India" located in the New Kingston area. Sukhi coordinated in different charitable concerts, she also did many performances there as well. She welcomed the young teenagers who wanted to give of what they could. Shakira & Indra Bennett, Shanti Badaloo, were also among these girls, she tried her tutoring skills again and was successful in many shows that were held there. Sanatan Dharma Mandir is the first Hindu Temple that was built in Jamaica. Heartfelt thanks to all the Founders, and everyone who gave their help, love and hard work in making this happen.

During the happy and exciting years of Spiritual & Cultural events at SDM… much spectacular events took place. Two girls were graced in a Beauty Pageant to get the title "Miss SDM. Beauty Queens. The first one who got the title as queen, was the late FAY PANCHAM, ! May her journey on be a Good one. The 2nd queen who got the title was SUKHI SINGH.! Looking forward to more of these fun times, nothing lasts forever, Sukhi had to move on to another country to be with other family members, who needed her support. She migrated to America, and continue her singing, dancing, and charitable work with the Mandir. SDM Sanatan Dharma Mandir is now managed by Mr. & Mrs. Errol Johnson among others. It stands tall and Majestic with beautiful Marty, vivid colors and filled with much tranquility and peace. Thanks to everyone who did their part. Special thanks to all the founders. Long live SDM.

May there be peace, peace, peace.!!

Wilfred and Clarice Calu

Sukhi Singh

Lorna Sukie

Timothy Suckie, born on the 27th of April, 1930 in the parish of Portland, was the son of James and Marian Suckie. James Suckie came from a town in India called Gorakpur, along with his 3brothers as indentured laborers. James and his family lived in Portland at a place called Fellowship. They soon settled in Kingston at 30 Olympic Way in Cockburn Pen . The couple had 4 sons, Ernest, Frederick, Timothy, Joshua, Sivert and 1 daughter named Gadis.

Timothy was the twin brother of Joshua but sadly Joshua died at an early age . His father James, also died when he was still a young man. As a grown man, Timothy had a passion for the sea which made him become a fisherman. He bought a small engine boat and named it Killa which eventually became his nickname.

Timothy worked at Metal Box Jamaica Ltd. making plastic sheeting for many companies. He married Hilda Baccas through an arranged marriage and had 7 children - Icylin, Carmellia, Orville, Lena, lorna, Dennis, and Rohan. They bought their home at 86 Woodpecker Avenue where they raised their children.

Hilda was born on the 8th of October, 1928. Her grandfather, Osama, an indentured labourer went to the estate called Killankoli in Saint Mary. Osama's children were Ishmael (Hilda's father), Rahim Abbie, Abraham, Miriam Beharrie and Cees Dean. While coming to Jamaica, Osama's ship developed problems and had to make a stop on Colon, a small island off the coast of India. Osama stayed on Colon where Ishmael was born . Ishmael came to Jamaica as a young man. He lived in Saint Mary, Annotto Bay. He became a merchant and opened a store selling materials and othergoods. All of Ishmael's brothers migrated to England.

Ishmael met his wife Sleetie and started afamily. Their children were Hilda, Ethlyn, Evelyn. Pearl, Norma, Ramses and Stanley. The family eventually moved to Kingston. Hilda went to Gray's Inn All Age school. She worked at Metal Box Ltd for 35 years. She was the head person on one of the many lines that made tin cans for many factories in Jamaica.

Timothy Sukie and Hilda Baccas

Lorna's granddaughter - María Fernanda Thomas Duran

Roy Sweetland

Roy Amritt Sweetland – is currently an Events Photographer & music producer with Sweetland Photographic Sweetland Sound. Professionally trained telecomm engineer with over twenty-eight years of service as a Microwave/Fibre Optics Telecom Transmission Maintenance Engineer with the Jamaica Telephone Company JTC/TOJ/C&WJ 1974-2003. Implementing and maintaining the conversion from analog to digital development phase, successfully completing hundreds of manufacturer's equipment, plant and management training courses in Jamaica, Canada, Japan, the USA and the UK.

Started photography as a hobby back in the 1970's, and professionally since 2003 covering weddings and parties and now operates a Caribbean Image Archive of Caribbean and events photography image service and providing events coverage services, a freelance special events photographer who have covered concerts, press launches, sporting events, etc. for various clients and media houses including VP Records, TADS Records,

NCB, VMBS, PULSE, Sagicor, Bob Marley Museum, Rita Marley Foundation, Air Jamaica Jazz & Blues, Carib Cement, JWN, Jamaica Pegasus, PUMA Jamaica, VH1, Headline Entertainment, Reggaeville, Buzzz Caribbean Lifestyle Magazine.

Achievements: Have taken album cover and Artiste bio photos for over 100 Reggae and other music genre Album of artiste including Delroy Wilson - Hit after Hit-, George Nook tribute to Dennis Brown, Gregory Isaacs, King Yellowman – Duppy Gunman, Buju Banton, Wayne Wonder, Wailing Soul, Frankie Paul, Sugar Minott, Channel 1 Anthology, Kiddus I, Rankin Toyan, Tarrus Riley, Lou Lepke, Denroy Morgan, Jackie Mittoo VP Records Tribute, Beres Hammond, Vybz Kartel-Pon di Gaza 2.0, Carl Dawkins, Derrick Lara, Don Carlos, DYCR, Reggae Golden Jubilee, Jah Cure -Thank You For Life, Twin Of Twins, Raja Sarangie – Pleasures for the soul, among others.

Covered and archives most of the Major events, Reggae Concerts and Party Brands in Jamaica and a few in N.Y. And Florida since 2003 including, Reggae Sumfest, Reggae Sunsplash 2006, Air Jamaica Jazz & Blues, Rebel Salute, East Fest, Sting, Follow Di Arrow, Fully Loaded, Magnum Kings & Queen Competition, DigiCel Rising Star Competition, Rockfest, Springfest, Stars "R" Us, Arthur Guinness Show, Conscious Reggae Party, Earl Chinna Smith's Inna De Yard, JAAVA & JARIA Tribute Shows and annual Reggae month events, Camp Fire, Best Of The Best, Marleyfest, 9 Miles, Smile Jamaica, Stone Love, Weddy, Shaggy & Friends, Beres Hammond Moment In Time, Third World, Comitted, Welcome To Jamrock, Western Consciousness, Jamaica & Bacchanal Carnival, Unifest, Palm Beach & Orlando Jerk & Caribbean Culture Festival, Grace Jamaican Jerk Festival, annual Indian arrival day in Jamaica

Sweetland's Images have appeared in numerous Books, Magazines, Newspapers including. Coffee table books "Moods of Jamaica" 2004 by Moods of Mann Ltd. "Beautiful Jamaica" 2013 Special Jamaica 50Th LMH Edition by Evon Blake, the 2007 Book America Fair award winning "Reggae Scrapbook" done jointly with world renowned Reggae Archivist Roger Steffens and photographer Peter Simon. "Inna Di Dancehall" By Donna P. Hope. Dancehall – Slaveship To Ghetto by Sonjah Stanley Nyah.

Among some of the Magazines, newspaper and other publications that have utilized his images include Source, VIBE, Billboard, Jamrock Magazine, The BEAT Reggae Magazine, Air Jamaica Jazz & Blues Event program booklet. Newspaper include The Jamaican Daily Gleaner, The Observer, South Florida Caribbean National WeeklyNespaper.

Was a member of the 40-year-old now defunct PCOJ Photography Camera Club of Jamaica winning over 28 awards in all Amateur categories entered the very first time entering the 2006 JCDC National Annual Visual Arts Competition including Gold for his Jamaican nightlife – Caesar's Girl image, Silver, Bronze and Merit certificates. Won a British Council honorable mention award for his 2002 "The Queens Theatre" Environmental Photo-journalism in the Jamaica Jubilee Photography Competition. Roy's work was part of the inaugural 2017 "Let There Be Reggae" photo exhibitions in South Florida during Miami Art week's Art Basel show in wynwood.

Currently the senior events photographer for the BUZZZ Caribbean Lifestyle Magazine since 2003 Based in Kingston Jamaica and covers events in the Jamaican Diaspora worldwide. He now does Album, Concerts, Events and Book reviews for the BUZZZ Magazine and is in the process of compiling his two major lifetime book projects "My Jamaica - Sweetland of Mine" and "This Is Reggae Music – Heartbeat of the people" Two book which speaks to the subjects by utilizing Images and writers intimately involved in the various areas for each chapters of each book including his own writings and images.

A citizen of the USA and Jamaica Roy resides in Ft Lauderdale Florida with wife Annett, daughters Candi and Sumitra, grand children Joshua and Vanessa and cat Nala Windy, he frequently returns to Jamaica for various Photo Assignments.

Mission: To capture moments, preserve memories and archive images of people, events and items seen and of interest for posterity. Goal: To support cultural events of mankind and complete two lifelong book projects on Jamaica and Reggae Music.

Wilbert Tallo J.P.

Wilbert Tallo was born on December 14, 1949. He was the seventh child for Mr. and Mrs. Percival Tallo. He attended Cockburn Garden Primary, St. Andrew Primary, Denham Town Senior School and St. Andrew Technical High School. Wilbert did skill training at St. Andrew Trade Training Center in Welding and Metal Fabrication. He received certification in Welding Craft Practice and Technology. Wilbert also attended the Vocational Training Institute in 1980, and the General Technical Institute in Linden, New Jersey. Wilbert attained A.S.M.E. Certification with the American Society of Mechanical Engineering in 1986. He also attended Principles, Techniques and Practice of Industrial Welding at UTECH in 1989.

Wilbert worked at the Red Stripe Brewery from May 1, 1967 to July 11, 1999 as a welding supervisor in the Engineering Department. Wilbert is the father of five children; two girls and three boys. He also has thirteen grandchildren. Being commissioned as a Justice of the Peace on May 29, 2000 and sworn in on July 11, 2000, he has presided in the Lay Magistrates Court at Half Way Tree since October 200 to present. He received training at the D.R.F. Mediation course in May 2005.

Wilbert served as a Director on the Board of the L.M.A.J. from 2002 to 2008, and continues to be faithful to his chapter without fear, favour, affection or ill will. Mr. Tallo was the recipient of the Parish award in July 2012. He works closely with the South St. Andrew Police at Hunts Bay. Wilbert visits lock-ups, presides at identification parades, remands detainees, writing caution statements, and performing question and answer sessions. He is a member of the interviewing panel of the Narcotics, Duhaney Park, Olympic Gardens, M.I.T., and Scene of the Crime Police Departments. Wilbert offers counsel and advice to the people in his community and other communities.

Vijay Thompson

Vijay Thompson was born on December 10, 1978 in St. Andrew, Jamaica. Born the first child of parents Basil Thompson and Joyce Thompson. Thus, becoming the eldest of five children.

Vijay spent his adolescent years going to Trenchtown high located in Kingston, Jamaica. When he graduated, he went on to participating in an apprenticeship with his Uncle to learn mechanical work.

After spending, most of their young years in Jamaica the Thompson family decided to migrate to the United States in search of a successful life. Thus, in this new life they started up a family business in the food industry. A local family friendly restaurant named Joyce's.

After settling in this foreign country Vijay decided to start a family of his own, marrying Kerriann Ramsay becoming Mrs. Kerriann Thompson. The loving couple produced five children similar to their parents and currently spends their days living in Brooklyn, New York.

SONNY WARD J.P. & FAMILY

Alberto Fernando Ward (Sonny) was born on September 5, 1922 to the parents of Charles and Ethel Ward. Sonny had one sister, Emma (Pearl) and one brother Alexander (Byron). Alberto was married on June 17, 1951 to Dhandie, daughter of Arthur and Mary Maragh. Dhandie was born on July 30, 1932 and she had seven siblings. Sonny and Dhandie had five children, Charles, Diana (Pam), Kenneth, Albelto (Freddy) and Michele. They were also blessed with five grandchildren and two great-grandchildren.

Sonny was an entrepreneur who was influenced by his parents at an early age to be self-sufficient. As a teenage boy, Sonny would often accompany his father on daily rounds for his various businesses in Kingston. As Sonny got older he helped his father, Charles to manage his bus company (Ward Transportation Line) and real estate properties in Kingston. In later years, Sonny and Dhandie established 'The Sugar Bowl Club' on Spanish Town Road where Dhandie managed the daily operation and he did the accounting whilst fulfilling his duties as a Justice of the Peace (J.P). Sonny had a pleasant disposition and enjoyed interacting and socializing with the people in the community. Both ensured that their children had a good education. Sonny was instrumental in the Indian Independence celebrations in Jamaica in 1947.

ALBELTO WARD AND FAMILY

Albelto Ward (Freddy) was born in June 1957 in Kingston, Jamaica to the parents of Alberto and Dhandie Ward. Albelto has four siblings, Charles, Kenneth, Diana and Michele. Albelto attended C.A.S.T. (UTECH) in Kingston, where he obtained a diploma in Mechanical Engineering (ME). He continued his education at Polytechnic University (NYU) where he graduated with a B.Sc. degree in (ME). Freddy is currently the Chief Engineer for a manufacturer of noise and vibration control products in New York.

Freddy married his high school friend Fern, who is the daughter of Robert and Miriam Pancham. Marva Fern was born in April 1958, in St. Andrew, Jamaica and is the sixth child of seven siblings including one brother. They are Lucilda Newman, Fay Maragh (dec'd), Beverly Rampersad, Ferdinand Pancham, Sheila Gallow and Indra Dalling. Fern attended Wolmer's High School for Girls, then later on obtained a B.Sc. degree in Natural Sciences in 1982 at The University of the West Indies (UWI) Mona. She worked as an administrator in the jewelry industry in NY. Freddy and Fern are the proud parents of daughter Fazia and son Faraz. Fazia was born in December 1987 and Faraz was born in February 1992 in New York. They both went to Division Avenue High School. Fazia graduated in May 2011, with a B.Sc. degree in Bioscience at Farmingdale State University and is currently a quality assurance specialist, at a pharmaceutical company on Long Island. Faraz received a 'Book Scholarship Award' in 2010 with SUNY Old Westbury Honors College, where he graduated with a B.Sc. degree in Computer Information Science in May 2015. He is presently a software developer, for a software solutions company on Long Island.

Fern and her sister, Sheila participated in many Indian cultural events in the form of plays (skits), film dances and traditional Indian folk dances. They, as well as, Sukhdevi Singh, Evelyn Cobb, Valda Williams, Marine Sukhoo, Grace Jackson, Annette Jackson and Marlene Punancy performed at venues including Vale Royal, The Institute of Jamaica and the Sanatan Dharma Mandir in Kingston, Jamaica.

Marley Kiah Agustus Williams

Call him Augustus, BreddaBonai, Boops, - Grandfather, Greasey, Marley Kiah, - Oley, Son or Uncle but to many he was King, a king in his own right. He was the eldest son of Anita Baccas (Mother Annie) and Father Williams. King was born at March Pen Road, Spanish Town St. Catherine. Since he had no true documentation of his birth date, by using comparisons of other family members and their ages we deduce that he could have been born about 1917.

As a young child he went to live with his aunt (his father's sister). Upon reaching his teenage years his aunt realized that his mother needed help to provide for her household. King had to work to support his family which now included his younger siblings, brothers, Bubu and Kurru and sisters Lyn and Shaggy. He turned to cultivation as a means of livelihood. After years of working hard and being the breadwinner for his mother and siblings, he decided to start his own family. He met and married his first love Betsy from Chapleton, Clarendon in 1942. He did not adapt well to the transition in Clarendon and yearned to return to his birth parish. Neither could Betsy adapt to a new residence in St. Catherine. The inevitable happened and they separated soon thereafter but not without leaving proof of their union, Evelyn Williams who was born in 1943.

Betsy and Evelyn remained in Clarendon while King returned to Spanish Town, St. Catherine where he engaged in rice cultivation. Somewhere during that time he met Louisa Hill (Puncie), whom he fell in love with. This was the beginning of his entry into the extended families of the Hills, Maraghs and Jaghais. He now juggled jobs between farming, gardening and carpentry and worked with the likes of people as Major Melville and Mr. Barnes, a building contractor from whom he perfected his skills in masonry, plumbing, electrician, building designs and engineer.

Puncie and King lived with Puncie's parents Minnie and John Hill at Lindsay Pen, now known as Lawrence Avenue. At that time, Myrtle Hill, Puncie's sister was only ten years old. King quickly became a loved brother in law, and caregiver to the Hill's children and adopted the role as an informal parent to Mitchie, Puncie's baby brother. King's career of growing other people's children began. So good was he with children, that Father Hill, Puncey's eldest brother, accommodated him and Puncie at his home in Norbrook to help with his eight children.

In the ambitious quest to have their own home, both King and Puncie went back to Spanish Town and lived there for a while but returned to St. Andrew and built a one room wooden structure at the back of the property at 9 Rosalie Avenue. Elizabeth Hill (Puncey's younger sister) and her family lived in the house at the front of the property.

He had made such an impression on the Hill family as a responsible and nurturing caregiver that when Elizabeth, and her husband, Butty Maragh, migrated to England in 1959, they could think of no better person to leave their five children with, than King. Fay was 9, Herman 8, Christine 4, Junior 3 and Tony, just a baby of 6 months. At 9 Rosalie Avenue, for three years King and Puncie looked after these children, working hard to provide food, shelter and most of all pouring unconditional love upon them. Between 1961 to 1962, the first three of the Maragh children were sent to England to join their parents. Junior and Tony were left behind. Tony, who was now three years old was their infinite source of joy. In 1963, both boys left Jamaica to join their parents.

One wet, chilly night in 1963, Myrtle Hill, and her husband Henry Jaghai, suddenly moved to 9 Rosalie Avenue. They had purchased the property previously from Ivan, Myrtle's brother, who had bought it from Butty Maragh upon his migration. Henry and Myrtle, had demolished the existing house and had started to build a new one. Up to that time it was not completed. Being the compassionate couple they were, King and Puncie moved out of their house at the back and opted to stay in Mr. Jaghai's unfinished house.

That memorable night King welcomed into his life the four Jaghai children, Patricia 4, Sam 2, Tony 1 and Andrea 5 months. This would be the beginning of a journey of 47 years of King's abundant love and care to these children, which extended to the two other sons who came after, - Peter and Paul. This expression of fatherly love flowed over to the neighbour's niece - Joan, of 10 Rosalie Avenue. He acted in every way a father would and even when Puncieleft Rosalie Avenue, he remained, because he knew he had a duty to his children - to love, care, protect and defend them. The grandchildren that came after were icing on the cake for him. They were his delight and joy. He was a constant companion to them on school outings, family events and overseas travels. When the parents or grandparents reprimanded Alicia, Stacy, Tira, Shari, or Shelley, King became highly upset. If Rajesh, Aaron, Alex, Adam, Andre or Matthew were physically punished, he would voice his displeasure. To Sasha, Tiffany, Jordan and Brandon, we share your grief of losing a treasured caregiver. Although the periods of time they shared with him were brief, King's biological grand children and great grandchildren will hold those precious moments in their hearts forever.

King was a hallmark of Rosalie Avenue. He was a jack of all trades and a master of all. The house and garden at Rosalie Avenue bears testament of his handiwork. His superior intelligence allowed him to quickly adapt and excel in any new occupation. He was instrumental in building the business, at Jaghai's Garage. Given the right education, King could easily have been a master engineer.

King did not suffer from any major illness; his only condition was old age. Just a couple of hours before he died he was conversing with family and friends about old times. He moved about in his wheelchair from the front to the back of the house several times – maybe reminiscing about his fifty-one years at Rosalie Avenue. When he got tired, he went to his room and fell into a quiet sleep - a sleep of eternal rest.

Vinroy Webb

Vinroy was born on July 23, 1944 to parents Lebert Webb and Louise Dusing. His siblings are Lloyd and Amy Moore, living in England. He attended Cockburn Garden All-Age School. Vinroy is married to Lorna James Webb. He is the father of seven children; Ann Marie, Jo Ann, Simone, Charlton, Lisa, Crystal and Sanjay. Charlton has a successful barber shop in New York, following in his father's footsteps. Vinroy owned and operated Webb's Barber Shop for over 54 years. His clients included prominent members of Jamaican society such as government officials. He is an active member of the Indo-Jamaican community starting out with the Prema Satsang Group. He was involved in the promotion of Indian cultural activities. This included live performances by the Indian Merry Maker band among others on the beach. People used to look forward to these shows.

Samuel Williams

Samuel Williams, his wife Alice and their children at his 90th Birthday party.

Samuel Williams was born on October 25, 1926 in Point Hill, Roaring River, St John's in the parish of St. Catherine to parents Charles Williams and Catherine Collis. He has one sister, Molly Williams. He attended the Point Hill Church School. On the weekends, Samuel along with his son, Tony rode on a bicycle to various parishes to sell dry goods, to make additional income to support his family. Samuel worked at R Hannah & Sons Ltd. in Kingston, Jamaica and upon migrating to the United States was employed at Winn Dixie Supermarket in Miami, Florida. He married Alice Sukie on July 30, 1961.

Alice Sukie-Williams was born on April 18, 1932. She lived at 6 Whitehall Ave, Kingston 8, Jamaica. She has two sisters, Gladys McPherson and Evelyn Hibbert, and six brothers, Sonny, Kenneth, Cleveland, Eric, Harry and Cedrick. Alice attended St. Johns Elementary School. She worked at Captain Morgan. Samuel and Alice have six children, three boys Toney, Paul and Richard, and three daughters, Judith, Marcia and Annette.

On October 25, 2016 Samuel celebrated his 90th birthday with his wife, children, family and many friends in Miramar, Florida.

Arjun's relatives in Rattapur

Jaghi's relatives and villagers in Bahadurpur

APPENDIX 1

Importing Countries of Indian Indentured Labourers
CARIBBEAN BRITISH COLONIES

Countries	Date	First Arrivals	Total Arrivals Number
Guyana	May 5, 1838	396	238, 909
Jamaica	May 10, 1845	261	36, 412
Trinidad	May 30, 1845	219	143, 939
Martinique	May 16, 1853	455	25, 509
Guadeloupe	1854		42, 326
French Guyana	1855		8, 500
Belize	1857		3, 000
Grenada	May 1, 1857	336	3, 200
St Lucia	May 6, 1859	318	4, 350
St. Kitts	1860		337
St. Vincent	June 1, 1861	260	2, 472
St. Croix	1862		321
Surinam	June 5, 1873	399	34, 309
Sub-Total (Caribbean British Colonies)			543, 579
Mauritius	September 9, 1834	36	453, 063
Seychelles	1840		6, 315
Reunion Island	July 25, 1860		26, 507
Natal-South Africa	November 16, 1860	342	152, 184
East Africa			32, 000
Fiji	May 14, 1879	31	60, 965
Sub-Total (Other BritishColonies)			731, 034
TOTAL			**1, 274, 613**

[23] (Source: en.wikipedia.org/Indian_indenture_system)

APPENDIX II

SHIPS WHICH CAME TO JAMAICA FROM 1845 TO 1917

Year	Number Arrived	Ship Name	Port of Embarkation	Date of Departure	Date of Arrival
1845	261	Blundell Hunter	Calcutta	-	May 9
1846	301	Scotia	"	Feb 8	June 7
"	288	Warren Hastings	"	Feb 19	?
"	317	Hyderabad	"	Nov. 22	Mar 5
"	293	Morley	Madras	?	?
"	276	Thetis	"	?	?
"	203	Tropic	"	?	?
"	345	Anne Armstrong	"	?	?
"	283	Winfred	Calcutta	?	?
"	224	Mandrin	?	?	?
"	336	Barossa	Madras	?	?
"	250	Athenian	"	?	?
1847	235	Success	Calcutta	Nov. 7	?
"	340	Barossa	Madras	?	Jan. 11
"	333	Athenian	?	Apr. 2	?
"	340	David Clark	Calcutta	?	July 11
1860	233	Rajasthan	"	Mar. 29	Aug. 13
"	363	Themis	"	?	?
1861	349	Clarendon	"	Mar. 12	June 28
"	282	Pearl	?	May 15	?
"	293	Wentworth	"	June 18	?
"	257	Ravencraig	"	Oct. 25	Feb. 1
"	311	Good Hope	?	?	?
1862	375	Scorsby	?	Oct. 8	Jan. 19
"	287	Marion	?	?	May 12
"	389	Hungersford	?	?	?
"	307	Empress Eugenie	?	?	Feb. 20
"	381	Sydenham	?	?	?
"	324	Gertrude	Calcutta	?	Jan. 4
"	389	Hougomont	?	?	June 14
1863	258	Norman Morri- son	Madras	?	Jan. 3
"	383	Lady McNaugh- ton	"	?	Mar. 4
1867	366	St Hilda	Calcutta	?	Apr. 29
"	384	Ganges	"	?	May 29

Year	Number Arrived	Ship Name	Port of Embarkation	Date of Departure	Date of Arrival
"	483	Corona	"	?	June 24
"	392	Salmanca	"	?	July 7
1869	448	Patrician	"	?	Mar. 28
"	545	Buckinghamshire	"	?	Apr. 17
"	396	Gainshorough	"	?	May 10
1870	437	Alnwick Castle	"	?	Feb. 10
"	469	Poonah	"	?	Mar. 23
1872	543	Hereford	"	?	May 26
"	385	Marchantman	"	?	Mar. 7
"	416	Salisbury	"	?	June 9
"	406	Humber	"	?	Sept. 9
"	318	Sea Queen	Calcutta	?	?
1873	319	Lincells	"	?	?
"	587	Stockbridge	"	?	?
"	301	Latona	"	?	?
1874	509	Woodburn	"	?	Jan. 28
"	360	Duke of Argyll	"	?	Mar. 31
"	490	Loch Lomond	"	?	Apr. 25
1875	435	Moffusilite	"	?	Jan. 23
"	452	Neva	"	?	?
"	363	Robert Lees	"	?	May 8
1876	340	Chetah	"	?	Mar. 10
"	408	Middlesex	"	?	May 3
1878	529	Silhet	"	?	Feb. 19
"	366	Chetah	"	?	Apr. 9
1879	167	Chetah	"	?	Apr. 20
1880	383	Chetah	"	?	Apr. 19
"	364	Lightning	"	?	June 4
1881	504	Howrah	"	Feb. 20	June 8
1883	396	Howrah	"	?	May 28
1885	570	Hereford	"	?	Feb. 25
1891	538	Erne	"	?	Apr. 1
"	535	Moy	"	?	June 4
"	1,043	Belgravia	"	?	Oct. 27
1893	476	Volga	"	Sept. 7	?
1895	683	Arno	"	?	Jan. 2
"	468	Avon	"	?	Nov. 28

Year	Number Arrived	Ship Name	Port of Embarkation	Date of Departure	Date of Arrival
1899	610	Rhine	"	?	June 24
1900	655	Rhone	"	?	May 6
1903	812	S.S. Dahomey	"	Feb. 10	Apr. 8
1905	812	S.S. Indus	"	?	July 27
1906	814	S.S. Indus	"	?	May 15
1907	609	S.S. Indus	"	Sept. 5	Nov. 11
1908	414	S.S. Ganges	"	?	Nov. 16
1910	273	S.S. Sutlej	"	Dec. 31	Feb. 4
"	852	S.S. Mutleh	"	?	Feb. 13
1911	813	S.S. Indus	"	Mar. 20	May 5
1912	408	S.S. Ganges	"	Feb. 27	Apr. 19
1913	428	S.S. Mutleh	"	Apr. 4	May 20
"	376	S.S. Indus	"	Nov. 27	Jan. 12
"	246	S.S. Mutleh	"	Dec. 25	Feb. 9
"	427	S.S. Chenabl	"	Feb. 1	Mar. 16
"	293	S.S. Mutleh	"	Oct. 10	Dec. 1
1916	617	S.S. Dewa	Calcutta & Madras	Apr. 7	June 9
1917	?	?	?	?	?
Source: Documents at Jamaica Archives, and other reports					

APPENDIX 111
ESTATES TO WHICH INDENTURED WORKERS FROM VARIOUS SHIPS WERE DISTRIBUTED

Jamaica Archives Ref.	Name of Ship	Estate	Owner of Estate	Parish
1B/9/2	Thetis	Alexandria	John Cass & H.B. Evans	Hanover
1B/9/3b	Hyberabad	Petersfield	J.O. Harrison	Westmoreland
		Friendship	C. Williams	
		Canaan	United Fruit Company	
		New Galloway	United Fruit Company	
		Hylersfield	United Fruit Company	
1B/9/3c	Success	Info unavailable		
1B/9/3d	Athenia	Good Hope	John Poyntz	Trelawny
		Patosi		
		Spring		
		Pheonix		
		Adelphi		
		Lima		
		Friendship		
1B/9/3e	David Clark	Copse	J. Cass	Hanover
		Georgia	J. Cass	
		Hayham	United Fruit Company	
		Goodhall	United Fruit Company	
		Pell River	United Fruit Company	
1B/9/4	Themis	Spring Garden	Mr Ross	Westmoreland
		Bellisle	John Warner	
		Corniswall	John Warner	
		New Hope	John Warner	
		Blue Castle	Anthony DaCosta	
		Masemune	J. Florentone	
		Black Health	Anthony DeGray	
		Charlottenberg	D. Meason	
		Eardly	John de Souza	
		Meyersfield	Charles Rojores	

Jamaica Archives Ref.	Name of Ship	Estate	Owner of Estate	Parish
1B/9/5	Gainsbor-oug	No info available		
1B/9/6	Gertrude	Areadia	William Sewell	Trelawny
		Barrett Hall	Overseer – John William; Owner – Thomas Boddington & Richard Davis	St. James
		Fontabelle	Overseer – George Bowman; Owner – Eden Ceolville	Trelawny
		Hampstead	Overseer – James Fisher; Owner – Richa Hectwood	Trelawny
		Hague	Overseer – John Powell; Owner – RichardMajo	Trelawny
		Green Park	Overseers – James Fletcher & John Perye Owners – Eleanor Liverpaul, Spinster & William Harrison	Trelawny
		Latium	Overseer – Ralph Brown; Owner – George Lawrence	St. James
		Running Gut	Overseer – Alexander Grant; Owner – George Whitehorne	St. James
		Hampden	George Lawson	St. James
		Windsor Lodge	Overseer – Ralph Brown; Owner – Robe Gordon	St. James
1B/9/6	Ravenscraig	New Works	J. McPhail	St. Thomas in the Vale
		Tulloch	J. Melville	St. Thomas in the Vale
		Pennants & Kupis	J. Melville	Clarendon
		Denbeigh	J. Melville	Clarendon
		Moreland	Vere Estate Co. Ltd	Clarendon
		Amity Hall	H. Mitchell	Clarendon
		Savoy	H. Mitchell	Clarendon
		Gibbons		Clarendon
		May Pen	J. Harvey	Clarendon
		Tarentum	J. Harvey	Clarendon
1B/9/6	Marion	Pusey Hall	DanielCallegham	Clarendon

Jamaica Archives Ref.	Name of Ship	Estate	Owner of Estate	Parish
		Whitney	Daniel Callegham	Clarendon
		Green Wickle	Francis Henry	Clarendon
		Dawks	George Solomon	Clarendon
		Moneymusk	Francis Henry	Clarendon
		Harmony Hall	Louis McKinnon	Clarendon
		Caswell Hill	Louis McKinnon	Clarendon
		Retreat	George Solomon	Clarendon
		Sevens Plantation	Louis McKinnon	Clarendon
		Amity Hall	Louis McKinnon	Clarendon
		Rock River	George Solomon	Clarendon
1B/9/6	Sydenham	Ballards Valley	Wilmot Westmoreland	St. Mary
		Gilbraltar	Wilmot Westmoreland	St. Mary
		Hopewell	James Stewart	St. Mary
		Fort Stewart	Wilmot Westmoreland	St. Mary
		Townpatton	James Stewart	Portland
		Lowlayton	James Stewart	Portland
		Gayle	J. Melville	St. Mary
		Frontier	Robert Clementson	St. Mary
		Birlington	G. Solomon	Portland
		Spring Garden	H. Jacobs	Westmoreland
		Woodstock	Hon. Hosack	Westmoreland
		Friendship	Hon. Lindo	St. Mary
		Lambkin Hill	George Geddes	St. Mary
1B/9/6	Wentworth	Water Valley	CDW Matthews	St. Mary
		Gray's Inn	Y.R. Scarlett	St. Mary
		Agualta Vale	I. Levy	St. Mary
		Gibraltar	A.C. Westmoreland	St. Mary
		Dover	I. Levy	St. Mary
		Charlottenburgh	W. Westmoreland	St. Mary
		Orange Hill	Gas G. Cohen	St. Mary
		Gayle	J. Melville	St. Mary
		Lambkin Hill	George Geddes	St. Mary
		Eden Estate	Gas G. Cohen	St. Mary
		Frontier	Robert Clementson	St. Mary
		Friendship	Hon. Lindo	St. Mary
		Trinity	JP Carter	St. Mary
		Ballards Valley	Wilmot Westmoreland	St. Mary
		Heywood Hall		St. Mary

Jamaica Archives Ref.	Name of Ship	Estate	Owner of Estate	Parish
		White Hall	Wilmot Westmoreland	St. Mary
1B/9/6	Good Hope	Cornwall	William Vickers	Westmoreland
		Roaring River	William Vickers	Westmoreland
		Belleisle	William Vickers	Westmoreland
		Friendship	William Vickers	Westmoreland
		Retreat	Daniel Sinclair	Westmoreland
		Mesopotamia	Richard Burgess	Westmoreland
		Blue Castle	James Fenton	Westmoreland
		Masemure	Tomlin Campbell	Westmoreland
		Charlottenburg	David Meason	Westmoreland
		Meylersfield	William Cooke	Westmoreland
		Blackhealth	Henry Stoly	Westmoreland

Jamaica Archives Ref.	Name of Ship	Estate	Owner of Estate	Parish
1B/9/6	Clarendon	New Works	John McPhail	Clarendon
		Denks	J. Solomon	Clarendon
		Rock River	J. Solomon	Clarendond
		Belmont	J. Solomon	Clarendon
		Bushy Park	J. Solomon	Clarendon
		Lodge	James Harvey	Clarendon
		Sutton Pasture	James Harvey	Clarendon
		Hill Side	James Harvey	Clarendon
		Parnassus	James Harvey	Clarendon
		Chesterfield	James Harvey	Clarendon
		Seven Plantation	L. McKinnon	Clarendon
		Caswell Hill	L. McKinnon	Clarendon
		Harmony Hall	L. McKinnon	Clarendon
		Kupuis	J. Melville	Clarendon
		Penants	J. Melville	Clarendon
		Tulloch	J. Melville	Clarendon
		Lloyds	B. Von Kittlehold	Clarendon
1B/9/7	Humber	Renningberg		
		New Ramble	Y.R. Scarlett	St. Mary
		Gray's Inn	Y.R. Scarlett	St. Mary
		Gibraltar	A.C. Westmoreland	St. Mary
		Burlington	H. Cork	Portland
		Spring Garden	H. Jacobs	Portland
		Orange Hill	Gas G. Cohen	St. Mary
		Water Valley	C.D.W. Wathlewis	St. Mary
		Ballards Valley	Wilmot Westmoreland	St. Mary

Jamaica Archives Ref.	Name of Ship	Estate	Owner of Estate	Parish
		Cromwell Land	John Pringle	St. Mary
1B/9/8	Borossa	No info available		
1B/9/10b	Howrah	Amity Hall	H. Mitchell	Westmoreland
		Hordley		
		Fontabelle	Hugh A. Vickers	Westmoreland
		Somerset	Michael Muirhead	Manchester
		Spawich	Charles Walter	St. Elizabeth
		Appleton Estate	Dikenson	St. Elizabeth
		Pusey's Hall	E.C. Elliott	Clarendon
		Whitney	Ernest C. Elliott	Clarendon
		Belleisle	William Vickers	Westmoreland
		Albion	Williams Richards	St. Thomas
		Cornwall	William Vickers	Westmoreland
		Lyssons	I. Demercads	St. Thomas
		Gray's Inn	James Stewart	St. Mary
		Agualta Vale	I. Levy	St. Mary
		Orange Hill	Isaac Levy	St. Mary
		Quebec	R.P. Simmond	St. Mary
		Denbeigh	James Melville	Clarendon
		Golden Grove	David John Davis	St. Thomas
Jamaica Archives Ref.	Name of Ship	Estate	Owner of Estate	Parish
		Golden Grove	United Fruit Company	St. Thomas
		Potosi	Henry Cork	St. Thomas
		Golden Vale	United Fruit Company	Portland
		Llanrumney	Y.E. Kerr & Co.	St. Mary
		Iter Boreale	J. Hosack	St. Mary
		Riversdale	A. MacIntosh	St. Catherine
		Gray's Inn	John A. Scarlett	St. Mary
		Worthy Park	J. Calder	St. Catherine
		Hill Side	W. Pearce & W. Harvey	Clarendon
		Fort Stewart	John Pringle	St. Mary
		Vinery	J.W. Hill	Portland
		Hopewell	John Pringle	St. Mary
		Latium	J. Farquharson	St. James
		Zuebee	H. Limmonds	St. Mary
		Charlottenburg	W. Westmoreland	St. Mary
		Burlington	Henry Cork	Portland
		Osbourne	R. Beubow	St. Mary

		Esher	A. Westmoreland	St. Mary
		Gibraltar	M. Westmoreland	St. Mary
		Trinity	John Pringle	St. Mary
1B/9/11	Dahomey	Chovey	John Pringle	St. Mary
		Windsor Castle	A. DaCosta	Portland
		Fort George	A. Ellis	St. Mary
		Claremont	R.I. Constantine	St. Mary
		Duckenfield	I. Michelin	St. Thomas
		Water Valley	Charles Isaacs	St. Mary
		Shrewsbury	J. Miller	Portland
		Agualta Vale	John Pringle	St. Mary
		Newey	John Pringle	St. Mary
		Orange Hill	John Gayle	St. Mary
		Fontabelle	Harriet Delisser Limmonds	St. Mary
		Mid-Layton	J. Wasou	Portland
		Green Castle	John Pringle	St. Mary
		Honingsberg	John Pringle	St. Mary
		Cape Clear	John Pringle	St. Mary
		Monymusk	Charles Ward	Clarendon
		Mesopotamia	Percival Greg	Westmoreland
		Longville	The Amalgamated Products Company Lt	Carendon
		Amity Hall	Henry Mitchell	Clarendon
		Nutfield	John Pringle	St. Mary

Notes: Research at Jamaica Archives done by Henry W. Jaghai, OD, JP, Patrick Jaghai, Wilbert Sirjue, and Doreen Sirjue. The parish, St. Mary, was formerly called Metcalfe

APPENDIX IV

Note: The indentureship scheme was terminated in 1917. The last ship of repatriated Indians from Jamaica to India, the SS Sutlej, departed from Kingston on November 23, 1929 and arrived in Calcutta January 20, 1930. The table below provides information on the number of Indians who took the last voyage back home.

	MEN	WOMEN	CHILDREN	INFANTS		TOTAL SOULS	
No of Immigrant	219	98	36	24	20	425	
No. died	5	2	-	-	-	-	7
No. Arrived	214	96	36	24	28	20	418

The records show that the poor living conditions on the ship resulted in the death of seven Indian repatriants and the serious illness of 70 others. These sick Indians had to be specially quarantined and treated for days at the Indian port of arrival. The names of those who perished on the journey home were Munni, Gulab, Mohabir, Hublal, Sheoratan, Suleeman, andSubratan.

(Source: Jamaica Archives Document Ref 1B/9/37)

APPENDIX V

DISTRIBUTION ROLL FOR SS DAHOMEY SHIP, 1903
TABLE SHOWING DISTRIBUTION ROLL OF INDENTURED INDIANS WHO SAILED FROM INDIA ON FEBRUARY 10, 1903 AND ARRIVED IN JAMAICA ON APRIL 8, 1903 ON THE SS DAHOMEY

Parish & District		Owner	Estate	Number
St. Mary	Albany	C. D. Wathlewis	Water Valley	20
	Annotto Bay	A. FG Ellis	Fort George	20
	Albany	JP Carter	Trinity	15
	Albany	H. W. Pringle	Chovey	35
	Annotto Bay	H. W. Pringle	Agualta Vale	15
	Annotto Bay	EEC Hossack	Fort Stewart	30
	Annotto Bay	EEC Hossack	Iterboreale	50
	Richmond	C. Abraham	Hopewell	10
	Richmond	R. Fraser	Homingsbury	10
	Annotto Bay	Gas. G. Cohen	Newry	10
	Annotto Bay	Gas. G. Cohen	Orange Hill	10
	Annotto Bay	Gas. G. Cohen	Green Castle	10
	Annotto Bay	Gas. G. Cohen	Nut Field	15
	Albany	J. E. Herr & Co.	Llaurmury	20
	Albany	R. Simmonds	P. Quebec	15
	Albany	McDougal	Fontabella	15
	Albany	F. L. Bathur	Esher	25
	Annotto Bay	A. C. Westmoreland	Gibralter	25
	Richmond	W. H. Westmoreland	Charlotten- burg	10
	Annotto Bay	Y. R. Scarlette	Grays Inn	30

	Location	Name	Estate	Number
	Annotto Bay	R. L. Benbow	Osbourne	10
	Richmond	R. L. Constantine	Clermont	8
	Buff Bay	John W Hill	Vinery	75
	Orange Bay	J Wasou	Midlayton	25
	St Marga-ret's Bay	Henry Cork	Berlington	15
	Buff Cross-ing	AEA DaCosta	Windsor Castle	12
	Hope Bay	James Millec	Strawberry	35
	Stearner	United Fruit Company	PhillipsField	25
	Riversdale	AR McIntosh	Rio Magna	10
	Ewarton	JV Calder	Worthy Park	10
	Spanish Town	Charles Hudson	G. Blair Pen	10
	May Pen (Vere)	FM Ellis	Hillside Raywood	25
	Montego Bay	JC Farquharson	Latimer	10
	Steamer	W. Stewart	Potosi	10
Sub-Total				670
Other workers distributed to other estates including Dr. John Pringle (Clonmell, St Mary) & W.F.P. Phillips (Phillips Field, Stearner, St Catherine)				142
TOTAL DISEMBARKED FROM SS DAHOMEY				812

Note: Sometimes last minute changes were made to the above allocations.

APPENDIX VI

VINERY ESTATE INDENTURED WORKERS
LIST OF INDENTURED WORKERS WHO WERE DISTRIBUTED TO VINERY ESTATE
IN PORTLAND WHICH WAS OWNED BY JOHN W HILL

Name	Age	Name	Age	Name	Age
Ghundoo	18	Rambhorosay	23	Bipat	18-months
Jaganath	20	Bhular	18	Kabutri	24F
Budhoo	19	Dhamesar	20	Baruddin	28
Mangriya	20	Ramdai	20F	Fazaldin	25
Bhanam	18	Idua	18F	Maharaji	19F
Diputy	20	Jaganath	20	Nobra	21F
Kalloo	20	Mechi	22F	Jahban	17
Kursud	21	Harki	18F	RambriebaSing	22
Peyari	20F	Champi	19F	Jabur	19
Radhaiya	25F	Phagu	26	Bakuidan	22
Ghirjee	22F	Janki	25	Malogi	27
Sitioo	30	Teejia	17F	Jharabag	24
Gania	20F	Binia	20F	Lalmohomed	24
Ori	24	Bhajwandas	28	Manohar	19
Khurdhan	3mths	Sarjoo	26	Munjru	18
Ramdai	22F	Ramlal	19	Hanoman Sing	26
Autar	26	Roorki	18F	Mohammedali Khan	16
Dedue	20	Jackey	25F	Ramphal	22
Maharajit	17F	Autoar	28	Gayadin	24
Rajbali	22	Mahuginia	24F	Ramjai	16
Bhageloo	22	Chandi	24	Autar	24
Lallai	24	Jamait	27	Algoo	24
Kalohal	22	Hardin	21	Malgia	17
Sarjo	24	Subedar	19	Sukal	26
Locckia	22				
MALES	50	FEMALES	21	INFANTS	2

Note: A male and a female were re-assigned to other estates.

APPENDIX VII

LIST OF INDENTURED WORKERS WHO WERE DISTRIBUTED TO FORT STEWART ESTATE IN ST MARY WHICH WAS OWNED BY E.E.C. HOSSACK

Name	Age	Name	Age	Name	Age
Ganesh	23	Ramdai	24F	Jairam	21
Sukhai	19	Isuvareyal	21	Mullood	20
Janki Singh	26	Raghubar	20	Sirichand	21
Karivian	23	Mullia	22F	Sukbrnia	19F
Sawdagar	20	Sheorani	22F	Sarjoo	19
Gajadar Singh	18	Lachman	25	Parbati	26F
Mukut Singh	18	LalBahadu	26	Jibodh	27
Seetal	20	Ramkunw	5F	Bhagwant	22
Nanni	20	Mahraji	20F		
MALE	19	FEMALE	7		

Note: Four workers of the original assignment were reassigned to other estates.

APPENDIX VIII

DISTRIBUTION OF WORKERS

BY PARISH ESTATES TO WHICH INDIAN INDENTURED WORKERS WERE ASSIGNED IN RESPECTIVE PARISHES

Parish	Owner	Estate
Portland	John W Hill	Vinery
	J. Wason	Middleton
	H. Cork	Berlington
	A.E.A. DaCosta	Windsor Castle
	J. Miller	Shrewbury
	United Fruit Company	Golden Vale, Fellowship, Paradise, Red Hassell, Tom Hope, Unity Valley, Williamsfield and Windsor
	H. Jacobs	Spring Garden
St. Thomas	I. Demercads	Lyssons
	D. Davis	Golden Grove
	United Fruit Company	Golden Vale, Tulloch and New Works
	H. Cork	Potosi
	I. Michelin	Duckenfield
	W. Richards	Albany
St. Catherine	A. McIntosh	Riversdale
	J. Calder	Worthy Park
	T. Cowley	Oberlin
	Charles Hudson	Blair Pen Dairy
	United Fruit Company	United Estates and Phillips Field
	James C. Lecesle	Harker's Hall Estate
Hanover	J. Cass	Alexandria, Copse, Georgia
	United Fruit Company	Hayman, Goodhall, Pell River
	L. Sanfleben and Sons	Santoy
Manchester	M. Muirhead	Somerset
Trelawny	J. Poyntz	Good Hope, Potosi, Springs, Phoenix, Adelphi, Lima, Friendship
	W. Sewell	Archadia
	E. Ceolville	Fontabelle
	R. Heetwood	Hampstead
	R. Majo	Hague
	E. Liverpaul	Green Park

Parish	Owner	Estate
Westmoreland	J.O. Harrison	Petersfield, Lincoln
	C. Williams	Friendship
	J. Warner	Bellisle
	A. DaCosta	Blue Castle
	J. Florentone	Masemure
	A. DeGray	Black Health
	L. Anthony	Shrewsbury
	W. Vickers	Cornwall, Roaring River
	D. Sinclair	Retreat
	R. Burgess	Mesopotamia
	J. Fenton	Blue Castle
	T. Campbell	Masemure
	D. Meason	Charlottenburg
	W. Cooke	Meylerfield
	H. A. Vickers	Fontabelle
	P. Greg	Mesopotauna
	Belleisle Estate Co.	Frome
	Mr Ross	Spring Garden
	J. Warner	Corniswall, New Hope
	United Fruit Company	Heylerfield, Canaan, New Gallo- way
Clarendon	H. Mitchell	Amity Hall, Halse Hall, Mamee Gully, Savoy, May Pen
	B. Von Kittlehold	Lloyds
	Vere Estate Co. Ltd	Moreland
	D. Callegham	Pusey Hall, Whitney
	F. Henry	Green Wickle, Monymusk
	G. Solomon	Dawks, Retreat
	L. McKinnon	Harmony Hall, Caswell
	Delisser Brothers	Sevens Plantation
	J. Solomon	Donks, Rock River, Belmont, Bushy Park
	J. McPhail	New Works
	J. Harvey	Lodge, Sutton Pasture, Hillside, Parnassus, Chesterfield, May Pen, Spring Garden, Tarentum
	J. Melville	Kupuis, Penants, Tulloch, Denbeigh
	E.C. Elliot	Point Hill
	Clarendon Amalgamated Co. Ltd	Longsville
	F.M. Ellis	Hillside, Raywood

Parish	Owner	Estate
St. Mary	W. H. Westmoreland	Charlottenburgh, Ballards Valley, White Hall
	Y.R. Scarlett	Grays Inn, New Ramble
	John Pringle	Clonmell, Cape Clear, Brimmer Hall, Coleraine, Lower Fort George, Upper Fort George, Cromwel Land, Noningsburg, Nonesuch
	R.L. Constantine	Clermont
	C.D. Wathlewis	Water Valley
	A.F.G. Ellis	Fort George
	JP Carter	Trinity
	H.W. Pringle	Chovey, Agualta Vale
	E.E.C. Hossack	Fort Stewart, Iterboreale, Lady Hole
	C. Abraham	Hopewell
	R. Fraser	Homingsbury
	Gas. G. Cohen	Newry, Orange Hill, Green Castle, Nutfield, Eden Estate
	J. Kerr and Co.	Llaurumury
	MacDougall	Fontabella
	H. Delisser	Fontsbelle
	A.C. Westomoreland	Gibralter
	I. Levy	Dover
	R. Clementson	Frontier
	Hon. Lindo	Friendship
	G. Geddes	Lambkin Hill
	H. Limmonds	Zuebee
	H. Graham	Halcot Farm
	J. Fletcher	Montrose
	E. Pigou	Rose End
	United Fruit Company	Wentworth
	T.M. Grey	Platfield
	C. Rojores	Meyersfield
St. ELizabeth	M. Dikenson	Appleton Estate
	C. Walter	Ipswich
	Williams Nuttall Campbell Farquharson	Holland Estate
St. James	J.C. Farquharson	Latimer
	T. Boddington	Barrett Hall
	G. Lawrence	Latium
	G. Whitehorse	Running Gut
	G. Lawson	Hamden
	R. Gordon	Windsor Lodge

APPENDIX IX

EAST INDIAN SETTLEMENTS

The settlement information below was supplied by the cooperative efforts of Mr. Henry Jaghai, Mr. Ram Ragbeir and Mr. Gam Bankasingh. All three resided at the Tewari owned lands and attended Ebenezer School, which adjoined TewariLands.

Gam Bankasingh – lived in the area between Ebenezer Lane and Back 'O'Wall Henry Jaghai – lived in the area between Ackeewalk and Newland

Ram Ragbeir –lived in the area between Maranga Lane and Grassyard

Ackee Walk: Abibulha, Arjun, John Barker, Damar, Debidean, Gurdean, Harri, Jaipaul, (Dancer Man) Jugarie, Baby Latchman, Arduwar Maragh, Balragh Maragh, Bangali Maragh, Bhoora Maragh, Durjan Maragh, Lalchun, Maata Phiharie, Parsard, Patunnaho, Piralilal, Raju, Ramparsard, Argobin Singh, Sriram, Sitaram and Sukamar Maragh the father of Pandit Ramadhar Maragh Williams.

Back 'O' Wall: Abdul, Badal, Beharie, Bihaari, Aladean, Dilaawhar, Gadragh Maragh, Gosaine Maragh, Guyah, Husman, Gopaul Maragh, Gopie, Madam Gopaul Maragh, Icilda Maragh, Jadusingh, Jyrahsingh, Junjhi, Kisoonsingh, Latchman, Latchmi Parsaad, Luthaawan, Matadeen, Mohan, Paalu, Peter Maragh, Nirahu, Ramlakhan Maragh, Samuel Bankersingh, Saman, Saroopsingh, Shankar, Sital, Suckoo, Suenaut, Sypo, Tantia and Tiajah.

BarchanPen: Zackie Ackbersingh, Maudlin Bechai, Tuckman Behari, Joe Durgasingh, Lucille Henry, Kuluman, Baba Maragh, Marjorie Matadean, Zeddie Matadean, George Mohamed, Samuel Ramgeet, Louisa Ramsay, Joseph Rattie, Joseph Roberts, Leonard Roberts, Beatrice Setaland, Bob Williams.

Cockburn Pen: Samuel Algho, Baccas, Mary Baker, Ram Baran, William Bedasse, Horie Boyd, Wilfred(Bada)Calu, John Cayman, Muralie Dar, Dean, Hasalat Gallow, Ginghor, Ramsamooj Graham, Jadusingh, Aston Jackson, Jagu, Jysingh, Lakhan, Alfred (Badrie) Latchman, Mackoo, Alfred Maragh, Ardewar Maragh, Jagat Maragh, Terry Macko, Willie Mangaroo, Pakeel, Pancham, Pancham (nagara drumplayer), Peru, Punancy, BahSiddo, Sukhai, andTalloo.

Granton Pen: Bacchas, Brass, Willie Brown, Arnold Budram, Damallie, Dubar, Gadur, Ginghai, Gopie, Harry, Masagad Gouraho, Hardial, Henry, Khunkun Theophilus Pandohie, James Purai, Mousa Ramdeen, Sewag, Mackay Singh, and Dyhal Tolan and Walter.

Grass Yard and Maranga Lane: Adean, Alladean, John Allan, Amir Bacchas, Bongo Brown, Botha, Bridgemohan, Budhai, Bunda, Calu, Dirpaul, Don, Dukanie, Edward, Elsie Nattee, Garboo, Gopie, Lawla, James Lewis, Latchman, Machan, Bandari

Maragh, Cappledoo Maragh, Goshaine Maragh, Tani Maragh, Pajhar, Raghbier, Raghu, Ramdeen, Santram, Sardarsingh, Syephoe, Dhanuk Dhari Tewari and DyhalTolan.

Hindu Town consisted of approximately 25 acres of land, which was part of the Waterhouse property. The entrance was accessed through Waterhouse Lane (now called Henley Road) which was situated on Spanish Town Road at Four Miles.

Dr. Varma had recognised the East Indians' need for residence and had bought the land from Dr. Bailey. He subdivided the land into half and one acre lots with two road access, one called Ashoka Road (named after his son, a lawyer) and the other, Varma Road (after himself). He offered the residents a ten-year contract for which they paid thirty pounds. Upon completion of the ten tears, they became owners of the lots. Residents included Joe Ajarie, Rama Budram, Ramdani Budram, David Edite, Charlie Gajadhar, Isaac Gorbharran, Gurnatan, Joseph Hill, Johnny Mohammed Khan, Ganga Parsard, Ramasre, Elizabeth Ramharrak, Margaret Ramharrak, and Sukah

Mona: Abibalha, Ali, Amair, Cecil Andru, Badal, Mary Byjue, Gadya, Gughai, Gulfarm, Guyadean, Jaghi, Jaghee, Martha Kalapnaut, Khani (Khani Barbers) Latchman, Manhu, Samuel Michael, Mangal, Manowgie, Mahaloo, Moonie, Rambaccas, Ramdeen, Ramjeawan, Madhu Singh, and Tantia.

Newland: Bacchas. Chetram, Harry, Mackbull, Munsi, Raheem, Sarju, Sumai, and Tatar.

Norbrook: - Bankey, Barbay, S.J. Dukharan, Basmatie Dukharan, Maragh, Puranda, Sarju, and Samaroo.

Long Lane: - Gulai, Tilak, Latchman, Codie, Ramharrack, Comal, Badarey, Serechan, Suraj, and Gulai

Payne Land: was approximately thirty acres of land is situated on Spanish Town Road at Two Miles. The land was leased to East Indians by Mr. Payne who also supplied the property withwater from his well. The residents maintained vegetable gardens. East Indians who lived there include Cecil Barker, John Barker, Louise Barker, Louise Bharosee, Beepat, Bhola, Gali, Marajin, Murat, John Mykoo, Patia, Ragbeir, Rampersad, Rhyman, Mahadeo Singh, Sahadeo Singh, Subran and Levi Thompson.

Swallowfield: Sunnath, Muckett, Patasar, William Bedasse, and Khouran

Whitehall: Maragh, Guptar, Puranda, Ramraj, Rajit, John Sukie, Benjamin Sukie, Ramlal Malgie, Bwia Baldeo, John Bhola, Jagasar, Turner, Lal Badal, Soberon, Alfred Sukie, Poulton, Tony Maragh, Luluman, Maragh, William Sukie, Marasie, Gurchan Sukie, Biju Malgi, Deena, George Sukie, Ramjeet Thomas, Guyah and Bagaloo.

APPENDIX X

When Jaghi and Autuaria went to register at Gorakphur in May 26, 1905, there were other people who registered too. All 48 of them became became friends while living in the holding area for two weeks. They went by train to Calcutta to join with the other villagers. There were 812 in all. They sailed on the S.S. Indus and arrived in Jamaica on July 27, 1905. They went to various estates but they kept in touch and lived like a big family when they met up at Indian functions. Some of them returned to India when the five year contract was up . The others remained and made Jamaica their home.

Name	Depot	Father's Name	District	Village/Town
Jagai	Gorakphur	Seojahan	Basti	Bahadurpur
Autaria	Gorakphur	Seobatak	Basti	Bahadurpur
Akalu	Gorakphur	Budhram	Basti	Galhaura
Sukhdia	Gorakphur	Kamohai	Basti	Galhaura
Uamraj	Gorakphur	Seojitam	Basti	Marauth
Jahesher	Gorakphur	Jalim	Basti	Marauth
Ram sarup	Gorakphur	Debi	Gonda	Khafigeon
Bhikha	Gorakphur	Adhin	Basti	Jainmpur
Baldeo	Gorakphur	Kasi	Basti	Naghrapur
Kubitra	Gorakphur	Sabind	Gonda	Khafigeon
Rammangal	Gorakphur	Bhaggu	Basti	Belhar
Bikarma	Gorakphur	Khelawan	Basti	Belhar
Mohan	Gorakphur	Taila	Basti	Katia
Phekni	Gorakphur	Sumesar	Gorakphur	Pipra
Rugali	Gorakphur	Ugar	Gorakphur	Pipra
Ulpatia	Gorakphur	Naik	Gorakphur	Gurwalia
Baindori	Gorakphur	Ramphal	Gorakphur	Gurwalia
Dukhni	Gorakphur	Gabarohan	Gorakphur	Gurwalia
Gatti	Gorakphur	Andhu	Gorakphur	Sekhuri
Fatinga	Gorakphur	Jhingur	Gorakphur	Dharampur
Rainjhari	Gorakphur	Chattu	Saran	Baletha

Jageshar	Gorakphur	Ram charan	Gorakphur	Siswa
Shew	Gorakphur	Dhurai	Gorakphur	Mahabir chhupra
Chhangur	Gorakphur	Kadai	Gorakphur	Lakarhia
Chaitura	Gorakphur	Suchit	Basti	Teusi
Mahabir	Gorakphur	Gaya	Basti	Kaunharia
Agar singh	Gorakphur	Prithi singh	Basti	Karauli
Garib	Gorakphur	Dauyal	Gorakphur	Madrahua
Patti	Gorakphur	Balli	Gorakphur	Sedhwa
Sabbhagia	Gorakphur	Dholai	Gorakphur	Sultanpur
Farid	Gorakphur	Khajay	Basti	Bebraey
Fahima	Gorakphur	Pardhi	Basti	Kirhirhia
Ramdhan	Gorakphur	Suhohain	Basti	Kirhirhia
Aotar	Gorakphur	Sukohain	Basti	Kirhirhia
Rameswar	Gorakphur	Pudsi	Gorakphur	Darghat
Surajbali	Gorakphur	Sukhu	Basti	Pachasi
Raghuni	Gorakphur	Merhai	Basti	Pachasi
Mahrajia	Gorakphur	Surajbali	Basti	Pachasi
Sarjudice	Gorakphur	Surajbali	Basti	Pachasi
Badri	Gorakphur	Merhai	Basti	Pachasi
Chhutkan	Gorakphur	Timal	Basti	Dhaurpara
Manraj	Gorakphur	Merhai	Basti	Dhaurpara
Bipet	Gorakphur	Timal	Basti	Dhaurpara
Jias	Gorakphur	Dular	Basti	Rajhunathpur
Budhia	Gorakphur	Seosaran	Gorakphur	Bakhra
Phulesri	Gorakphur	Janki	Gorakphur	Sakra
Phulesri	Gorakphur	Sibaran	Gorakphur	Kurmawal
Sarju	Gorakphur	Nadlu	Gorakphur	Sisai

www.ingramcontent.com/pod-product-compliance
Lightning Source LLC
Chambersburg PA
CBHW081346080526
44588CB00016B/2386